Polar Winds

To Jeremy –
Happy reading +
happy birthday!
Danielle

Polar Winds

A Century of Flying the North

Danielle Metcalfe-Chenail

DUNDURN
TORONTO

Editor: Michael Melgaard
Design: Courtney Horner
Printer: Webcom
Cover design by Jesse Hooper
Cover image courtesy of Erich Osterberg.
Top cover photos, left to right: Preus Museum, Elaine de Blicquy, Adam Morrison.

Library and Archives Canada Cataloguing in Publication

Metcalfe-Chenail, Danielle, author
Polar winds : a century of flying the North / Danielle Metcalfe-Chenail.

Includes bibliographical references and index.
Issued in print and electronic formats.
ISBN 978-1-4597-2379-5

1. Aeronautics--Canada, Northern--History. 2. Air pilots--Canada, Northern--Biography. 3. Canada, Northern--History--20th century. 4. Canada, Northern--Biography. I. Title.

TL523.M48 2014   629.130971   C2014-904272-8
C2014-904273-6

1   2   3   4   5   18   17   16   15   14

We acknowledge the support of the **Canada Council for the Arts** and the **Ontario Arts Council** for our publishing program. We also acknowledge the financial support of the **Government of Canada** through the **Canada Book Fund** and **Livres Canada Books**, and the **Government of Ontario** through the **Ontario Book Publishing Tax Credit** and the **Ontario Media Development Corporation**.

Care has been taken to trace the ownership of copyright material used in this book. The author and the publisher welcome any information enabling them to rectify any references or credits in subsequent editions.
J. Kirk Howard, President

The publisher is not responsible for websites or their content unless they are owned by the publisher.

Printed and bound in Canada.

VISIT US AT
Dundurn.com | @dundurnpress
Facebook.com/dundurnpress | Pinterest.com/Dundurnpress

Dundurn
3 Church Street, Suite 500
Toronto, Ontario, Canada
M5E 1M2

Small cover images, left to right:
Roald Amundsen's Dornier-Wal flying boat; Lorna de Blicquy, pioneering northern pilot, in Resolute, NWT; A Trans North helicopter in the Yukon.

Main image:
A Helio Courier taking off from a glacier in the Yukon.

For my parents

Table of Contents

Acknowledgements

To write this book, I drove two thousand kilometres along the Alaska and Dempster Highways in winter, mostly in a rental car without snow tires. I flew another 1,200 kilometres along the "Big Dipper Route" from Whitehorse, to Dawson, to Old Crow, and to Inuvik aboard Air North's turboprop airliners. I also got amazing aerial views of Yellowknife and Great Slave Lake in a 1930s Norseman bush plane and Buffalo Airways Douglas DC-3 — both times with "Buffalo" Joe McBryan at the controls. These travels gave me a great sense of this amazing region: the span of the Mackenzie Delta, ice fog in November, and the endless days of July. Even more importantly, they allowed me to meet a number of people connected to northern aviation in the air and on the ground.

These research trips would not have been possible without grants from the Canada Council for the Arts, the Edmonton Arts Council, and the Fox Moth Society of Yellowknife. The Writers' Trust of Canada also provided three months at the Berton House Writers' Retreat in Dawson City, Yukon. My time there afforded me the chance to immerse myself in the North and to access communities, archives, and libraries across the Western Arctic and Subarctic. It also allowed me to soak up inspiration from two of my historical heroes, Pierre Berton and Charlotte Gray, the latter of whom has since become a wonderful source of encouragement.

During my jaunts, I relied on a lot of northern hospitality. Thank you to Yvonne Quick, Bruce Barrett, and Judy Forrest-Barrett for putting me up, and putting up with me, and to Deb Nehring, Betty and Dan Davidson, and Michael and Kathy Gates for their help along the way. Thanks to the following people for coffees, beers, and meals in addition to great information and contacts: John Chalmers, Doug Davidge, Don Klancher, Jack Van Norman, Sherron Jones, Murray Biggin, Garry MacLean, George Balmer, David Neufeld, Bill Kendrick, Isaaq Appaqaq, Chris Lennie, Paul Laserich, John Zigarlick, and Jimmy Essery. Some of these people passed away during the creation of this book, and several far too soon, but not before they contributed to northern aviation in important ways.

In addition to those whose names appear in the rest of the book, I would like to thank the knowledgeable members of the Canadian Aviation Historical Society who were generous with their assistance: George Fuller, Hugh Halliday, Rod Digney, Roger Beebe, Leo Kohn, Tony Hine, and Alan Rust. Lech Lebiedowski, Rod MacLeod, and Tom Hinderks at the Alberta Aviation Museum were very helpful, as were the following people and institutions: Cheryl Charlie at the Yukon Archives; Leighann Chalykoff at the MacBride Museum; Robin Weber and Ian Moir at the Prince of Wales Heritage Centre; Laura Mann at the Dawson Museum Archives; Casey McLaughlin at the Yukon Transportation Museum; Megan Williams, the heritage manager at the Government of the Vuntut Gwitchin First Nation; Braden Cannon at the Provincial Archives of Alberta; Monika Sjue at the Preus Museum; and the many people who helped me at the various branches of the Yukon and Edmonton Public Libraries.

Thanks also to my agent, Carolyn Forde at Westwood Creative Artists, as well as Michael Melgaard and Margaret Bryant at Dundurn, for their help bringing this book into the world. And thanks to David and Rose Scollard for brunches, editorial insights, and their early encouragement.

I am also grateful to Robin Brass for creating the map for the book, and to Neil Taylor of Edmonton who was kind enough to read the entire manuscript and offer his valuable feedback.

Then there are the wonderful friends and writers who have seen me through this long journey: Caitlin Crawshaw, Ashley Dryburgh, Erinne Sevigny, S.G. Wong, Caterina Edwards, Jean Crozier, Mar'ce Merrell, Lorie White, Debby Waldman, and Jessica Kluthe. Your critiques and support have been invaluable.

A huge thanks to my incredible husband, Doug, who always believed in me and this project (and subsidized my writing habit), and to my son, Andre, who has been connected to this book from the beginning, and shows every indication of loving aviation as much as his namesake.

Finally, this book began on the shelves of my parents' curio cabinets and bookcases. There, I found my father's Inuktitut lesson books and the soapstone carvings my mother brought back from business trips to the Arctic. Thank you and merci for looking north and nurturing my dreams — I dedicate this book to you.

Author's Note

While researching and writing this book, I encountered several challenges. Right away, I had to make the difficult decision of where the region we call the "North" begins and ends. Following the example of several other historians, I used the political division of the 60th parallel as my lower limit, but I recognize this is quite arbitrary, as anyone who has spent time at the northern edges of the Canadian provinces can attest.

I have also run headfirst into the challenges associated with naming the North and its peoples. Names are culturally and politically significant, and unless it is in quoted material, I tend to use the contemporary place name with the older name in brackets afterward. Also, while the separate territory of Nunavut now exists, it did not for the time span of this book, so when I refer to the Northwest Territories, it encompasses the whole region before it was split in 1999.

Regarding the names of the various indigenous peoples of the North, I have tried to be as specific as possible. Too often non-indigenous authors have defaulted to "Indian" or "Native," ignoring geographic, linguistic, and cultural diversity. Even with this in mind, I tend to use the blanket term "Inuit" unless I am writing specifically about the Inuvialuit in the Western Arctic. I do recognize, however, that there are regional differences and that in Nunavut alone there are seven dialects of Inuktitut. For the spellings of Inuktitut words outside of quoted material, I largely followed the North Baffin Island spellings found in Shelagh Grant's *Polar Imperative* and *Arctic Justice* and Nancy Wachowich's *Saqiyuq*.

Even something as seemingly easy as aircraft have resisted common punctuation and spellings, and I know from working in the field that rivet counters can be particular about these things. I have employed the most common usages, and have generally deferred to spellings used by the Canada Aviation and Space Museum and aviation historian Larry Milberry. In the text, I have often omitted specific manufacturers, makes, or models, for readability, but these can be found in the index under the specific manufacturer names (i.e. de Havilland Canada DHC-2 Beaver).

The long time span of the book also posed problems in terms of numbers. Canada officially switched from the Imperial to the metric system during the twentieth

century, and we still straddle the two. This is especially the case in aviation, it would seem, where many pilots still talk about gallons, miles per hour, and feet. I have followed the current metric convention throughout the text, except in quoted material, which I have left as is.

Finally, when I mention money, especially in the earlier chapters of this book, I use the basic calculator on the website *www.measuringworth.com*, to calculate what the amounts would be roughly equivalent to today.

INTRODUCTION

Gamblers and Fortune Seekers

"They were all gamblers and fortune seekers. They did things on their own — were independent people who wanted to be free to roam. They were good people, but, of course, some were loners or escapists. They all depended strictly on their wits." Joe McBryan, pilot and owner of Yellowknife-based Buffalo Airways, sat at his family's old mining camp on Gordon Lake in the Northwest Territories when he said this on a hot July day in 2011. He was talking about gold prospectors in the 1940s, but McBryan could just as easily have been describing the aviators who have flown northern skies for over a hundred years.

Some of those fortune seekers wanted to make money, like the American "balloonatic" who soared above the crowds of Dawson City, Yukon, looking for his share of Klondike gold in 1899. Most simply wanted to make their mark — and maybe a living while they were at it. It was not easy

or even glamorous work much of the time, despite attempts by dime novelists and the media to make bush pilots out to be mythic heroes. And while crashes, mercy flights, and search and rescue operations provided drama, it was the day-to-day experience of northern aviation that made the most impact. In the early years, airplanes brought letters and newspapers, and sometimes even wives-to-be, from "Outside." In recent times, planes have become a way to get out on the land, to have your washing machine delivered, or to fly your dog team down to Whitehorse for the Yukon Quest. This flying can be quite routine, but it has been central to life in the North.

For those of us living south of the 60th parallel, aviation in the North conjures images of freedom, adventure, and escape — as well as potential tragedy in the Northwest Territories' "Barren Lands" or the bush. For the roughly one hundred

Aviation has been central to getting people from point A to B in the North for decades. In 1969 these three pilots — Paul Slager, George Fink, and Joe McBryan — were chartered to fly school teachers from Fort Smith, Northwest Territories, to Uranium City, Saskatchewan, for a weekend teacher's convention in a Cessna 185, Cessna 206, and Beaver.

thousand people living in the Canadian North, however, it is not wilderness, but home. Unsettled weather, freeze-up and breakup, and vast distances are daily realities.

The history of polar aviation is a long one and encompasses all peoples. The majority of northerners are Inuit, Métis, and First Nations. Though they have been left out of many other accounts, from the earliest days they have been central to flying in the North, as spectators and crew. By the end of the twentieth century, they owned and operated major airlines. Women were important players in early northern aviation as well, not only as wives keeping the home fires burning while their husbands were off flying (although this was very important),

but as business partners, flight attendants, pilots, and agents. Women were among the first brave (or some might say, foolish) passengers to clamber into open cockpit planes as well. This book seeks to use all these different, often under-represented, voices to tell the story of polar aviation.

The North is a massive region — there are 3.9 million square kilometres north of 60 degrees latitude in Canada alone. A team of researchers could spend years in various archives examining every document and trying to track down every bush pilot, air maintenance engineer, and Royal Canadian Air Force member for interviews, and still they would not have the full story. And that is not even including the pilots and explorers from other countries who have ventured into Canada's north over the years, flyers from the United States, Russia, Norway, United Kingdom, and Japan. This book tries to make sense of patterns and provide a bird's-eye view of the history; it is not an exhaustive history, but a representative one.

The growth of aviation gave newcomers greater access to the top of the continent. They came, sometimes in trickles — as in the case of small planes delivering mail down the Mackenzie River — and sometimes in floods — like during the mega-projects of the Second World War. Many people — from Hudson's Bay Company (HBC) traders, to missionaries, to Mounties — went north with the best of intentions; some, unfortunately, also acted, in cultural historian Daniel Francis's words, with "breathtaking arrogance," especially with regards to the indigenous peoples.

These contacts, at times, led to outbreaks of diseases — in the case of tuberculosis, government policy dictated flying individuals out to southern sanitaria, sometimes for years at a time. The "Flying School Buses" used to take indigenous children to residential schools are perhaps the most dramatic — and tragic — example of the intersection of aviation and assimilationist thinking. The Canadian government, churches, and Royal Canadian Mounted Police (RCMP) have all issued formal apologies for their role in removing indigenous children from their families and placing them in difficult, and at times downright abusive, circumstances. Writing about these topics can make non-indigenous writers feel as if we are "trespassing upon Aboriginal experience," as John S. Milloy, author of *A National Crime*, describes it, but these stories are part of our collective past, and we all need to understand them better.

This book explores the many ups and downs of aviation in this region — everything from exploration in airships, to flying ultralight pleasure craft, to industrial exploration in helicopters, to passenger travel in jetliners. It recounts not only what happened, but what aviation has meant to the North, its peoples, and the international cast of characters who took to the air from the Klondike Gold Rush through to the end of the twentieth century. Inevitably, all this flying in northern skies impacted those on the ground in significant, but not always foreseeable, ways.

Like *Saqiyuq*, the North Baffin Island Inuktitut word for a strong wind that suddenly shifts direction, the story of northern aviation has many twists and turns. It is not an easy story to tell, and at times it is as fraught as it is fascinating. Even so, as Salomon August Andrée, a Swedish balloonist who set off for the North Pole in 1897, said: "The thing is so difficult I cannot help but attempt it."

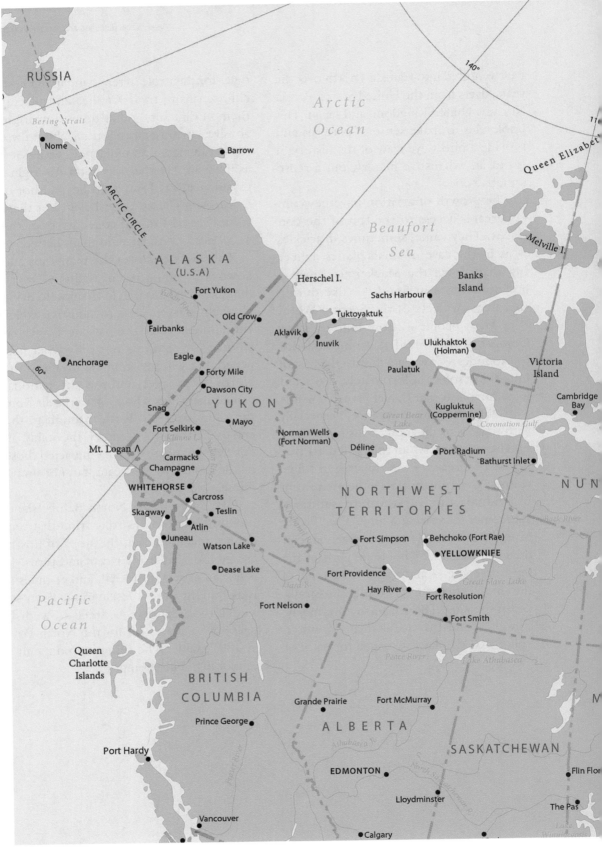

RUSSIA

Bering Strait

Nome

Barrow

Arctic Ocean

ARCTIC CIRCLE

ALASKA
(U.S.A)

Fort Yukon

Herschel I.

Beaufort Sea

Banks
Island

Sachs Harbour

Melville I.

Queen Elizabeth

140°

110

Yukon River

Old Crow

Tuktoyaktuk

Fairbanks

Aklavik

Inuvik

Ulukhaktok
(Holman)

Eagle

60°

Anchorage

Forty Mile

Dawson City

YUKON

Paulatuk

Victoria
Island

Cambridge
Bay

Snag

Mayo

Great Bear Lake

Kugluktuk
(Coppermine)

Fort Selkirk

Norman Wells
(Fort Norman)

Déline

Coronation Gulf

Klunne L.

Mt. Logan Λ

Carmacks

Port Radium

Bathurst Inlet

Champagne

Yukon River

N U N

WHITEHORSE

Carcross

NORTHWEST

Skagway

Teslin

TERRITORIES

Back River

Atlin

Juneau

Watson Lake

Fort Simpson

Behchoko (Fort Rae)

YELLOWKNIFE

Dease Lake

Fort Providence

Great Slave Lake

Pacific Ocean

Liard R.

Hay River

Fort Resolution

Fort Nelson

Fort Smith

Queen
Charlotte
Islands

Peace River

Lake Athabasca

BRITISH

Grande Prairie

Fort McMurray

COLUMBIA

Prince George

ALBERTA

Athabasca R.

SASKATCHEWAN

M

Port Hardy

Fraser River

EDMONTON

Flin Flon

North Saskatchewan R.

Lloydminster

The Pas

Vancouver

Calgary

Lake Winnipeg

Map by Robin Brass

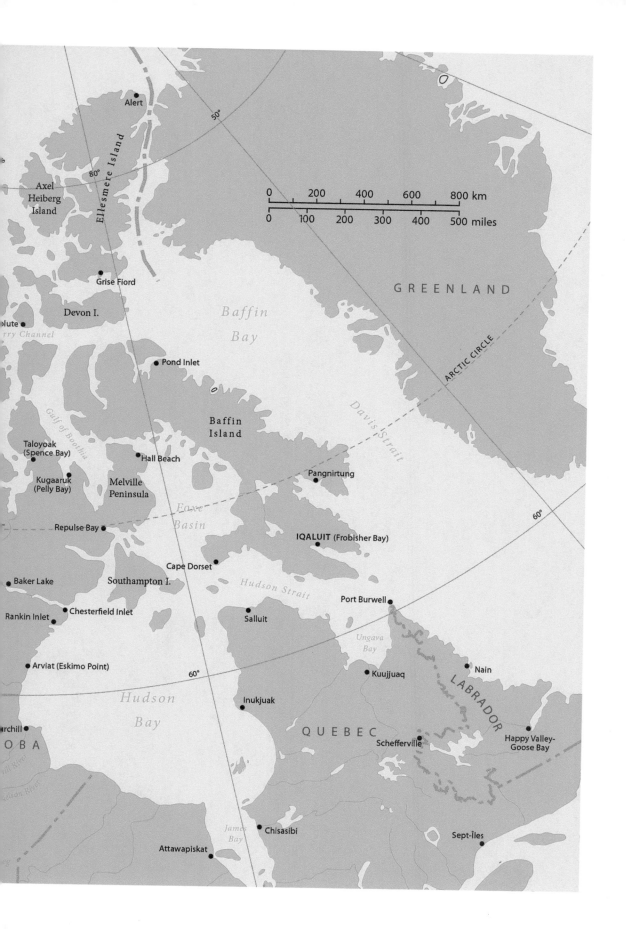

Alert

Axel
Heiberg
Island

Ellesmere Island

80°

50°

Grise Fiord

Devon I.

olute

rry Channel

0   200   400   600   800 km

0   100   200   300   400   500 miles

G R E E N L A N D

Baffin

Bay

Pond Inlet

ARCTIC CIRCLE

Gulf of Boothia

*Baffin
Island*

Taloyoak
(Spence Bay)

Hall Beach

Davis Strait

Kugaaruk
(Pelly Bay)

Melville
Peninsula

Fox e

60°

Basin

Pangnirtung

Repulse Bay

IQALUIT (Frobisher Bay)

Baker Lake

Southampton I.

Cape Dorset

Hudson Strait

Port Burwell

Rankin Inlet

Chesterfield Inlet

Salluit

*Ungava
Bay*

Arviat (Eskimo Point)

60°

Nain

Kuujjuaq

L A B R A D O R

Hudson

Inukjuak

rchill

Bay

Q U E B E C

Schefferville

Happy Valley-
Goose Bay

OBA

ll River

son River

*James
Bay*

Chisasibi

Sept-Îles

Attawapiskat

g

CHAPTER 1

Gold, Glory, and Spectacle

The Klondike Gold Rush sparked the imaginations of millions around the world, including a fair number of people who looked to the sky instead of the ground as a way to get rich. Inventors, entertainers, and hucksters profited from gold fever directly and indirectly by selling airship schemes to investors and "balloonatic" thrills to crowds. By the time the rush was over, however, many of those dreamers had seen their plans fizzle, and stockholders had seen their investments disappear. But the idea of flight in northern skies had taken hold.

BY AIR SHIP TO THE KLONDIKE

In July 1897 the ocean steamer *Portland* docked at Seattle, Washington, carrying prospectors dubbed the "Klondike Kings" along with a reported seven hundred thousand dollars' worth of gold (about twenty million dollars today).[1] This was the first time word of the massive gold strike in the Yukon Territory reached "Outside" — the northern word for anything south of the 60th parallel — and it triggered a stampede of prospectors looking to get rich quick and avoid working for low wages in dim offices, factories, or stores. But getting to the Klondike, in the distant reaches of Canada's Northwest, was anything but quick.

Two American prospectors, Bill Haskell and Joe Meeker, acted on rumours they heard sitting in a Colorado Springs bar and beat the main rush by a year. Still, they could not avoid the arduous three-month journey. The voyage began easily enough, with a twelve-day trip from San Francisco to the port of Dyea, Alaska, aboard a steamship. Once they reached their destination, Haskell and Meeker quickly unloaded their one and a half tons of provisions — enough to last them for a year — before the tide came in. They then wasted no time dividing it into sled loads, and each made four trips, pulling their sleds to the first stopping point, Sheep Camp. From there they went on foot, carrying their heavy supplies for six kilometres up the increasingly steep hills of the Saint Elias Mountain range, and finally up the incline to Chilkoot Pass, one thousand metres above sea level. The twenty-seven-kilometre trip — which included a two-week snowstorm delay — took them twenty-three days to complete. And they were still eight hundred kilometres from the gold fields.

Once on the other side of the Chilkoot Pass, the going, if anything, got even rougher. Because the lakes in the region were still frozen, the men once again had to pull their load on sleds. When the countryside finally began to thaw on May 1, they built a boat to take them the rest of the way. Far from a pleasant river cruise, their time on the water included navigating the White Horse rapids, "where the white foam on towering waves curled like a horse's mane" and dozens of people lost their lives during the gold rush. Then they had to paddle the fifty-kilometre length of Lake Laberge through more rapids, and used poles and tow lines to drag the boat along the Yukon River to their final destination, Dawson City. The entire way they were tormented by mosquitoes and blackflies, their "faces so swollen by insect bites that they could barely open their eyes."

This route, which was the best-known way into the Klondike gold fields, was referred to as the "Trail of '98." It was by no means the only way in, although it was the fastest and, in some ways, the easiest. There was also the "all-Canadian route," which another would-be prospector, A. E. Lee, took in 1898, at the height of the rush. Lee set out from Edmonton and it took him two years to reach Dawson City, "by which time all the gold was gone as well as a good deal of his patriotism."[2] Another 3,500 people attempted the "all-American Route," disembarking north of Dyea at Valdez, Alaska, to avoid paying duty to Canadian customs officials.[3] Their path was blocked by the huge Valdez glacier, however, which meant that only a fraction of them managed the trip successfully. In all, roughly one hundred thousand gold seekers like Haskell, Meeker, and Lee attempted

to reach the Klondike. An estimated forty thousand made it to their destination — the rest abandoned the journey or, in a few cases, died en route — and four thousand actually saw their dreams of gold pan out.

This huge influx of people into the Yukon meant opportunities abounded for the indigenous porters, steamship operators, and others who provided transportation services.[4] This massive expenditure of resources and money — some say fifty million dollars was spent trying to reach the Klondike — also inspired a series of creative solutions as to how people and their cargo could be moved into the region. Plans emerged to construct a railway from Chesterfield Inlet on Hudson Bay across 1,126 kilometres of Arctic tundra to Great Slave Lake, a "region almost totally unexplored, unmapped, and unknown" by non-natives. Others proposed a "snow train, propelled by a giant sprocketed wheel, that [would bear] a remarkable resemblance to the modern snowmobile (but which never worked)."[5] There were even rumours of plans for a reindeer postal service along the lines of the Pony Express, as well as a bicycle path.

Then people of science, business, and government began to ask: why not by air? It had been more than fifty years since the first manned balloon flight in Canada had taken place, and many now accepted that air travel would be viable in the not-so-distant future.[6] After all, the Swedish balloonist Salomon August Andrée had launched one of the first attempts to reach the geographic North Pole by air in July

A poster from "The Air Ship: A Musical Farce Comedy," a stage show that ran at the Grand Opera House in New York City in 1899. It featured scenes of an airship expedition to the Klondike and Dawson City in winter, much to the delight of theatre-goers.

1897, just as the Klondike Kings arrived in Seattle with their tales of adventure and sacks of gold.[7] Instead of trying to conquer the landscape through trails or rails, why not just float above it? A *New York Times* editorial pursued this line of thought: "Suppose an airship to be now perfected and practical," the author mused. "The riches of the Klondike would at once lie patent to mankind. The difficulties of reaching that lonely valley would vanish at once."[8]

In August 1897 the *Times* began reporting on a series of American schemes to make this idea a reality. Charles A. Kuenzel, a mechanical engineer of German extraction who had served as a soldier in the balloon department of the Kaiser's army, had been working on a balloon for years out of his home in Hoboken, New York. After hearing news of the Klondike rush, he formed a company with the intent of building a ship to fly north. The balloon cost him four thousand dollars (about one hundred thousand dollars today) to build, he told reporters, and contained the "lightest engine ever made." This gas-powered aluminum engine would help get him from New York to San Francisco and then to Dawson City in under a week. Despite his confidence that he had solved the problem of navigation in polar winds, he prudently planned to take three weeks' provisions for himself and the other five men who would work the ship. "On the first trip, we may get lost away up in the air somewhere," he admitted. "The Western and Klondike country is strange to me, and I may make some mistakes in steering. There are no charts for the air. But I'll land all right. I only want to be sure of having enough to eat and drink if we get stuck or stranded five or six miles above the earth." Kuenzel apparently never made it

to the Yukon, but he continued to promote his inventions, and received a patent for his airship design in 1911.[9]

There were others who pursued the idea as well. Hiram S. Maxim, superintendent of construction of the Atlantic and Pacific Aerial Navigation Company, for example, announced in November 1897 that his company was also building an airship bound for the Klondike.[10] He estimated that the three-thousand-cubic-metre, hydrogen-filled balloon would weigh 2,250 kilograms total, including about a metric ton of passengers and provisions, a four-hundred-kilogram engine made of aluminum, and enough gasoline to "drive the vessel around the earth without replenishing the supply." At roughly the same time, a man in Michigan made plans for a regular balloon route into the Yukon, which would make a return trip in a fortnight.[11] As *Klondike* author Pierre Berton notes, "People all over the country wrote to [him] offering ridiculous sums for passage or even 'a berth in steerage.'" Another American, Leo Stevens Jr. of New York, who adopted the more romantic name Don Carlos Stevens, raised $3.5 million in today's dollars to build the biggest balloon in the world to transport gold seekers from Juneau over the mountains.[12]

This idea was not limited to Americans. In Dublin, Ireland, one dreamer announced he was building a balloon big enough to take fifty passengers to the Klondike.[13] Even the Canadian government got on board, declaring that "it would start a line of airships at once through Western Canada to the Klondike." The scheme was first proposed by Joseph de l'Etoile of the Department of the Interior, who had invented an airship that was in the planning stages. According to him, with a financial investment he could build the airship and be ready for trial flights out of Ottawa within four weeks.[14] He stated that if his plan was successful, he would "at once offer the right of manufacture to the War Departments of the various Governments." His motivation was not all patriotic, however. He also noted that the City of Washington had a standing offer to award the equivalent of one million dollars to the first person to sail an airship into that city, and he expected to collect it "before many months."[15] However, he conceded, "I know many persons will laugh and jeer when they hear of my scheme. But that does not deter me from making the trial, which I believe will be a success."[16] There is no record he ever built the ship, let alone flew it.

Out of all the would-be aeronauts who promoted airships to reach the Klondike, only one had the credentials to make a serious attempt. Dr. Jean Antoine Variclé, an inventor and aeronaut, began formulating a plan in his native France to provide balloon services to the gold seekers. He was independently wealthy, having already invented a sardine-tin lid opener, a telegraph instrument, and a combination key used by the French government for time locks on post office property.[17] The *Victoria Colonist* newspaper might have been exaggerating when it stated that Variclé was "an authority second to none in Europe," but he certainly had training and experience, having studied under balloon maker and pilot Maurice Mallet.[18] In fact, in October 1897, before setting out for the Yukon, Mallet and Variclé (along with the latter's son, Marcel) left Paris in a balloon called *Fram*. By the time it touched down in a village near Hamburg, Germany, they had travelled 1,287 kilometres

and stayed aloft more than twenty-four hours, breaking the existing record for time spent in the air.[19]

With this voyage accomplished, Variclé set off for New York City in April 1898 aboard the *S.S. Bretagne*. Travelling with him was his balloon, which he told reporters would bring him and his twelve companions from Juneau, Alaska, to the Klondike. The balloon — to be transported cross-country and then filled with hydrogen at Juneau — was cylindrical in form, with an electric lighting system, including a searchlight. It had modern "marine instruments of geographical and topographical science" as well as carrier pigeons to send out news on the expedition's progress. This ship could reportedly carry a load of 3,300 kilograms and had several newly invented design improvements, including

A portrait of inventor and aeronaut Antoine Variclé published in *The Northern Light* by M. Wilma Sullivan, July 1904. The Paris-born Variclé made it to Dawson City, but instead of his plans to operate an airship between there and Skagway, Alaska, he staked mining claims and worked as a dentist.

Glenbow Archives M-9460-35-pg14

an "autolesteur," which a reporter roughly translated as an "automatic ballasting apparatus." This would help him direct the balloon "to a certain degree," but even with the addition of a rope and steering sail, it was unlikely he would actually be able to exert his navigational will on the balloon.

Variclé's reputation and status meant this was a well-funded and publicized event. The balloon was partly financed by the French Geographic Society, and counted among Variclé's group were a chemist and a geologist, as well as Arthur Tervagne, expedition secretary and correspondent for the French newspaper *Le Figaro*.[20] Despite their intellectual pedigrees and planning, the group was delayed and eventually disbanded.[21] Variclé did make it to Dawson City later that year, but instead of taking to the air, he staked claims and worked as a dentist for dance-hall queen Diamond Tooth Gertie and the other colourful characters in town.[22]

"A GLITTERING EXHIBITION OF AERONAUTICAL ENGINEERING"

Variclé was still in Dawson City on August 29, 1899, when another aeronaut, "Professor" John Leonard, made the first balloon ascent in the Yukon. A young man who had recently arrived in the territory, Leonard cut a dashing figure with his dark hair and moustache, laced-up boots, and his belted leotard. He looked like he would have been at home under the big top as a circus act, and in many ways he was one. Leonard was not an inventor, engineer, or even likely a professor. He was an entertainer, who told Yukon reporters he had been working as an aeronaut around North America since 1883.[23] "Do I like the business?" he asked

rhetorically. "Well, I know of no other that would suit me so well; having travelled all my life it would be hard indeed to settle down and watch the world pass by the door. I like to meet strange people and see uncommon sights."[24]

There was certainly no shortage of those in Dawson City. Thousands gathered along the city's waterfront with faces turned to the sky where Leonard's balloon hovered 1,520 metres above the crowd. After the "Professor" had performed acrobatic feats on a trapeze, he "unhitched his parachute and dropped, striking the river with a splash, while the parachute collapsed and floated upon the surface of the water." A heart-stopping moment later he reappeared from the icy water of the Yukon River, and swam to shore. "In the meantime, the balloon slowly floated up the river, rising as it went, and circled around over the city, when the gas began to escape rapidly and it finally disappeared over the hill opposite Mission Street." A group of volunteers then hiked into the bush to recover the balloon and bring it back to his base at the Villa de Lion Hotel in West Dawson.[25]

While his audience that day was sizeable, Leonard had missed the Klondike's zenith by a few short months.[26] Dawson City had been rebuilt after a fire that April, but in June 1899 an exodus had begun toward the next gold strike at Nome, Alaska. By that fall the population had dropped to fifteen thousand, half what it had been at its peak. Though the main frenzy was over, there were still crowds to entertain and money to be made in the "San Francisco of the North." Dawsonites prided themselves on being "up to date on attractions of all kinds," and by the turn of the century, any decent Victoria Day celebration, agricultural

DCM Archives/1975.2.1.24, Frances Cogdon collection

"Professor" Leonard, a self-professed balloonatic, made his first ascent in Dawson City, Yukon in 1899. These displays were very popular at the time, and Leonard managed to make a substantial amount of money by taking up a collection from his audiences.

society exhibition, or fall fair had to feature a balloon ascent — preferably with aerial acrobatics and a parachute jump.[27]

These diverse and cosmopolitan people, like their counterparts Outside, were drawn to balloon shows by a variety of motives. "For many," historian Jonathan Vance tells us, "idle curiosity or the prospect of a pleasant diversion brought them out on a sunny afternoon; some likely nursed the secret hope that they might witness some dreadful accident."[28] There were also many in August 1899 who had never seen a balloon before and were riveted by the sight. The local Tr'ondëk Hwëch'in, as well as Tlingit and Dene individuals who had travelled into the region during the rush, were sophisticated consumers and traders of non-native goods.[29] Even so, many had never come into contact with this new technology. After his performance, Leonard remarked of these indigenous spectators, "I am always sorry I do not understand their language[s] so as to get their opinions of ballooning."[30]

On Labour Day, Leonard did another jump in Dawson City. As the local newspaper reported, "To say that he gave a glittering exhibition of aeronautical engineering is no exaggeration."[31] Unfortunately, the spectacle ended when Leonard landed on the roof of a warehouse. As he wrote to his friend, John "Packer Jack" Newman — a well-known figure in Skagway, Alaska, at the time — he touched down on the corrugated iron roof only to slip and fall seven metres to the ground. "Received an awful strain," he wrote, "but didn't rupture." Even so, he was forced to cancel his upcoming show in the short-lived town of Grand Forks, Yukon, while he recuperated in bed for two weeks and then hobbled around Dawson on crutches.[32] By December he was well again, but wished he was Outside instead of facing a winter of "working on the creeks," where he took a big pay cut from the equivalent of ten thousand dollars he had been paid for his two Juneau jumps. Even passing the hat at his Dawson City performances netted him more than manual labour.[33]

By the next May he was back in the air, making ascents to mark Queen Victoria's birthday and collecting donations from Dawson crowds. On May 25, 1900, over two thousand people gathered to watch as Leonard hung by his ankles from the balloon. He put on such a successful show the town asked him to repeat it the next evening. Perhaps eager to impress, Leonard poured gas on the wood fire to hasten the inflation for the next show. The balloon "suddenly caught fire and burst, sending a sheet of flame high into the air

This glass lantern slide shows Professor John Leonard dangling from a trapeze high above the crowds at Dawson City. After his acrobatic display, he would deploy a parachute and plunge into the river, or, on one unlucky occasion, onto a corrugated iron roof.

and consuming the fabric." John Diston, a workman who was assisting Leonard, burned his face. Luckily, though Diston's injuries were painful, they were not serious, and Leonard escaped all harm. The balloon, on the other hand, was completely destroyed.[34]

Within a week, Leonard had built a new, stronger balloon and planned to give a performance on the afternoon of Saturday, June 9. However, the show was delayed so that Leonard could coat the balloon with a varnish, using a "sort of glazing process." The town dug a large furnace on First Avenue to inflate the balloon when it was ready. At last, on June 11, with clear skies and no wind, Leonard set to work readying the balloon. Once again it caught fire, but he and his assistants extinguished it and applied a patch over the damaged area. At 9:00 p.m., the balloon lifted above the town and Leonard completed his trapeze and parachute act, landing gracefully halfway up the hill behind Dawson. "The aeronaut," the newspapers reported, "was rewarded with a generous contribution from the crowd which appeared to be well satisfied with his performance." When he left Dawson a week later, bound for Nome, Alaska, Dawsonites gave him a miniature balloon with a parachute attached, as well as a bar pin made of "three handsome nuggets."[35]

Leonard returned for his fourth and final tour of the territory in May 1903 with his new balloon *Island Mail* in tow. He told reporters he intended to make an ascent in Dawson City, another at Grand Forks, and a third "somewhere else."[36] That "somewhere else" turned out to be the small town of "White Horse," which would not become the territorial capital we

know today until 1953. In Leonard's time, it was mostly a tent city with a population of about one thousand people. It may have been a small town, but every man, woman, and child appeared on the dirt streets that May 25 evening, and newspapers reported, "no more highly enthusiastic assemblage ever gathered" to witness the "Prince of the Air" perform.

The balloon "hung suspended like a large tent" in the middle of the street when Leonard appeared at 7:30 p.m. He called out to the men in the crowd to assist him with the final inflation, and about twenty came to his aid. Then, once everything was in position, he lit "the fire in the furnace and the splendid balloon began to show its graceful outlines." A half-hour later, it "floated in the air, straining at her moorings." With a flourish, Leonard ordered the helpers to let go, then "grasped the bar of the parachute and away he went" to an altitude of six hundred metres, where he released the parachute and "aeroplaned it the entire breadth of the river" before touching down on solid ground.

After this triumph Leonard practised his "high art" again at Dawson, on June 25, and once again went for a dip in the Yukon River, which still had a "silvery border of ice." This time, "he was compelled to cut loose from the balloon at a point just over the worst part of the river current" when the balloon began to lose altitude." Luckily his swim was relatively short, as a canoe was waiting nearby to retrieve him. "The ascension was quite a successful one," the newspapers noted. "The icy plunge making it even better than expected, for really the biggest thing about a balloon ascension is the close shaves."

One thousand spectators had lined First Avenue to watch the show. It was certainly a respectable number and on par with the crowd at Whitehorse, but it was a huge drop from the nearly fifteen thousand who were in the area when he had first come. At the end of the summer season, he told the Yukon papers he was headed for the St. Louis World's Fair, where he was to "have a flying machine built on the same principle as Count Von Zeppelin's famous contrivance." The opening of the fair, however, was delayed by a year. When it began on April 30, 1904, Leonard — whether he was actually slated to perform or not — was once again laid up. Shortly before, he had "suffered internal injuries and the breaking of both his legs" when his balloon hit a wall during a performance in Seattle.[37] Was it the accident that ended his northern career, or did the territory's waning population make a return trip unprofitable? Either way, the "Prince of the Air" disappears from Yukon history as abruptly as he appeared — but not before making his mark on the northern stage.

"THE THING IS SO DIFFICULT THAT I CANNOT HELP ATTEMPTING IT"

Leonard holds the distinction of being the first and only "balloonatic" north of 60, but Variclé, that seasoned aeronaut, had not given up his dreams. In 1900 he told reporters he would try to make the trip from Skagway to Dawson City the following spring, and hoped to one day fly over the Sahara.[38] First, though, he said he would make an aerial attempt to reach the North Pole.

Variclé was far from the only one trying to reach this "soul-stirring" spot on the map.[39] On July 11, 1897, Variclé's friend, the Swedish balloonist Salomon August Andrée, made one of the first aerial attempts at the pole when he departed Danes Island, Spitsbergen (Norway), with two companions in their balloon, the *Eagle*. They vanished, and it would be thirty-three years before their final camp was discovered on the arctic ice. Their diaries and photographic film told how fog and frost had brought down the balloon, and how they had all died after a two-and-a-half month trek across the unstable ice.[40]

The loss of Andrée and his companions did not deter others from making the attempt. For adventurers like the American journalist Walter Wellman, who made bids for the Pole in 1906, 1907, and 1909 in his airship the *America*, ego and determination trumped fear. Wellman may have also operated in blissful ignorance. As pilot and author John Grierson writes, Wellman "did not have a scientific background" and did not understand "the inherent danger of trying to fly low through Arctic fog, where moisture and hoar-frost were bound to spell disaster to a gas bag."[41]

National pride and the potential of acquiring territory for one's country were also central to the race for the North Pole and exploration of the area more generally. Canada's claims in the region appeared vulnerable at the time due to the vague terms Great Britain had used when it transferred jurisdiction over the area to its Dominion in 1880. The Alaska boundary dispute had also simmered from 1821 to 1903 and coloured this period with fears of a Russian or American land grab — even if the North Pole was more holy grail than terra firma.[42]

Preus Museum Archive

Mechanic Oscar Omdal with Roald Amundsen's Dornier-Wal *N25* flying boat in 1925. Amundsen received the first Norwegian pilot's licence in 1912 after learning to fly near Oslo, and made several attempts to reach the North Pole using heavier-than-air craft, including a Junkers J13 all-metal monoplane, a Curtis-Oriole biplane, and *N25*. In the end, Americans Floyd Bennett and Richard E. Byrd asserted they reached the Pole in 1926, but historians still debate their claim.

Of course, the potential for riches was another motive, or at least a way for explorers to gain the support of their governments and investors. Variclé, for example, created the International Yukon Polar Institute on August 5, 1905, for the "exploration and development of the Polar Regions" — although by then he had decided dogsleds would be more successful than airships. While he cited the scientific importance and aims of the organization, he mostly promoted "the fact that great wealth has lain dormant in the frigid zone for centuries, and that but a very small portion of this wealth has yet been retrieved."[43] In the end, Variclé did not reach the North Pole by air or

land. He left the Yukon to promote his Institute and died in 1907 in a Seattle hospital.[44]

Two years later, Americans Robert E. Peary and Frederick A. Cook both claimed to have reached the pole on foot. This discouraged further aerial attempts at the time, except for the ever-determined journalist Wellman, who tried once more with his airship *America* in August. When he had to abort that trip after two hours, he finally decided against further bids for the Pole.[45]

It would be more than a decade before others once again took up the challenge of reaching the North Pole by air.[46] Roald Amundsen, the Norwegian explorer who had successfully reached the South Pole in

1911, tried to fly across the Arctic twice in the early 1920s. First, in 1923, he and fellow Norwegian Oscar Omdal made an attempt in a Curtiss Oriole, *Kristine,* a two-seat open cockpit biplane on skis. They left from Wainwright, Alaska, but had to abandon the plan when the aircraft was damaged. Then, in May 1925, Amundsen and an American, Lincoln Ellsworth, used two Dornier-Wal flying boats — called simply *N24* and *N25* — to head for the Pole. Engine trouble forced them down onto the ice. After a harrowing time, during which they had to repair the engines and construct their own runway, they managed to fly themselves to safety.[47]

The year 1926 saw several bids for the Pole. Amundsen, Ellsworth, and an Italian Army colonel, Umberto Nobile, were in King's Bay, Spitsbergen with the *Norge* airship making preparations. At the same time, an Australian, George Hubert Wilkins, readied to depart Point Barrow, Alaska, with pilot Carl Ben Eilson, aboard a Fokker F.VII Trimotor called the *Detroiter*.[48] On May 9, 1926, an American Navy Lieutenant, Richard E. Byrd, departed King's Bay in the same type of Fokker Trimotor ski plane — the *Josephine Ford* — piloted by Floyd Bennett. He returned 15.5 hours later "reporting that he had successfully reached the North Pole," and cited his use of a sun compass, drift indicator, and two chronometers set at Greenwich Mean Time for factual accuracy.[49] Many, however, have cast doubt on his claim, saying the Fokker did not have the necessary range to complete the 2,400-kilometre round trip, nor enough speed to cover the distance in the reported time. As author Bruce McAllister

notes, "To this date, nobody has conclusively proved that Byrd and Bennett did or did not fly over the North Pole that fateful day."[50]

Regardless, Amundsen, Ellsworth, and Nobile decided to turn their attention to being the first to fly across the entire Arctic.[51] On May 11, 1926, they and a team of about a dozen men set off from Spitsbergen aboard the *Norge* airship. Sixteen hours later, "after battling wind, cold, snow, fog, and frozen water in the engine fuel lines, the *Norge* reached the North Pole." While there, the international crew dropped flags: Amundsen and Ellsworth left behind small Norwegian and American flags, while Nobile, much to the irritation of the others, unfurled and released a much larger Italian one. Their voyage ended approximately seventy hours later, when they set down at the Inuit settlement of Teller, Alaska — 5,117 kilometres from their point of departure.

In the following years aeronauts continued their attempts, often with loss of equipment and life. Perhaps one of the most tragic instances occurred May 23, 1928, when Nobile once again left for the Pole, this time in the airship *Italia*. The *Italia* crashed and tons of supplies as well as ten men spilled out onto the ice. "Suddenly lightened," author Stewart B. Nelson writes, "the *Italia* soared upward and disappeared forever, with six men still aboard." Nobile, who was severely injured, was fortunate that an operable emergency radio was among the items dumped on the ice pack. Even so, it was twelve days before a Russian farmer using a ham radio picked up their distress signals. Immediately Norway, Sweden, and Russia sent ships and two Italian flying

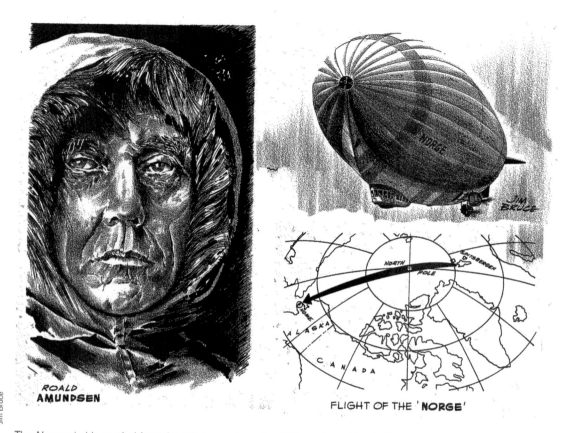

ROALD
AMUNDSEN

FLIGHT OF THE 'NORGE'

Jim Bruce

The *Norge* airship carried famed explorers such as Roald Amundsen, Lincoln Ellsworth, and Umberto Nobile across the Arctic from Spitsbergen to the North Pole on May 11, 1926, after travelling sixteen hours. It would be another seventy hours before they touched down at the Inuit settlement of Teller, Alaska.

boats — a Dornier-Wal and Savoia-Marchetti S.55 — to aid in the search. Amundsen even came out of retirement to help, leaving from Tromso, Norway, in a French Latham 47 flying boat to aid in the search. In a sad twist of fate, he vanished during this rescue mission and was never seen again. Finally, on June 20, an Italian airplane spotted the survivors, but it took a month and an international rescue effort to pick up Nobile and the few remaining *Italia* crew.

While pilots continued to chart courses for the North Pole and the Arctic in heavier-than-air craft, the time for airship expeditions soon ended as high-profile accidents coincided with the rise in popularity of airplanes. The end of the airship era came on July 31, 1931, when the *Graf Zeppelin* returned to Friedrichschafen, Germany, after a largely uneventful rendezvous with the Russian icebreaker *Malygin* at Franz Joseph Land. One crew member described it as nothing more than a "circus flight" to attract public attention, and served no real navigational or technological ends. Even so, Nobile and Ellsworth, who were among the first explorers to set their sights on the Pole, were fittingly involved in the airship's swan song.[52]

THE ORIGINAL AERONAUTS OF CANADA'S NORTH were much like the prospectors drawn to the Klondike. Many were inventors, dreamers, and schemers looking to hit pay dirt with an airship route to the gold fields, or perform their "balloonatics" to dazzled crowds. Others were explorers seeking personal and national glory in Arctic skies. Like the Klondike gold rush, aviation at this time was limited to tiny postage-stamp-sized areas: Dawson City, the North Pole, and its international launching grounds in Alaska and Norway. Soon, the aeronauts and balloonists trying to make a name for themselves — and make some money — in the North would give way to the first bush pilots and military-backed expeditions.

CHAPTER 2

The Era of Expeditions

During the first two decades of the twentieth century, aviation in the Canadian North shifted from international airships and aeronauts, to homegrown initiatives. Buoyed by J.A.D. McCurdy's *Silver Dart* and the success of Americans such as the Wright brothers, northern flyers went to great lengths to gain altitude. Many of these early bush pilots were veterans of the First World War and had seen first-hand how useful aviation could be for scouting terrain and transporting people and supplies. They also quickly realized that flying in the North required careful planning and made-in-the-bush solutions.

YUKON AIR-MINDEDNESS

A decade after the Klondike gold rush, Dawson City was still a mining centre — albeit a much smaller one. Its population had continued to fall after the days of Professor Leonard and Antoine Variclé, and by 1910 there were about two thousand people in town. As resident Laura Berton recalled, while the hotels were doing well, the dance-hall era was over and Second and Third Avenues were "on the verge of becoming a desert of second-hand shops and junk yards. Some of the buildings were already vacant and the windows boarded up."[1] Nevertheless, Dawson was a cosmopolitan city with citizens from every continent, and stores carried the latest Paris fashions and Japanese kimonos.

As in the gold rush days, getting Outside was still a challenge. The Yukon River was the main form of transportation, and at the turn of the century, British Yukon Navigation Co. steamers travelled back and forth between Dawson and Whitehorse, taking two days downstream and three and a half days up. The steamers ran while the water was open, from mid-June to the end of October, while in winter, travel was restricted to a trail the government had constructed between the two cities in 1902. The White Pass & Yukon Route (WP&YR) ran a tri-weekly stagecoach service using Concord coaches until there was enough snow for a sleigh. As Berton remembered, the overland stage to Dawson in February was far from luxurious. She and thirteen other passengers rode in the open sleigh for a week, often braving temperatures of forty below, stopping every thirty-five kilometres at roadhouses along the way. But at least it meant movement of people and goods: when the river was impassable during freeze-up and breakup, the town was essentially cut off from the outside.

DCM Archives/1998.22.734

Dolar De Lagrave constructed and tested this glider in 1927 in Dawson City, Yukon. He had joined the Klondike Gold Rush in 1899, and never returned to his family in Quebec, opting instead to remain in Dawson as a tailor and inventor.

It was these ongoing transportation challenges — as well as a growing sense of air-mindedness — that encouraged Yukoners to create new aviation schemes. In 1909 J.A.D. McCurdy executed the first heavier-than-air flight in the British Empire when his aircraft, the *Silver Dart*, took flight in Baddeck, Nova Scotia. It may have been over seven thousand kilometres away, but it inflamed the imaginations of those living in the territory. Dolar De Lagrave was the first in the Yukon to turn this interest in aviation into an actual flying machine.[2] He had left his family behind in Quebec to seek riches during the Klondike gold rush and never returned, opting instead to stay in Dawson and work as a tailor and inventor. In the fall of 1910 he constructed a biplane glider with a wingspan of 4.5 metres to test aeronautical theories. His methods of testing, however, were more foolhardy than scientific: "Mr. De Lagrave," noted the *Dawson*

Weekly News, "simply puts his arms through supports, and plunges off the prow of the hill, letting the wind assist the air."

At the time there were also reports he was building an airship with the support of his fellow Dawsonites, and he may have been behind the March 1918 plans for a fifty-seat flying machine to go between Dawson and Skagway.[3] Nothing came of either of these schemes, unfortunately, but he continued to build and test gliders in Dawson until his death in 1938.

THE FIRST ALASKA AIR EXPEDITION

De Lagrave may also have been inspired by early brushes with aviation in the Yukon. He was in Dawson in June 1913, for example, when the first airplane arrived in the territory, although he never saw it fly. Indeed, no one did: the Gage-Martin tractor biplane and its pilot, James V. Martin, travelled by train to Whitehorse and then on to Fairbanks by stern wheeler. The airplane was crated the whole time it was in the Yukon.[4]

He and other Yukoners likely had their first contact with airborne planes in August 1920. That month, the First Alaska Air Expedition arrived in the Yukon with much fanfare. The expedition involved eight U.S. Army airmen flying from New York to Nome, Alaska, in four open-cockpit D.H.4Bs, which were left over from the First World War. As author and pilot John Grierson notes, this was "an extremely ambitious target for any aeroplane in those days, even over the flattest and easiest flying country."[5] And the section of the trip from Edmonton to Nome was anything but easy. It involved some very challenging topography, which the pilots tackled with rudimentary maps, no radio, and very little information about the weather they might encounter.[6] The U.S.

and Canadian governments were willing to take these risks, however, to explore the feasibility of establishing air routes to the North for civilian and defence purposes.

The two countries had begun preparing in June. Captain H.T. Douglas of the U.S. Army Air Service and Captain H.A. LeRoyer of the Canadian Air Force travelled by steamer to make arrangements at Whitehorse, Dawson City, and various places in Alaska for refueling sites. At Whitehorse, the only place considered suitable for landing was the golf course west of town, which sat on government land leased to lumberman Antoine "Tony" Cyr. Councillor Robert Lowe oversaw the project to turn the course into an airfield, which involved a team of about ten men, including Cyr, clearing "scattered clumps" of pine trees and brush to make a landing field of roughly 450 by 115 metres and "slashing" the trees on the north and south ends to make the approach easier. By July 2, the Air Force signed off on the work, and the landing field was ready for use.[7]

Councillor Robert Lowe gives a welcome speech following the landing of Captain Streett at the Whitehorse, Yukon, airfield on Discovery Day, which fell on Tuesday, August 17, 1920. The other three U.S. Army Air Service aircraft of the First Alaska Air Expedition had landed the previous day, becoming the first heavier-than-air craft to land in the territory.

When the planes departed New York on July 15, local interest — which was already high — reached a fevered pitch. Newspapers updated Yukoners on the expedition's progress and the many hazards the flyers faced between Edmonton and Whitehorse: burst oil pipes; a forest fire over the Pembina River country; the grounding of the fleet in Prince George, British Columbia, after a hard landing, among others.[8]

On August 16, three of the aircraft finally arrived in Whitehorse (the fourth had to stay behind because of a nicked propeller). Whitehorse was still a sleepy little town that had shrunk to three hundred people after the boom years at the turn of the century, but the population turned out in force. After all, the arrival of a steamer or train was big news, so the first airplanes were not to be missed. Laura Berton remembered that "the entire village flocked up the hill to look at the strange machines, which seemed to be all wire and struts."[9] Another resident, Frances Watson, wrote her friend that she had a perfect view of the landing field: "I stood on the balcony of the old hospital where I was nursing and was thrilled to see the three [airplanes] coming in formation." She observed that local indigenous people had been getting ready for a funeral "just as the planes came in." When the procession spotted them, however, "the group of young men quickly placed the casket in a nearby wooded area and went up to the airport. As soon as the planes left they returned and carried on to the burial ground." After all, Watson remarked, "No hurry there."[10]

When the town learned the fourth and final airplane was due to arrive the next day, there was another rush of people to the aerodrome.[11] The *Weekly Star* reported on the scene: "Three cheers burst from the crowd as the captain, smiling and happy, stepped from his cramped quarters and shook hands with the excited assembly, many of whom were old timers of Yukon and had never seen an aeroplane before."

From Whitehorse, two of the pilots departed for Dawson City, where four thousand people had gathered for a Discovery Day celebration to mark the Klondike gold rush. Minto Park, on the south side of town, was decorated with flags and streamers and the celebration was well under way when two of the aircraft came into sight mid-afternoon. Someone in the crowd yelled, "Here they come, here they come!" and everyone looked to the sky. They then quickly deserted the park for the ferry landing to catch a ride across the river to Dr. G.M. Faulkner's Field in West Dawson. Dawson's power, telephone, and telegraph wires made it dangerous for the pilots to land near town.

The following day the weather was overcast when Captains Streett and Crumrine, who had stayed in Whitehorse to repair a blown tire, flew to Dawson to rejoin their comrades. On his way in, Streett had a very near miss: the ferry the spectators had used the day before employed a cable strung about thirty metres above the river. Streett, according to the *Yukon News,* "had not been told about the overhanging cable as no one had figured any of the flyers would be coming in that low." Luckily, he saw it just in time: "He keeled over on one wing, dipped under the cable and flew on to land safely." Apparently, even once he was out of his plane and on the ground, the veteran airman was trembling from his experience. He admitted it had been the closest call of his life.

LAC/ PA-101569

One of the U.S. Army Air Service's D.H.4B open cockpit biplanes takes off from the hastily constructed airfield in West Dawson on August 17, 1920. It was the First Alaska Air Expedition's final Canadian stop en route to Nome, Alaska.

After they had steeled their nerves and rested their weary bodies overnight, the flyers left for Fairbanks and then on to Nome. While it was the final destination of their arduous cross-continent trek, they still had to get their machines home again. Locals were again delighted when the pilots flew through the territory a week later, and made them honorary northerners by inducting them into the Yukon Order of Pioneers.

"A MAN OF EXCEPTIONAL SKILL AND PLUCK"

In 1922 the Yukon received its next aerial visitor, who was also flying to Nome from New York. However, instead of a well-organized military operation, it was a solo pilot relying on the generosity of the crowds he entertained en route. Clarence Oliver Prest was a twenty-nine-year-old Iowa native who had been in the "flying game" for over

a decade.[12] He told Yukon reporters he had been an instructor for the American Flying Corps during the First World War, and afterward, had gotten into auto racing and motorcycle stunting. Then, like many out-of-work pilots after the war, he started flying from town to town barnstorming — that is, performing aerial feats and selling airplane rides to local residents. The year before, he had made his first attempt to reach Alaska in a modified Standard J-1 biplane, *Polar Bear*. He had managed to fly without incident from Tijuana, Mexico, up the coast to Prince Rupert, British Columbia. There, however, he not only got thrown in jail for illegal exhibition work, but his plane cracked up in a heavy wind and he was forced to start over.

On his second attempt, in 1922, Prest left from Buffalo, New York, in early June, flying a brand-new J-1 biplane, the *Polar Bear II,* across the U.S., making enough money at each stop to fund the next leg of the journey. At Seattle he and his airplane boarded a ship and sailed for Juneau, Alaska, where he did a fifteen-minute exhibition that included the loop-the-loop, side-slip, and a number of other stunts. Then on July 6, he made the first aircraft landing at Skagway before departing for Whitehorse, where he set down at "Cyr's airfield" — the same spot the Alaska Expedition had used in 1920. There, Prest was met by the local RCMP, who had been warned about his legal tangle in Prince Rupert the year before. This time, however, he had registered the aircraft with the Air Board in Ottawa before his departure. After filling out a ship's "Bill of Health" form — since there were no aircraft forms yet available — and applying Canadian registration letters to the fuselage, he was allowed to continue on.

There was one snag: the Canadian officials informed him he could not do any exhibition work or carry passengers because it would be unfair competition to Canadian flyers. This was a major blow to Prest and his ability to fund the rest of his flight. When residents of Dawson City heard of this, though, they petitioned to allow him to perform there. Prest could not "disadvantage Canadian aviators" in the territory, they argued — there were none!

Lucky for Prest and would-be spectators at Dawson, the Air Board agreed. With all the bureaucracy sorted out, he departed Whitehorse in his plane, now sporting registration N-CACH, on July 10, bound for Dawson. On his way he stopped at Selkirk — the first aircraft to do so — and decided to stay there until he was sure the landing site at Dawson was ready. The next day, after he received the all-clear, he took off. It

was overcast, but he was not too concerned as the ceiling was high and the Yukon River provided many beaches and sandbars for emergency landings.

As Prest flew toward Dawson, people in places like Quartz Creek kept an eye on the skies and telephoned his position. In Dawson, the telegraph and *Dawson Daily News* offices posted bulletins for the excited townspeople. Dawsonite Archie Turnbull hurried to the landing field in West Dawson when he heard the plane was nearby. Turnbull, who had been with the American Flying Corps as well, had been charged with preparing the runway as no airplanes had used Faulkner's Field for two years. The north end, which the U.S. Army flyers had used, was covered with heavy hay, so Turnbull placed a white cross made of cheesecloth on the south end to mark where the plane should land. He also lit smudges so Prest could watch the smoke for wind direction.

At the same time, the fire chief sounded the fire bell and war siren to alert the town to Prest's impending arrival, and in spite of the early hour, a number of citizens took the ferry across the river. A special reception committee and RCMP constables were also on hand, but unlike at Whitehorse, they had been engaged to stand guard over the plane — not Prest. While he was thrilled at the warm welcome, the pilot had to tell the disappointed crowd he would not take up any passengers while in Dawson to conserve his plane: "I'm carrying practically no spare parts ... and I have to go easy with the machine." He reassured them, however, that he would perform a twenty-minute exhibition that Saturday evening.

On the appointed day, people came from across town and even the gold creeks

Claude Tidd, YA/007794

American aviator Clarence Prest and RCMP officer Claude Tidd stand by Prest's Standard J-1 biplane, nicknamed *Polar Bear II*, in a field near Whitehorse in July 1922. To avoid legal tangles, Prest had to fill out a ship's "Bill of Health" form and apply Canadian registration letters, switching N-CACH to G-CACH on the fuselage.

to watch the show. At 8:30 p.m. Prest took off from the newly cleared beach in front of Dawson and rose to a height of about six hundred metres. Then, "turning over the north end of town, the flyer pointed her prow downward, in the dare-devil nose dive, and shot so close to the ground" that spectators worried he would crash. Instead, the local newspaper reported, "he gave a graceful twist that sent the plane skimming on the horizontal and she shot by with a thrilling 'zoom' and soared away into the distance above the Klondike and the Yukon rivers." On his way back, he did a "beautiful spiral" and landed, by all accounts, quite gracefully on the beach. Everyone was thrilled with the performance, and fêted him at the tourist dance held afterward. In addition to giving and receiving

a short address to honour the occasion (as well as a purse the equivalent of $6,500 collected by the audience), the press noted the young pilot danced with "many of Dawson's charming young ladies."

On July 15 he left Dawson bound for Fairbanks, Alaska, with a quick stop at Eagle.[13] With him, he took letters destined for those Alaskan locales as well as copies of the *Dawson Daily News*. He also took on board what was apparently the Yukon's first international cargo shipment: a bottle of cough syrup sent from Chief Isaac of the local Tr'ondëk Hwëch'in to Porcupine Pane, an indigenous man at Eagle.

Yukoners respected Prest, saying only "a man of exceptional skill and pluck would venture, as he is doing, to cross Yukon and Alaska alone in an airplane."

Nevertheless, some wondered if he had overestimated his abilities. This was especially the case when he and his plane went missing in the bush 120 kilometres from Eagle. He had been forced to make two landings to deal with engine troubles on his way to Eagle, and once there he told reporters he "planned a general overhauling of the engine on arrival at Fairbanks," but insisted on pressing on. "Prest took unusual risks in attempting to cross such a wide stretch with an engine in unsatisfactory condition and with little or no food," observed the reporter for the *Dawson Daily News*. "Few experienced woodsmen or northern travelers familiar with … local conditions will plunge into such a region without food. Some few have been known to live off the rifle," he conceded, but Prest did not have one.

Luckily, Archie Turnbull had given Prest a thirty-two-calibre automatic pistol in Dawson in case of emergency, and the pilot put this to good use. When his plane went down in bad weather, it miraculously crashed into a herd of caribou. He shot one with the pistol and was able to butcher it with a pocket knife. After roasting the steaks over a fire he had started with aviation gasoline (or avgas as it is commonly known), he took shelter from the rain in the tail of the airplane. The miserable weather continued, and when a strong wind flipped the machine over so he could no longer sleep in it, he decided to try to make his way to Eagle on foot. His incredible luck continued: he picked up a trail and found an empty dry cabin on his third night, and then ran into one of the search parties on the trail, seventy-two kilometres from Eagle. He was tired and sick of eating caribou, but otherwise unhurt.

The aircraft, however, was a write-off, and according to Prest, "utterly impossible" to move. Even with this second crack-up, and agonizingly close to his goal, Prest was undaunted. He told reporters he would try again the next year, but, having seen all the rivers and lakes in the Northwest, he would fly a "hydroplane" instead so he could land on water. Yukoners were also unphased by what could have been seen as a major setback for aviation in the territory. Even after his crash, the editor of the *Dawson Daily News* suggested the high-profile search had given the territory positive international exposure: "The whole Prest exploit gives the Northland a great and gripping advertisement far and near."[14]

"MADE IN THE BUSH"

In their rhetoric about Prest's expedition, journalists drew parallels with another aviation undertaking north of 60: the 1921 Imperial Oil flight into the Northwest Territories. Both flights, the *Dawson Daily News* argued, directed "fresh attention to the possibility of regular air service in the Northland." They also showed that aviation facilities and demand were sorely lacking — at least for the moment.

On August 27, 1920, Imperial Oil drills had struck black gold at Fort Norman (now called Tulita) and the world's focus turned north. The local Dene First Nation had known about the oil's presence for centuries and used its "residue to smear and waterproof their canoes."[15] In 1789 explorer Sir Alexander Mackenzie had also noted oil in the area, but outsiders did not search for the resource until the early twentieth century. The First World War interrupted their work until 1919, when Imperial Oil sent in two geologists and a six-person drilling team. The information they gathered during that trip was enough to set off what could have been a "speculative spree," even though it took eight weeks to travel by rail and dog team from Edmonton in winter, or five to ten days in summer by boat with several difficult portages.[16] To prevent a free-for-all, the federal government introduced regulations to make small mineral claims unappealing, and the RCMP put restrictions on winter travel down the Mackenzie River.[17]

Imperial Oil also took steps to protect its interests by quickly setting up its own air service. This, it was hoped, would get employees to the well before the rivers were navigable and before would-be competitors, such as Northern Canada Traders Ltd., could send its own aircraft to Fort Norman.[18] In September 1920, Imperial Oil hired May-Gorman Aeroplanes, owned by war veterans Wilfrid "Wop" May and George W. Gorman, to establish operations. The Edmonton pilots, along with air mechanic Pete Derbyshire, began their work by flying to the railhead at Peace River, likely to find a suitable base of operations.[19] Gorman was tasked with choosing which type of aircraft Imperial Oil should purchase, and decided on two Junkers-Larsen JL-6s, which were the world's first all-metal transport aircraft. He and May then had to get the aircraft from the factory in New York to Edmonton in January 1921 — a frigid cross-country trip.

At this point, May took his leave from the operation to pursue other projects, but Gorman continued to work with Imperial Air Services on careful preparations for the upcoming flight to Fort Norman. The company designed and built skis for *Vic* (G-CADP) and *René* (G-CADQ), as the two aircraft were now called, and undertook the first ski flights in western Canada. There were major risks involved in flying north from Edmonton, as Canada's former Director of Civil Aviation J.R.K. Main noted: this was the "first winter operation of any magnitude undertaken in Canada," and "little was known about the steps needed to make winter flying safe."[20] But the Imperial Air Services crews were determined. On March 22, 1920, the flyers — Elmer Fullerton, George Gorman, George Thompson, and air engineer William J. Hill — departed to stash fuel at the Hudson Bay Company post at Upper Hay River, Alberta, about halfway to Great Slave Lake. This flight went off without a hitch, and the men were cautiously optimistic when they left for Fort Norman on March 24.[21]

Their optimism was soon tested. The multi-day journey was fraught with bad weather, heavy winds, detours, and unknown landing conditions. At Fort Providence, for example, they landed in a field adjoining the HBC post in a metre of snow. In order to get out the next day, they and several Dene men had to tramp down a runway using snowshoes. A landing at Fort Simpson presented them with an almost insurmountable challenge. As the pilots neared the settlement in a light snowstorm, they looked for a place to set down. The surface of the Mackenzie River looked "extremely rough," so they aimed for a nearby field. Unfortunately, it was riddled with snowdrifts. *René* nose-dived into them, damaging its propeller, undercarriage, and wingtip. Fullerton, who was piloting *Vic*, saw what happened and landed safely in a nearby channel.

NWT Archives/Fred Jackson fonds/N-79-004:0075

In March 1921, Imperial Oil sent two Junkers-Larsen JL-6 airplanes from Edmonton to Fort Norman, Northwest Territories, to secure its claims at what would become Norman Wells. En route, the planes encountered a series of calamities and bush solutions. Pictured is G-CADP, nicknamed *Vic*, at the Fort Simpson Roman Catholic Mission with the flight crew, RCMP officers, and possibly Chief Antoine of the local Dene.

The next day they decided Fullerton would go on to Fort Norman, but *Vic* had developed engine trouble over the previous days' flights, so they cannibalized *Vic*, fitted the parts to *René*, and decided to send it on instead. When Gorman attempted to take off, however, "it rocked, nose-dived, and shivered the second propeller to atoms." The crews were able to draw on local help to get the machines up and running again, which involved one particularly stunning piece of bush-flying ingenuity: Hill and Walter Johnson, the HBC boat's engineer and general handyman, spent two weeks making a new propeller out of sleigh board and moose glue. This was done in the relative comfort of the Roman Catholic Mission workshop, where Father Decoux, O.M.I. offered them tools and whatever they could find to use as clamps.

By the time the propeller was ready, installed, and tested, the Dene at Fort Simpson warned the aircrews that the ice on the Liard River might go out before their planned departure date of April 24.

Fullerton and company ignored them, which nearly cost them all their hard work. Luckily, a local Métis man, Henri Lafferty, woke them early on the morning of the twenty-fourth, shouting that the ice was breaking up. They jumped into their clothes and snowshoes, and hurried over to *Vic*, taking off just in time and landing the plane on a still-frozen lake nearby. According to HBC post manager Phillip H. Godsell, "only about 400 feet of solid ice remained for a take-off — while a foot of muddy water was already swirling above the skis." That evening, Godsell and the other HBC workers ferried Gorman, two mechanics, and their guide, Jack Cameron, to *Vic* in a canoe. By then they had received word from Imperial, however, to return to Edmonton, as the well at Norman had failed to make any fuel for the Junkers. So they headed south in *Vic* while *René* remained at Fort Simpson with Gorman, Hill, and Johnson to await parts.

In late May Imperial sent Fullerton and *Vic* back to Fort Norman to take geologist Theodor A. Link up for a reconnaissance flight of the district. They were plagued with engine and radiator trouble as well as bad weather, but finally managed to do the flight on August 6, completing "a survey that would have taken months on foot." *Vic* rejoined *René* at Fort Simpson, and by August 21 the airplanes were ready to depart for the south in convoy.

Their troubles were not over yet. One final insult (and injury) occurred when *René* came in for its landing at Peace River: while trying to avoid a cable ferry at the last minute, the right pontoon struck a log or rock beneath the water's surface and there was a "terrific crash." All the people aboard were safe — Gorman, Hill, Johnson, reporter Chester Bloom, and Imperial employee Ronald W. MacKinnon — but one of the two husky puppies they had with them drowned.

René was salvaged the next day, but it was a write-off. *Vic* was fine, but Imperial Oil still decided to shut down its air service. It put *Vic* into storage in Edmonton, along with parts from *René*, and sold everything the next year. The experiment had cost them quite a bit in machines, men, and hangar construction at Peace River, but it had shown that surveys by aircraft — when they worked — were useful and efficient. The trips had also illustrated the importance of good ski technology and proper float training.

AIRPLANES TO THE ARCTIC

In the 1920s Canada also began undertaking aerial expeditions even further afield. In response to an increased American presence in the Arctic, the Canadian Coast Guard ship *Arctic* had begun a series of patrols to the far North at the beginning of the century.[22] The country's attention turned

elsewhere during the First World War, but by 1922, the Federal Department of the Interior looked north again, both over sovereignty concerns and with the aim of enforcing a Canadian-style justice system over Inuit. In that year, it decided it would set up RCMP posts in the region, and asked for the co-operation of the Air Board.

Before dispatching any planes, the RCAF wisely sent Squadron Leader R.A. Logan to do reconnaissance. Logan, a land surveyor familiar with northern conditions and an experienced flying officer who knew meteorology and navigation, departed Quebec City July 18, 1922, aboard *Arctic*. During the next two and a half months, Logan and his team visited Baffin, Bylot, the north of Devon and Ellesmere Islands, and began marking the site for the "world's most northerly air strip" on the latter.

Logan recommended setting up detachments and investigating the use of airships, which he thought would be ideal in the Arctic. These would allow Canadian authorities to watch the movement of ice and report conditions to ships. As Logan wrote in his report, perhaps concerned about the relatively recent Bolshevik Revolution in Russia, it would also be useful for the defence of Canada, Great Britain, and Europe, against what he called "the Slavs." He also reported airships could be used to transport surveyors and track animal populations.

Unlike many of his contemporaries, Logan was able to appreciate local expertise. He recommended that a local Inuk ride along on each flight in case of forced landing and suggested that personnel should wear clothing as "similar in every way to that worn by the natives of the islands." Shoes should be the waterproof *kamiks* made of sealskin he had encountered, and socks should be

R.S. Finnie/LAC

American Navy Lieutenant Richard E. Byrd's Loening COA-1 amphibious biplane approaching the stern of the SS *Peary*. The ship and airplanes were used by U.S. Navy as part of the MacMillan Expedition to claim territory in the Arctic in August 1925, and were the first heavier-than-air craft in the Canadian Arctic.

sealskin with the fur inside. Because Inuit women traditionally repaired clothing, he advised the RCAF employ them at each base. Finally, Logan said station personnel should learn the local dialect of Inuktitut.

The next step, Logan said, would be to send two small, specially equipped aircraft and their crews with an Arctic expedition. They could then "establish an air base, and conduct flying operations throughout the year" to observe local conditions and gather data. Unfortunately, while the Air Board agreed with his findings, by then it had merged with the Department of National Defence, and Canada's aviation policy had changed direction. Ships continued to patrol the Arctic — indeed annual expeditions were sent between 1922 and 1926 — but the RCAF would not be involved.[23]

Instead, the first flyers in the Canadian Arctic were Americans. In August 1925, the U.S. Navy sent three identical Loening COA-1 amphibious biplanes by ship to Greenland under Lieutenant Commander Donald MacMillan.[24] The MacMillan Expedition, as it became known, landed the planes on Ellesmere Island's Hayes and Flagler Fiords — without prior Canadian approval. As historian Shelagh Grant notes, the Americans considered much of the archipelago as *terra nullius,* and sought uncharted lands near the North Pole to potentially use as an advance defence post. The Canadians, in an attempt to assert sovereignty over the region, first had the RCMP undertake a major sled patrol from Craig Harbour across Ellesmere Island to Axel Heiberg in the winter of 1925. The next year, the government created the Arctic Islands Game Preserve to underline its claims.

HUDSON STRAIT

The RCAF did not get its first polar air experience until 1927, when it launched the Hudson Strait Expedition.[25] A railway had been built to carry grain within Manitoba from The Pas to Churchill on the coast of the Hudson Bay. From the railhead, ships would bring the cargo through the Hudson Strait to markets in Europe. The trouble, as author Larry Milberry notes, was the Canadian government "knew little of navigation conditions" in the area and "rushed to correct the situation" using the RCAF, Royal Canadian Corps of Signals, and the Department of Marine and Fisheries.[26]

The RCAF expedition was commanded by Squadron Leader Thomas A. Lawrence and consisted of six officers, twelve airmen, four personnel from the signal corps, three RCMP constables, and nineteen civilians who were to build the bases.[27] The six aircraft selected were rugged Fokker Universal monoplanes, with registrations from G-CAHE to G-CAHJ. They also had a small experimental biplane, the D.H. 60X Moth (G-CAHK), for initial base-finding flights. The whole contingent sailed north from Halifax in July 1927 aboard the icebreaker CGS Stanley and steamship Larch, and over the next year the expedition established bases at Port Burwell, Wakeham Bay (Kangiqsujuaq), and Nottingham Island (Tujjaat). The RCAF used Fokkers on skis or floats to conduct regular patrols and take oblique photographs, which Logan had championed, then wrote detailed reports about conditions.

Lawrence also believed in engaging Inuit for northern operations and each aircraft carried an Inuit guide. This proved an excellent practice, and helped avoid tragedy. On February 17, 1928, RCAF pilots A. Lewis and N.C. Terry were on patrol with their guide, a one-eyed Inuk named Bobby Anakatok. They were travelling from Port Burwell to Resolution Island, and then on to the Grinnell Glacier on Baffin Island. On the return flight the crew became lost in a heavy snowstorm and reported back to base that they were out of fuel. Darkness was closing in, and Lewis was unaware of his exact location and radioed he was going down on the icepack. He dodged towers of ice and looked for a place to land: "The pinnacles were so numerous, however, that we could not avoid hitting one head-on."

They had crashed on the frozen ice of the Labrador Sea well east of Ungava Bay. They built an igloo in half an hour, brought their sleeping bags and other emergency equipment inside, and made tea. The next day they carried what they could as they began trekking toward what they hoped was salvation. After not sighting land, Lewis realized they were actually eighty kilometres out in the Atlantic. They immediately reversed their direction and headed west, and seven days later, after travelling over rough ice conditions and crossing open lanes of water in their inflatable rubber raft, they reached the stark coast of Labrador, starving and exhausted. "The greatest hardship of all," Lewis recalled, "was the complete absence of fresh water." They were surrounded by ice and snow, but it had a thick crust of sea salt on it.

These three Fokker Universals, purchased by the Department of Marine and Fisheries for sixteen thousand dollars each, were used during the Hudson Strait Expedition in the summer of 1927. The planes and their crews were critical in establishing bases, conducting patrols, and taking aerial photos – as well as learning about flying conditions in the North.

The crew members, having consumed all the food in their emergency kit, lived off raw meat from a walrus Anakatok shot with their rifle. After four days of trudging northward up the barren coast, suffering badly from hunger and exposure, they came across an Inuit family who helped them to a village and gave them "some beautiful salmon-trout." The men recalled later: "Seldom had anything tasted so delicious. Then, still parched for fresh water, we proceeded inland under our hosts' direction for about a mile to a frozen lake, at the edge of which a spring bubbled." The next day, the family woke them early for a "hectic komatik [sled] dash from

moonlight to moonlight" to reach their home at Eclipse Harbour. Lewis and Terry bid farewell to their hosts the next morning with "promises to return and visit them with a 'tingiook' [aeroplane]."[28]

Even with this close call and the fact the RCAF Moth was lost when it "overturned at its mooring in a storm," aviation authors consider the Hudson Strait expedition a "striking success."[29] The RCAF learned much, not only about the conditions in the Strait, but about flying in polar regions. The airmen learned how to start the Universals in the deep cold of an Arctic winter by draining and warming the oil and heating the covered engine with blowtorches — a method bush pilots would use for many years. The RCAF also realized the importance of creating accurate maps and charts for the region, something that would become central to the RCAF's activities in the coming years.

THE BOUNCING BRUNO

Meanwhile on the civil front, interest in prospecting north of 60 was high as increased demand for Canada's mineral products spiked prices. Prewar railway building had brought new "large tracts of mineral-rich country" into the range of prospectors, and both the general public and large mining syndicates took advantage of the maps and reports put out by Geological Survey of Canada field parties.[30]

It took until 1925 for the first aerial prospecting to take place in the Yukon — and for the first Canadian pilots to touch down in the territory. That summer, Seattle-based Dease Lake Mining Co. leased Laurentide Air Service's Vickers Viking Mark IV (G-CAEB) flying boat, nicknamed *The Bouncing Bruno,* to scout for minerals in northern British Columbia.[31] The mining company also hired a Laurentide flight crew to operate the plane: J. Scott Williams as pilot and C.S. (Jack) Caldwell as co-pilot and engineer. From their base at Dease Lake, Williams and Caldwell explored the southern Yukon, landing at the small HBC post at Frances Lake where "the Bruno created a sensation."[32]

The next summer Caldwell and the *Bouncing Bruno* were back north. This time they (along with air engineer Irénée "Pete" Vachon) were searching the southern fringes of the Northwest Territories — all on the vague directions of a grizzled prospector with a mason jar full of gold. The previous fall, the prospector had arrived at the offices of the Northern Syndicate Ltd. in Calgary, Alberta, with this jar, saying he had collected it from a deposit near Great Slave Lake. He refused to give the exact location, but said he had "marked it with a rough cross cut in the bush by the side of a large lake" and left his Dene wife to watch over it. They would be able to find the spot from the air easily, he said, and they would all be rich.

While the Northern Syndicate was making preparations for this flight, however, the prospector got in a bar brawl and fractured his skull. The blow affected his memory, unfortunately, and his health would not permit him to go as a guide. The Syndicate decided to proceed without him, and in mid-June the *Bouncing Bruno* was shipped to Lac La Biche in northern Alberta and overhauled. Then, on June 25, Caldwell and Vachon left for Fort Fitzgerald using the same route *Vic* and *René* had taken in 1921. Unlike the Imperial Oil crews, however, they had excellent weather and only one aircraft glitch — a cracked crankcase. But that was all the luck they had: they spent July flying in ever-widening circles while Northern Syndicate-employed prospectors examined the ground on foot. But they never found the site.

THE MACALPINE EXPEDITION

Even with its disappointing results, the Northern Syndicate saga underlined the usefulness of airplanes for mineral prospecting, and several other mining syndicates turned to the era's best bush pilots and airplanes.[33] In 1928, for example,

Clennell H. "Punch" Dickins flew 6,500 kilometres across the Barren Lands in the Northwest Territories — the first to do so — in G-CASK, a Western Canadian Airways Fokker Universal. He did this while under contract with Dominion Explorers (Domex), which, based on reports of mineral wealth in the area, had begun setting up prospecting bases along the northwestern shore of Hudson Bay.[34]

As Dickins told writer and fellow bush pilot Tim Sims, the eight-hundred-kilometre section from Baker Lake to Athabasca illustrated what he and other pilots were up against in the region: there were "no weather reports, no maps worth a damn, no distinctive water systems or mountain ranges, no radio aids, in fact no radio — period." When Sims asked Dickins how he navigated, the latter replied "dead-reckoning. Having started from some point, I made as careful a check of maps as possible, laid out general compass headings to within a few degrees, and then kept a check on progress by map reference, or by landmarks that I had spotted and marked on previous flights." Dickins noted responsible pilots also only attempted new flights in good weather: "failing to do this, and the 'press-on' syndrome, caused many an aviation tragedy."

The next year Domex was involved in what became the most famous aerial undertaking of the decade — and the largest ongoing aviation search in Canadian history.[35] In August 1929 two Western Canada Airways (WCA) airplanes, a high-winged Fairchild CF-AAO piloted by Stan McMillan and another Fokker Universal, G-CASP (which was later replaced by SK after a mishap), left Winnipeg for the vast tundra of the Northwest Territories called the Barrens. On board were eight prospec-

tors, including Richard Pearce, editor of *The Northern Miner*, and the leader of the expedition and head of Domex, C.D.H. MacAlpine. The group went in search of mineral riches; instead, they found themselves trapped in an unforgiving landscape without proper equipment or training.

Dickins, who later searched for the missing men, notes the Barrens in summer is "surprisingly … beautiful country with lots of brilliantly coloured flowers." But by September, summer is decidedly over and the weather changes dramatically.[36] McMillan, who was ex-RCAF and had a year's experience flying throughout the Northwest Territories, was caught in the turning weather. With his compass affected by the magnetic pole, he got lost and flew to the limit of his fuel, and was forced to land above the Arctic Circle. MacAlpine, who knew communications in the North were usually spotty at best, had left orders that no search was to be undertaken unless they had been missing for ten days. On day ten, WCA pilot Andy Cruickshank and Domex agent Guy Blanchet deployed all available RCAF and civil aircraft in the search. While those involved read like a who's who of early Canadian bush flying, author Larry Milberry notes efforts were hampered by "limited fuel supplies, the need to change over to skis, and several costly accidents." Besides these, few of the air crew had had experience flying over the Barren Lands.

The search went on for ten weeks, and as time wore on, McMillan admitted, "there were times when we got depressed." They were understandably impatient to return home — especially after one of their number was forced to have "field treatment" for an abscessed tooth — but they had to wait for the ice to thicken so they could walk the 112 kilometres to Cambridge Bay. "The Inuit told us it was not [ready], but we insisted," McMillan recalled later. "We got out a couple of miles and ran into open water, slush, and slob ice." In the end, they relied on an occasional "slug of Scotch," cigarette, or piece of chocolate — and of course local Inuit — to keep their spirits and strength up during the long wait. Finally, they ran across the partially frozen ice to the HBC post at Cambridge Bay where they sent word to Domex and WCA to send planes to evacuate them.

In the end, the search parties spent over three hundred flying hours and covered 46,670 kilometres in what was often bad weather. Luckily, neither the members of the MacAlpine Expedition or their rescuers were critically injured or killed during the saga, but Domex's Dominion Explorers' share in the search costs was roughly five hundred thousand dollars at a time when the world was headed toward the Great Depression. After another year of aerial prospecting in the Northwest Territories, it stopped all aviation operations on January 14, 1931.

THE FIRST WORLD WAR WAS A CATALYST FOR aviation and provided, in the words of historian Jonathan Vance, "a large cadre of experienced, skilled pilots who could put aviation to practical good."[37] Before the war, northerners like Dolar De Lagrave had put their ingenuity to the test with limited resources and no first-hand experience with flying machines. By the second decade of the century, he and others living in the Yukon and Northwest Territories had watched the Alaska Air Expedition or aerial prospectors land on their fields or lakes, been dazzled by Clarence Prest's aerobatic displays, or spotted *Vic* and *René* flying overhead toward northern oil wells. There had been many close calls, forced landings, and crashes, but for the moment it appeared aviation in the North held nothing but promise.

CHAPTER 3

Hope in the Sky

By the 1930s the promise of aviation in the North dovetailed with a mineral boom that turned campsites into towns within months. Bush pilots loaded (and often overloaded) planes with prospectors, canoes, and a variety of colourful cargo. At times they learned the hard way about weather conditions, appropriate gear, and which lakes, rivers, and fields made for good landings. Even so, aviators pushed ahead to create mail routes, test the Great Circle Route to China, and help the Mounties "get their man" in the distant reaches of the Western Arctic.

NORTHERN RICHES

It may have been the Great Depression, but there were riches to be found in the North and a lucky few made a fortune — often with the help of airplanes. In 1930 a new prospecting rush was touched off in the Northwest Territories when pilot Punch Dickins dropped off Gilbert LaBine near Great Bear Lake, about 140 kilometres north of Yellowknife.[1] LaBine found a large mineral deposit of pitchblende, also known as Uraninite. Radium could be extracted from the pitchblende and used for cancer treatment and on instrument dials; it was worth more than gold at the time — the Belgians, who until then had a monopoly on the mineral, had charged up to two hundred thousand dollars a gram. By 1932, the worst year of the Depression, three hundred men had staked claims in the region and LaBine's mine at Port

Radium — aptly named Eldorado — "became the hope of a stricken nation."

While radium was incredibly valuable, it did not have the same romance as gold. So when rich deposits of the yellow metal were discovered near Great Slave Lake in the early 1930s, it sparked the imaginations of prospectors everywhere, and individuals as well as large companies like Cominco and Consolidated Mining and Smelting, turned to aviation to reach the new gold fields.[2]

Mining engineer George M. Douglas was one of those heading north in 1932. He was no stranger to the area, having undertaken six prospecting trips in the region over a span of twenty years. In February 1932 he was amazed at how much transportation had changed: in 1912 it had taken him eighteen months to travel from Toronto to Coppermine, hauling all his own supplies. Twenty years later, his heavy freight was flown in by Paul Calder

Claude and Mary Tidd fonds, YA/7395

Everett Wasson poses with Treadwell-Yukon's Bellanca CH-400 Skyrocket, CF-AOA, at Mayo, Yukon, in 1932. 'AOA crashed near the Queen Charlotte Islands (now called Haida Gwaii) off the coast of British Columbia in October 1941.

of Canadian Airways Limited (CAL), and after three days on a train to Edmonton, Ronald George flew him north aboard a CAL Bellanca (likely a Pacemaker, CF-AKI). Douglas's biographer, Enid Mallory, writes, "As they flew over the Athabasca, Douglas, with his nose pressed to the cabin window, could recognize each rapid which cost such labour and frustration 20 years earlier." From their first stop at Fort McMurray in Alberta, Walter Gilbert flew him to Great Bear via Forts Rae and Resolution. Douglas noted in his diary, "Four other planes loaded with prospectors and their gear were at Fort Rae following the same course to Great Bear." They reached their destination of Fort Smith in the late afternoon of March 7. Instead of taking a year and a half as in 1912, the journey lasted only a week.[3]

This compression of time and space through aviation made it much easier to reach the area, and Winnipeg journalist Allen Bill was right when he forecasted that it would be a frenzy of activity once the lake ice broke up. Three oil wells at Fort Norman, as well as another to the north, had been reopened to provide fuel for the Eldorado mine's operations, and while much was freighted by water in summer, aircraft were pressed into service in all seasons. Pilot Duncan McLaren remembers that he and "Con" Farrell routinely flew 1,500 kilometres a day during the summer for CAL. Every Monday they would depart Edmonton bound for Yellowknife. The next day, they would reverse direction, "we hoped, terminating in Edmonton." They were supposed to have Sundays off, but

McLaren noted, "with weather delays and side trips, we often ended up flying the seventh day to make up for lost time."[4]

In the summer of 1932 Yellowknife was, as Douglas and prospector Rene Hansen remembered, "a collection of tents surrounded by construction."[5] From their campsite on an island across the lake, they watched it grow: "Frantic building, planes more than I've ever seen in one place before — RCAF, Can Airways, Mackenzie Airways, private planes — water taxis running between the town and the mines." As they paddled back to their campsite after being in the bush for a month, "they sat in their canoes blinking at the transformation. A helter-skelter, hodge-podge city had replaced the tents." There was even a hastily built thirty-two-room hotel, which had opened just in time for Ontario Premier Mitch Hepburn's visit, and a brothel commonly known as "The Library" operating out of a log building.

By 1935 there was a full-on boom centered on Yellowknife, which meant air freighting of all kinds. McLaren recalled flying out of Yellowknife at the time with Rudy Heuss in CAL's Fairchild 82, CF-AXE, hauling "mail, dogs, passengers, food, mining equipment and dynamite.... Rudy always wrapped the dynamite caps in his sleeping robe to minimize the risk of inadvertent explosion and we tried to fly the caps and dynamite on separate flights."[6] Once they moved a complete sawmill. Wop May, who became superintendent of the Mackenzie River District for CAL, told a radio interviewer: "One chap asked us to bring rings for his marriage and bring the lady as well. One lady insisted she bring her canary along for the ride. We even carry ice cream beyond the Arctic Circle."[7]

One of the most common — and most welcome — air cargoes in the North was liquor. "There were then no liquor outlets in the Northwest Territories and all of us who were able to come up with an NWT address were entitled to a liquor allotment each year," McLaren explained. Yellowknife was technically "dry," he noted, so there were many bootleggers — twenty-six in the winter of 1937–38 — and those working for the air services got involved too. "Those of us who could, ordered our annual allotment for shipping to Yellowknife C.O.D.," said McLaren. "When the order was picked up at the freight office by the designated individual, the C.O.D. charges, including the air freight, were paid in full. Unlike other C.O.D. merchandise, our Canadian Airways agent Al Pierce had no storage problems with the liquor shipments. They were always a fast-moving commodity."[8] They never ran afoul of the law, either, as engineer Sammy Tomlinson noted, "We were taking it to the damn Mounties!"[9]

Pilots and air engineers also had loads that were more challenging. Often they would fly teams of sled dogs, and crews had to be careful not to get bitten; after all, these were high-strung working animals, not coddled pets. After a few close calls, McLaren perfected a system for avoiding snapping teeth while unloading them after he landed: he would carefully grab the dogs by the scruff of the neck and the tail then throw them out the cabin door into the lake. In another case, prospector Don "Tiny" Ferris recalled the time he had to transport the first forty-kilogram gold ingot from the Consolidated Mine: "I tried to load it into a Norseman and I had it in a silk sack as I stood with one foot on the dock and the other foot in the door of the aircraft, when the damn

Marlie McLaren Kelsey

Rex Terpening and Duncan McLaren in 1937 at the Cooking Lake float plane base near Edmonton, Alberta. The two worked for Canadian Airways at the time as air engineers, and both went on to long and distinguished careers in civil aviation.

thing went through the bottom of the sack into 18 feet of water! I think I was in after it before it touched bottom! I couldn't get it out, so they had to tie a rope around me and then pull me and that $150,000 worth of gold up out of the drink."[10]

Stan McMillan faced near-drowning in the Northwest Territories as well. He was flying the *Eldorado Radium Silver Express*, a Bellanca Aircruiser (CF-AWR) operated by Mackenzie Air Service for Eldorado Mines, "carrying mail, machinery, food and men to the mine on Great Bear Lake and bringing out a return load of at least two tons of uranium concentrate per trip to Fort McMurray." In 1936 McMillan recalled that, "with a load of surveyors and their equipment … I cast loose from the bank of the South Nahanni River, in the calm water just a few yards from the lip of the raging 'sluice box' immediately above Virginia Falls. My engine had quit and, after three attempts

with the hand crank on the inertia starter, it finally took hold — just in time!" If it had not, McMillan's engineer and co-pilot, Archie Vanhee, was apparently ready to dive into the water and swim ashore with a line, hopefully before they reached the waterfall.[11]

Landing could be as tricky as taking off in the region. Pilots worked with many small-time prospectors trying to hit the mother-lode, some with only vague ideas of where they were going — and what landing conditions would be like once they got there. Fred Meilicke recalls leaving Great Bear Lake in a Fairchild 71 with a prospector who wanted to go to a small lake about eighty kilometres away. This prospector assured him someone had gotten into the lake before with another single-engine floatplane, a D.H.83 Fox Moth, but when Meilicke tried to land he found it was an extremely tight fit. "The bloody trees were coming at me at one hell of a rate when, by the grace of God, one ski

Leigh Brintnell, owner of Edmonton-based Mackenzie Air Service, and its Bellanca Aircruiser, CF-AWR, dubbed the *Eldorado Radium Silver Express*, c. 1935. 'AWR transported minerals from the Eldorado mine site in the Northwest Territories until January 1947, when it crashed in northern Ontario and was abandoned. In 1973 the fuselage was recovered by the Western Canada Aviation Museum and is currently being restored.

snagged a frozen caribou skeleton just enough to ground loop the plane," he noted. "We stopped with the wingtip no more than 50 feet from those trees!"[12]

In the summer months, pilots like Meilicke often started flying at 5:00 a.m. and went till midnight, trying to take advantage of every last minute of daylight. Page McPhee, who worked for Mackenzie Air Service, once averaged three hours of sleep per night and logged seventy hours of flying time in one week. The pace caught up with him, though. On one trip from Hay River to Fort Smith he flipped the control column to engineer Ernie Mills to get caught up on his books. "It might not have been quite legal, but I figured if they were going to ride along they might

as well know how to handle the aircraft," he said. "Suppose something happened and they had to take over? Anyway, it worked out nicely and it helped them pass the time. Well, I started in and the next thing I knew, we were over Fort Smith and Ernie had a big grin on his face. I looked at the logbook and saw that I'd done only a line and a half — I'd been so beat, I'd fallen asleep!"[13]

In winter, though the flying hours were much shorter, aviators and engineers had to deal with darkness and frigid temperatures. There was often no avoiding working "bare-handed, doing repairs, or refueling from drums, with a hand-operated wobble pump."[14] The layers of clothes pilots like Duncan McLaren wore to keep warm could also make moving, let alone flying, tricky:

From the skin out it went like this: light-weight pure wool underwear with long legs and long sleeves, a cotton shirt, a sleeveless wool sweater, another shirt of heavy material, melton ski pants, wool windbreaker, two pairs of heavy socks or a pair of duffle socks, felt insoles, moosehide moccasins, parka, wind pans and assomption sash. Usually I wore a ski cap with ear flaps or if it was extremely cold, a leather flying helmet with a strap under the chin. By dressing in this manner, one could easily adjust the layers of clothing to suit the temperature. Later, the ski pants were displaced by wool breeches and the moccasins by mukluks. The assomption sash was multi-coloured....the purpose, aside from being colourful, was to keep the wind from blowing up under the parka....Mitts were usually moosehide and duffle lined, which were worn over woolen gloves or mitts. To prevent the loss of an outer mitt the two were roped together with a cord which went over the shoulders and around the back of the neck.[15]

Some challenges existed regardless of season. The smart pilots learned from experience or instruction to have the proper equipment on hand should they go down in the bush or the Barrens. Wop May had perfected his tool box and ration kit through years of bush flying, and always carried survival gear such as a Woods three-star sleeping bag, gun, fishing line, and a "tightly sealed case of wax-coated matches." Getting fuel could also be a life or death issue. Commercial Airways sent avgas up the Mackenzie River by boat as their pilots had to refuel at each of the thirteen stops. Those flying into the Barrens, such Mackenzie Air Service, would cache barrels of fuel at different spots and mark their locations on a map for future use. A bath — while perhaps less crucial — was almost as hard to come by. McLaren recalled it usually "had to be delayed until returning home, except on the rare occasion when there was a stopover at a town with running water and hotel bathroom facilities."

They could, however, usually rely on the kindness of the small northern towns they served. Wop May once told a radio interviewer, "The pilot is the only link between the inhabitants of the North and the outside world, except of course the radio." The pilots would get room and board; in return, the families received news from Outside and an entertaining guest.[16]

SKED RUNS AND MAIL ROUTES

Pilots were especially welcome when they carried letters, a precious cargo to southerners living and working in the North. In fact, mail was arguably almost as valuable as gold or radium at times. George Douglas fondly recalled the day when Wop May and Lou Parmenter circled his campsite in a CAL single-engined Junkers and set down on the water. "They had just flown from Fort Resolution, and Wop was anxious to get back there before it got any darker.... Within half an hour of the plane's landing, it had taken off again ... leaving me alone, but with a big bunch of letters."[17]

Residents of Whitehorse had tried to get airmail as early as 1920. When the Alaska Expedition flyers left for Dawson City that year, they had a petition for air service aboard for the Commissioner of the Yukon. "On this historical occasion," Whitehorse citizens wrote, "we wish to express a fervent hope that our Government will keep pace with other countries in the establishment of a regular aeroplane service throughout our Dominion and especially in Yukon where it is so much needed." Canadian airmen had shown amazing skill and bravery during the Great War, they argued, and were now back home and available for domestic flying duties. The Expedition flyers delivered the petition, and the Commissioner was apparently in complete agreement. Even so, the Yukon would not get its airmail for almost a decade.[18]

It was not for lack of trying. During the 1920s several companies — including Laurentide Air Service of Quebec — tried to establish airmail service in the territory, but for a variety of reasons failed.[19] Finally, in 1927 Andy and Esmé Cruickshank set up Yukon Airways and Exploration Company with their Ryan B-1 Brougham monoplane — sister ship to Charles Lindbergh's *Spirit of St. Louis*. With the *Queen of the Yukon* (as G-CAHR was known), the husband-and-wife team launched the first scheduled airmail and passenger route in the North.[20] On November 11, 1927, they made Dawson City's first airmail delivery. While Andy flew the *Queen* low over the town's main street, Esmé dropped a mail sack out the plane's window to the grateful crowd below. Unfortunately the operation lasted only a year; it folded after the *Queen of the Yukon* and two of its successors crashed.

Yukoners would not be deterred, however, and other pilots and companies were waiting in the wings: Klondike Airways, formed by T.C. Richards and W.L. Phelps, soon picked up the Yukon airmail con-

tract.[21] The decade also saw big American companies like Pan American Airways make stops in Whitehorse, with its shiny twin-engined, all-metal Lockheed 10 Electras, while flying the route between Fairbanks and Juneau, Alaska. There were others from Outside making inroads as well: Pacific Alaska Airways, Canadian Airways, and United Air Transport Ltd., all entered the northern fray during the 1930s.[22] Seeing the future importance of aviation, local companies such as Treadwell Yukon Co., North Canada Air Express, and White Pass Airways vied for contracts. Even entrepreneur George Simmons of Carcross, in the Yukon, who had had "no interest at all in flying" according to pilot Stan McMillan, created Northern Airways and switched from running horse carts and dogsleds to airplanes.[23]

To help establish early airmail routes for Western Canada Airways, Punch Dickins undertook several plane trips following the Mackenzie River from Edmonton in 1929. Beginning in January, he flew ten mail trips between Waterways in northern Alberta and Fort Simpson in his Fokker Universal, and also attempted an exploratory flight from Edmonton to Aklavik in the Northwest Territories that month.[24] While landing at Fort Resolution in forty-below temperatures, however, Dickins hit a hidden ice ridge and damaged the aircraft: "All I could think of, though, was the fact that this one [bad] landing might put mail delivery in the North back a long time. This trip was important to me — but a lot more important to those isolated little places along the way." He managed to limp back to Waterways in the Fokker and in late June made the first successful flight to Aklavik, one he remembers being "the most satisfying I ever made."

Eldon Bjerke collection, YA/83_20_1

The S.S. *Tutshi* lake sternwheeler and Canadian Airways Ltd. Junkers W-34, CF-ABK, at Carcross in southeastern Yukon in 1933. The small town was a transportation and tourism hub from the Klondike Gold Rush days through this period.

"The weather was good," Dickins recalled, "and I really enjoyed the whole thing. I stopped at every village on the way down the river to show the flag for Western Canada Airways. The greetings I received were always enthusiastic, particularly because the farther I went, the less chance that anyone had ever seen a plane." On July 1 — Dominion Day — he arrived at Aklavik. "The roar of the plane as I flew over and landed brought the entire village out to greet me," he noted. "There were a couple of Mounties, some priests, nuns, and local fur traders, as well as thirty-five or forty Inuit. None of the Inuit had ever seen a plane before, and they were quite curious about it." That trip he logged thirty-nine hours flying time over eleven days and about 6,500 kilometres — a trip that Dickins estimated would have taken two years by boat, canoe, and dog team. "It was then that I knew that the airplane was going to change the entire way of life of the people of the North."

By this time, WCA had established the first scheduled route from the railhead at Fort McMurray in Alberta to Fort Simpson. Once a week, Dickins made the flight, stopping en route at other Northwest Territories communities such as Fort Resolution, Hay River, and Fort Providence. Dickins thought, understandably, after these pioneering flights WCA would get Canada Post's first airmail contract for the Northwest Territories. Instead, it went to Dickins's childhood friend and friendly rival, Wop May of Commercial Airways, who had recently flown a well-publicized mercy flight from Edmonton to Fort Vermilion to deliver diphtheria serum.[25]

On December 9, 1929, May and two other Commercial Airways pilots flew the "Red Armada" — so called because of their three red Bellancas — over a distance of almost three thousand kilometres to settlements along the Slave and Mackenzie Rivers with five tons of mail. The pilots reached Fort Good Hope on Christmas Day, with a frozen bottle of rum and nine-kilogram turkey. Locals provided homebrew till the rum thawed, and the WCA pilots, after trying to cook the turkey by throwing it right into the woodstove, chopped it with an axe and filled pans with snow to make turkey stew instead. The last leg of the trip to Aklavik took them two weeks instead of the two months it would have taken by dogsled. After a town-wide celebration that lasted several days, the Armada returned home.[26]

Like their counterparts in the Northwest Territories, Yukoners enjoyed living and working in the territory, but many grew tired of the isolation — and getting newspapers three months after they had been printed. "The only connecting link between Whitehorse and the Outside," Laura Berton wrote in her memoir, "was the little narrow-gauge railway running over the White Pass to Skagway. The train came in twice a week during the winter, unless, as seemed perennially the case, it was snowbound, blocked by a rockslide or a flooded river. When this happened … there was no

fresh milk, for all the cows were in Skagway. There was no mail and usually no telegraph service, for in periods of bad weather the wires were down. There was no undertaker, for he too came from Skagway."[27]

"OUR ROUTE WAS NEW"

Routes within the North were valuable, but Pan American Airways (known simply as Pan Am to most) was already looking farther afield. The airline — the largest in the United States at the time — wanted to find a commercial route to China using the so-called "Great Circle Route" from New York to Hankow (now Hankou), and funded an exploratory flight through the North in 1931.[28] It was none other than Charles Lindbergh, Pan Am's technical advisor, and his wife Anne Morrow Lindbergh, who undertook the 11,425-kilometre flight in their single-engined Lockheed Sirius on floats (registration NR211). While Canadian authorities tried to convince the Lindberghs that flying the Arctic was dangerous, nothing could sway them.

They were as prepared as possible for emergencies over land or water, having packed parachutes, camping supplies, and a rubber boat with a sail and oars. They also brought survival gear and enough food for thirty days. The aircraft was equipped with new instruments, including a radio direction finder and extra fuel tanks. They were also very aware of the aircraft's weight limits. "Every object to be taken," Anne wrote, "had to be weighed, mentally as well as physically." Even with all this careful preparation, there were many unknowns. Anne later wrote in her book *North to the Orient*: "Our route was new, the air untraveled; the

LAC/ PA-062878

Charles Lindbergh and his wife, Anne Morrow Lindbergh, piloted this Lockheed Sirius across the Canadian North to China on a scouting flight for Pan American Airways in 1931. Originally, the Sirius was an open-cockpit landplane, but the Lindberghs modified theirs with a sliding canopy and Edo floats for this journey.

conditions unknown; the stories mythical; the maps, pale, pink, and indefinite." At their first stop in the Northwest Territories, they were faced with a reminder of the precariousness of their journey: on the beach "was a broken pair of pontoons which had brought some flier in to Baker Lake but never took him back." Even so, they pulled their plane up on the shore and anchored it to fifty-gallon gasoline drums.

Their next leg was from Baker Lake to Aklavik, which they did in twelve hours without stopping. Throughout the flight Anne took drift and ground-speed observations and communicated with the ground. "I could hear through my ear-phones the noisy chatter of the big cities over the edge of the world," she wrote. Anne and

Charles also alternated napping, one taking the controls while the other slept. During one of these naps, Anne was "jerked awake" when the engine stopped while Charles switched fuel tanks over the wide expanse of Coronation Gulf. Other than that little hiccup, the Lindberghs had a smooth trip, arriving in Nanjing in September. They had proved that air traffic could fly the Great Circle Route to the Far East, and in 1935, Pan Am inaugurated its *China Clipper* flights between San Francisco and Manila, Philippines using a Martin M-130, four-engined flying boat.

In 1934 a colourful young Royal Air Force pilot named John Grierson also attempted an international flight over the Canadian Arctic, but had considerably more trouble.[29] Grierson's original plan had been to fly around the world by the so-called "Arctic Route," but he had run into trouble with Soviet authorities in 1932 and was told that "owing to [his] inexplicable propensity for landing in prohibited areas, we are unable to accede to this request." He redirected his efforts to make a flight from London to Ottawa via the Arctic instead, converted his D.H.60G Gipsy Moth (G-AAJP), the *Rouge et Noir*, into a seaplane and learned how to fly on floats. He also added navigational and communications equipment, packed the survival gear the Canadian government required (a .256 Mannlicher with fifty rounds of ammunition, pemmican for ten days, and suitable fishing tack) and paid a deposit to the Danish government in case a search party was needed.

On August 4, 1933, Grierson departed in his underpowered and overloaded airplane and ended up capsizing off the coast of Iceland. As the captain of the ship who came to his rescue said, "I am sorry for you but in a way, I am very glad. I believe this crash has saved your life." Grierson concurred, realizing that "such a slow machine might have been dangerous for crossing Greenland in any but the finest weather." On his next two attempts, he switched to a Fox Moth (G-ACRK), which he nicknamed *Robert Bruce*. His third try was luckier, and in late August 1934, Grierson made a series of stops along Baffin Island. He made his first at Loks Land Island on the eastern tip of Baffin Island's Blunt Peninsula. Then he continued toward the HBC post at Lake Harbour (now called Kimmirut), but had trouble locating it. He was soon put on the right track. "When I saw several tents and a boat moored in the bay I landed only to find Eskimo women, who waved their arms in an opposite direction towards Lake Harbour," he noted. "I soon found the houses of the post which I had mistaken in the distance for grounded icebergs." From there he departed for the posts at Puvirnituq and East Main in northern Quebec, and finally to Ottawa. In the process, he became the first to complete a London–Ottawa flight, as well as the first to fly solo across the Greenland ice cap.

In the 1930s the U.S.S.R. also went in search of world records.[30] During the summer of 1937, after two years of secret preparations, it sent several of "Stalin's Falcons" (as the Soviet pilots were known) over the North Pole in search of air routes to the United States. In June pilot George Baidukov made the first trans-Polar airplane flight from Moscow to San Francisco in an unpressurized, unheated cabin while battling massive icing. He was largely disdainful of the operation, calling the area between the North Pole and Canada the "Pole of Inaccessibility" and noting that "to the airman the Pole doesn't really mean a damned thing. We have passed over it, and that is that."

The next month several others made a record non-stop flight over the same route. Finally, in August 1937, pilots Sigismund Levanevsky and Nikolai G. Kastanayev along with their crew left Moscow in a DB-A, a four-engined transport bearing U.S.S.R. registration N-209. They were headed for New York, with a refuelling stop scheduled at Fairbanks, Alaska. They had attempted this flight in 1935 in a single-engined Ant-25, but after ten hours the aircraft had sprung an oil leak and they had been forced to turn back. This time they were determined to complete their mission. N-209 was outfitted with the latest direction-finding equipment, enough food to last the crew ninety days, and eighteen tons of fuel — enough, they thought, for the seven-thousand-kilometre journey to Fairbanks. The crew expected the trip to take just over a day to complete, but nineteen hours into their flight on Friday, August 13, the crew reported they were over the North Pole in heavy cloud. That was their last clear transmission.

Radio operators across the Arctic listened for a distress signal, and the renowned Arctic explorer Vilhjalmur Stefansson coordinated an international search that included Canadian, American, and Soviet pilots who flew nearly twenty-one thousand kilometres in a thirty-day period. Efforts resumed over the winter, with many of the North's greatest bush pilots and air engineers taking part, but even with these massive efforts, no trace was ever found. Finally, in March 1938, the Soviet Ambassador announced they were calling off the search.[31]

"YOUR AVIATORS, GOD BLESS THEM!"

This expansion of air services in the North led to other casualties, unfortunately. In the crash of the *Queen of the Yukon II* (CF-AHD) on November 2, 1929, pilot John Melvin "Pat" Patterson became the Yukon's first aviation fatality. The "curse of the Queen" also touched Andy Cruickshank, who died — along with engineers Harry King and Horace Torrie — in the Northwest Territories' first fatal plane crash on June 29, 1932. He had been flying Western Canada Airway's Fokker Super Universal (G-CASL) from the mining camp at Great Bear Lake to Fort Rae when the

engine, which he had felt was not airworthy, died. The plane cracked up on impact.[32]

Luckily, there were also happy endings. There were numerous mercy flights in the 1930s, including several to Letty Harbour near Paulatuk, Northwest Territories, on the Arctic coast. On January 25, 1935, Stan McMillan of Mackenzie Air Service rescued the captain and crew of the *Margaret A* from their icebound ship in the harbour. The next year pilot Matt Berry and engineer Rex Terpening answered the prayers of the Catholic mission at Letty Harbour after Bishop Fallaise sent an SOS saying they were almost out of food. Berry and Terpening came to the rescue in CF-ARI, a Canadian Airways Junkers W-34, braving marginal weather and freezing temperatures; they were the first to fly that far north in winter. As author Bruce McAllister notes, "[the] resourceful flight crew had their own survival gear on board, including custom Arctic sleeping bags and a Remington rifle. There were no maps for their destination, so they had to draw their own maps and rely on the few landmarks that were available." When they arrived, they loaded everyone into the aircraft and headed to Aklavik. Their troubles were not over, however: they hit bad weather en route and were grounded at a fuel cache for ten days.

While bush pilots were wary of "pushing" the weather, they would take calculated risks. This was the case in November 1939 when Punch Dickins, who was by then superintendent of CAL, received an urgent telegram from Montreal: "Msgr. Turquetil wants badly injured missionary rushed out from Repulse Bay with minimum delay as otherwise man will be maimed for life. Realizes difficult condition but very anxious we make attempt." The missionary, Father Buliard, had apparently been hunting alone on the ice five kilometres from the mission. He struggled back for an hour in -22°C weather before he was seen and carried to shelter, but his hands had already frozen and now gangrene was setting in. The only chance to save the twenty-five-year-old from getting his fingers or hands amputated was to get him to medical help fast.

The company generally refused to fly the west coast of Hudson Bay between freeze-up and April. Rex Terpening, along with pilots W.E. "Bill" Catton and A.J. Hollingsworth, however, volunteered to make the 2,200-kilometre journey through "the worst flying country in the North." Still, they had to wait for the weather to improve, and to receive word about ice conditions and fuel supplies along their route. They also needed to an Inuit interpreter to accompany them. Reports from the RCMP and telegraph service warned them unequivocally against making the trip.

They were determined, though, so when the weather improved on November 27, 1939, the longest ambulance flight in Canadian history departed Lac du Bonnet, Manitoba. The crew flew CF-ASN, another of the company's Junkers, as far and fast as they could during the brief winter days. They had to stop several times en route to change over to skis or because of bad weather. At the community of Ilford, for example, "fog and icing held them on the ground for two days, watching the sky" until they could make the next jump to Churchill, Manitoba. From there, they had the trickiest section to fly: 450 kilometres of "vast whiteness" with no distinguishing landmarks or navigational aids to Tavani, Northwest Territories.

When they landed at Chesterfield Inlet — still 482 kilometres away from their destination — it was too late to go farther that day. While they were close (at least by northern aviation standards) they could not leave for Repulse for a week because of blizzards and gales. On December 9, they finally landed at the Notre Dame des Neiges ("Our Lady of the Snows") mission; the next day they began their journey to the St. Boniface Hospital in Winnipeg, encountering more rounds of punishing weather, delays, and forced landings. On December 20, 1939, they finally made it — and Father Buliard's hands were saved. Msgr. Turquetil, who had written the original telegram begging for CAL's help, was overjoyed, writing to the company: "Your aviators, God bless them!"[33]

THE FUR TRADE TAKES TO THE AIR

Like mission societies, the famous Hudson's Bay Company — whose acronym was sometimes half-jokingly changed to "Here Before Christ" — also had posts scattered across the North. As early as 1840, it opened its first post north of the 60th parallel at Peel River Post (Fort McPherson) near the border between what is now the Northwest Territories and the Yukon. By the end of its expansion in the 1920s, it operated over 200 posts in the North, including more than a dozen in the Arctic.

It is not hard to see why the HBC was so interested in the North: reports from 1921 and 1931 show that trappers in the Yukon and Northwest Territories sold about two million dollars in furs those years. This was roughly equal to what minerals had netted, and would be at least twenty-five million dollars today. Along the Mackenzie Delta and Crow Flats in the northern Yukon, Gwitch'in and Inuvialuit began trapping muskrats, beavers, marten, lynx, and wolverine once prices rose — and once the HBC had enough trade goods to make it worth their while. Charlie Peter Charlie of Old Crow recalled, "That last year I trap for him [Lazarus Charlie] I killed one hundred ten marten and ninety-five lynx. The lynx is over one hundred dollars each." In the Arctic, Inuit trappers caught silver fox and Arctic fox, whose furs were very fashionable in cosmopolitan centres and fetched top dollar. Some Inuit were reported to have made the equivalent of more than one hundred thousand in today's dollars in one season. Inuit, according to HBC managers, traded their furs for flour, sugar, butter, and canned food at the posts, and the most successful bought gramophones, cameras, sewing machines, high-powered rifles, and outboard motors.[34]

Getting fur from remote areas to the posts, however, was hard work and time-consuming. Charlie Thomas remembers it took him "about six days from Old Crow to Fort Yukon (Alaska)" by dog team, and Dick Nukon noted it still took his dad four days in his motor boat.[35] By the mid-1930s, that length of time was significantly shortened when Alaska Airlines began flying mail in to Old Crow and bringing fur out. Despite the promise of aviation for the fur trade HBC "refused to participate in a new scheduled air service between Edmonton and the Mackenzie Valley," as Peter C. Newman noted in *Merchant Princes*. The company had nonetheless begun cautiously investigating aviation's potential in the North. During the winter of 1930, HBC paid

Punch Dickins's expenses to do a mercy flight to Coppermine, and hired him on contract to fly fur out of Fort Good Hope. Then in September 1932, HBC Governor Patrick Ashley Cooper and three colleagues made the company's first inspection tour of the Northwest Territories. With Walter Gilbert at the controls, the party covered a distance of almost two thousand kilometres in Canadian Airways' Fokker Super Universal, G-CASK. What would have taken ten days by water transport only took 10.5 hours by air.[36]

During that same time, other CAL pilots were flying on charter for the HBC on the west coast of Hudson Bay.[37] While separated by thousands of kilometres, the two operations had one thing in common: bad winds sweeping across the northern part of the provinces and Northwest Territories. Governor Cooper and his party had wisely waited them out for a day; the pilots flying out of Hudson Bay had not — a decision CAL and the HBC would come to regret.

The contract had begun in late June 1932, when pilot W.J. Buchanan flew CAL Junkers JU-52, CF-ARM, to Arviat (Eskimo Point). From there, he was to haul freight from the post to Padley Lake, 250 kilometres away, and only recognizable in the tundra landscape because of a row of six spruce trees. With freeze-up looming, which would make the float-equipped 'ARM inoperable, CAL sent up crews with two smaller planes (Junkers W-34 CF-AMZ and Junkers W-33 CF-AQW) to help finish the job. Working during the brief northern summer was anything but easy, but the crews managed, operating from open tidal waters without docking facilities. They were down to their last few loads when the gale-force winds hit.

NWT archives/ Edmonton Air Museum Committee Collection/N-1979-003-0170

Matt Berry and Frank Hartley with a load of white fox fur from the Northwest Territories, c. 1936. Likely in front of Canadian Airways Junkers W-34, CF-ARI, which crashed in northern Alberta shortly after take-off on January 25, 1940.

The gusts began at 4:00 a.m. on September 14. The crews, worried about their aircraft, left their beds and walked down to the beach. Even in the early morning darkness, they could see that 'ARM had broken its anchor chains and blown onto the rocky shore. Buchanan cautiously boarded it, started the engine, and taxied to a small shelter about three kilometres away to prevent further damage. When the sun came up a few hours later, he saw the floats were torn up by rocks and completely waterlogged. He later wrote in his report that "only the excessively high wind held the machine up." While the crews worked to beach the battered machine, 'AMZ, which had dragged its anchor as well, drifted into 'AQW, and "broke in two." Now all personnel feverishly got to work trying to prevent further harm to the remaining aircraft.

The winds continued for two days, preventing the crews from reaching 'ARM to send out a message by radio to CAL or fix the aircraft. When the wind abated a little, the men walked to the damaged 'ARM to attempt repairs. They realized this would be no easy feat. "Here was a machine which, with float equipment, weighed approximately five tons," Buchanan wrote. "And it was resting on the floats which had to be repaired. There were no cranes, derricks, or any facilities with which to lift it up so that we could get at the floats. The only feasible solution was to dig a hole among the boulders." This turned into a Sisyphean task: "Every hole we dug the tide filled in for us, and the water would seep in … One man was fully occupied baling out each hole while the man in the hole drilled the under surface of the floats to put on patches."

Dick de Blicquy

CF-ARM was a Junkers 52/1 M flown by Canadian Airways and was known as the "Big Junkers." CAL used it on contracts around the country, including north of 60. In this photo taken at Sioux Lookout, Ontario, in the 1930s, a mildly sedated horse is being loaded for transport to a Red Lake mine. It turned out, however, that the sedation was a little too mild, and when 'ARM landed at the mine, there were three or four hooves sticking out the side.

They spent the next day finishing the repairs to 'ARM, using "every spare piece of sheet metal and every bolt that was available in the settlement." They also unloaded and cached the remaining freight from 'AMZ before dismantling it and loading the wrecked machine onto a tugboat. Finally, at 4:30 a.m. on September 19, Buchanan and his exhausted crew were ready to fly 'ARM

south — only to find that the patches had leaked overnight and the floats were once again full of water. While disappointed at this turn of events, they quickly regrouped for a new plan of action: over the next few days, as they watched the lakes around them ice up, they dragged 'ARM over to the HBC post, covered the two floats with duck canvas, and replaced the useless patches with sealskin. On the night of September 22, it began to snow hard and they saw their window rapidly closing. After a few failed takeoff attempts, they decided to try a new strategy to get the plane out by the next tide: they dug two trenches into the ocean that were fifteen metres long, over a metre wide, and half a metre deep. Their final herculean effort worked, and they carefully towed the machine along the shore to the HBC post, reaching it at 1:30 a.m. They did this by hand because they were afraid if they put the engine on the speed might strip the canvas. On September 24 Buchanan noted they were finally able to fly 'ARM out, "we got off, but only just."

Though the HBC saw ups and downs during the Depression years due to changing animal populations, weather, fur prices, and fashions, it persevered. It also got over its initial hesitations and expanded its use of planes during the 1930s; it continued to send its managers on aerial inspection tours, ship freight in to posts, and furs out of them. Within a few years a *Beaver* article would even note that these flights, which had so recently been "items of front pages news value," had become "plain jobs o' work."[38]

THE MAD TRAPPER OF RAT RIVER

Despite becoming more common, there were still some northern aerial exploits worthy of the front page. Starting in January 1932, one event in particular was splashed across every newspaper in North America and glued people to their radios as a story more terrifying and thrilling than Depression-era radio plays unfolded.[39] A man of apparent superhuman strength had shot several Mounties in the Western Arctic and was evading capture in some of its toughest terrain during the depths of winter. The questions on everyone's lips, from cab drivers in New York City to farmers in Saskatchewan: Who was he? Why had he become violent? And would the Mounties ever get their man?

Events had been set in motion a month earlier, when someone calling himself Albert Johnson moved to the Yukon. He seemed quite ordinary, people said. No one knew much about him, but they respected his wish for privacy — the North saw its fair share of outsiders down on their luck from the Depression, men who sometimes "simply walked away and, for all intents and purposes, disappeared" from their previous lives. Unfortunately, these outsiders did not always understand or respect the local codes of conduct. As Alfred Charlie, a long-time resident of Old Crow remembers, Johnson "came to Aklavik with a raft and moved to Rat River. He put a cabin right on somebody's trapline. That winter somebody went to set traps and Albert Johnson went on that guy's trapline and sprung some traps."[40] When the Vuntut Gwitch'in trapper saw this, he left for the RCMP Detachment in Aklavik to report the tampered-with traps.

An RCMP patrol set out to investigate.[41] They departed Aklavik by dogsled on December 30 for the 130-kilometre trip, and made the rounds of cabins. When they came to Albert Johnson's, they had no reason to suspect him of any wrongdoing. They knocked, just as they had at the other cabin doors. But unlike the others, despite being able to hear someone inside, no one replied. Suspicious, they returned to Aklavik for a search warrant and assistance in the form of two other constables.

This time when they approached the cabin, Johnson fired on them, hitting one of the Mounties — Constable Alfred King — in the chest. The other Mountie on the patrol, Constable Robert McDowell, raced him back to Aklavik by dogsled in a punishing twenty-hour trip, saving his life.

With this violent turn of events, two more patrols set out. These were made up of Inspector Alex Eames, Constables McDowell and Edgar Millen, five special constables, and a local guide, Peter Alexis. This time they were prepared to take Johnson dead or alive. Johnson was apparently ready as well, and he held his ground, besieged in his cabin, for two days. Even after the Mounties launched dynamite at the cabin, Johnson continued to fire at them. The patrols, unable to budge Johnson from his position, finally decided to regroup back at Aklavik. When they returned to the site five days later, the trapper had burned down his home and was nowhere to be seen.

The "Mad Trapper" as he would come to be known by the media, had a solid head start on his trackers. It also appeared he knew at least a few evasion tactics, as he left misleading trails and kept his fires as small as possible to avoid detection. He was also incredibly adept at wilderness survival and apparently very fit. As Sheila Reid notes in her book *Wings of a Hero,* "he had no bed-roll, no tent, no stove, no provisions. Only the high-powered hunting rifle he had used against them at the cabin.... [and] he was travelling quickly and continuing to keep well ahead of them in heavy snowshoes in temperatures that remained bitterly cold."

While the manhunt was thrilling fare for outsiders, those living in the region were understandably frightened. Hannah Netro of Old Crow was a child at the time. Her

family was living at a winter bush camp on their trapline and she recalls her father told her and her siblings that if Johnson came while he was out hunting, they should "talk nice to him and give him tea or whatever." Luckily he never came calling. Dick Nukon was also just a child in nearby Whitestone River. He recalled his father going to visit two non-indigenous trapper friends, sixteen kilometres to the south of their camp. "When he came back he brought the news," Nukon recalls. "He got big radio, this guy.

Peter Alexis guided the RCMP patrol that sought to apprehend the "Mad Trapper of Rat River," Albert Johnson, in early 1932 in the Western Arctic. Vuntut Gwitchin from Old Crow like Alexis were key members of the patrols, working as special constables and guides.

Arthur Thornwaite fonds, YA/83_22_450

He hear it on radio, when he come back he told us ... a man name Johnson he shot that RCMP last night in Aklavik.... So, next day we just left."[42] Nukon and his father strapped on their snowshoes and hit the trail for Eagle, Alaska, to warn their friends and relatives there.

The patrols pursued Johnson for weeks in the unforgiving Richardson Mountains to the west of the Mackenzie Delta. Then on January 30, 1932, the patrols cornered him. While outnumbered and worn down from cold, hunger, and exertion, Johnson did not give up. Instead, another firefight ensued and he shot and killed thirty-year-old Constable Edgar Millen. The next day, determined to seek justice for their fallen colleague and realizing they were evenly matched on the ground, the RCMP contacted Canadian Airways for assistance. Punch Dickins, who was working at CAL, received the message at Edmonton. He quickly wired one of the company's top pilots, Wop May. May had been listening to reports from the Aklavik radio station at the Fort McMurray base, and knew the

Jack Bowen, Frank Riddell, and Wop May pose in front of Canadian Airways Ltd's Bellanca CH-300 Pacemaker, CF-AKI, in 1932, during the hunt for the Mad Trapper of Rat River. 'AKI crashed four years later in a snowstorm at Lake Athabasca, Saskatchewan.

situation. He readied CAL's ski-equipped Bellanca, CF-AKI, to fly north for whatever was needed: bringing in dried fish for the dog teams, assisting with aerial tracking, or anything else CAL might be called on to do.

As it turned out, one of his first tasks was a sad one: transporting Millen's frozen body from the remote patrol camp back to Aklavik. That flight, while unhappy, was at least relatively smooth. As May discovered, flying in the northern Yukon in February was anything but easy. He encountered whiteouts and fog that grounded the Bellanca on at least one occasion. Even when the weather co-operated more, visibility was poor. "It was very hard to see as there was no sun," May recalled later. In fact, because it was so hard to see his tracks in the snow, May hoped Johnson would try and fire on the Bellanca during his reconnaissance flights and disclose his position, "but he was too wise for that." Nevertheless, May's flights in the area saved the patrols days of work as he was able to advise them about Johnson's attempts to elude capture through doubling-back and other manoeuvres.

One day the sun finally appeared and May was able to make out a snowshoe trail leading through Chute Pass in the Richardson Mountains to the Yukon side. "He was fooling us actually," May notes. "He was using the Caribou trail, running along the centre of the river. He had taken his snowshoes off and was following this Caribou trail so that we couldn't trace him." Using his aerial vantage point, May could see Johnson was on the Eagle River. He signaled the location to the RCMP patrol team via radio and the next morning the Mounties left to intercept Johnson.

Denny May

"I could not get out as early as I wanted to because of the fog," May said later.[43] The ground team left trees down to guide him, though, and once the fog lifted he hurried to join them. Then on February 17, May saw the final encounter between the RCMP and Johnson: "I was overhead when [Inspector] Alex Eames was coming round the bend of the river and Johnson was in the middle of the river. He tried to run up the bank to get out of his way, but he didn't have his snowshoes on; he couldn't make it so he came back into the centre of the river, dug himself into the snow and the fight started. We were up on top and circling, watching the fight and taking pictures of it."

In the final standoff, Constable Hersey was shot and a bullet passed through his elbow, knee, and chest. May landed near him, and with the help of the other Mounties, carried him to the plane. "He was in bad shape and the blood was just spurtin' out and there was nothing we could do for him but get him in the aircraft and get him back to Aklavik where there was a hospital." May jumped back in the Bellanca and while he hit heavy winds and a snowstorm over the mountains, he managed to make it back to Aklavik in under an hour.

Because of May's fast flying, Hersey's life was saved. Johnson did not fare so well. According to local accounts and recent forensic tests on his body, he was shot several times during a final firefight. Author Barbara Smith notes, "The trapper was no longer physically capable of fleeing, but still he managed to continue resisting capture, dropping to the frozen river and shooting as many rounds of ammunition as he could at his pursuers."[44] RCMP special constable John Moses, a Vuntut Gwitch'in man from Old Crow, delivered the fatal blow.[45] After forty-eight days, the Mad Trapper saga was finally over. Interest in the story continues, however, and Johnson's real identity, motives, and ability to elude capture for so long still baffles locals, historians, and scientists. What is clear was how important May and his Bellanca were in supplying the teams, evacuating wounded Mounties, and tracking Johnson's movements from the air.

DURING THE 1930s CANADA'S BUSH PILOTS, especially Wop May, Punch Dickins, and the like, became household names. In a time of dire financial straits across the continent, they offered the hope of reaching gold, radium, and furs. While to many in the South the ground meant drudgery and dust bowls, aviators left those worries behind when they took to the air and were able to fly away to new adventures and new opportunities. No one wanted to hear that flying was hard work and that many pilots lived a hand to mouth existence. To a population that was hungry for escape — and often simply hungry — the bush pilots meant hope.

CHAPTER 4

The Northern Front

Bush pilots were important to early aviation, but they were not alone in northern skies. Canadian military and RCMP flyers were also active in the region — albeit doing civilian work. Soon, however, these "bush pilots in uniform" would be called up to serve in another world war. Many pilots, soldiers, and civilians would flood into the North, bringing with them improvements in technology and transportation, but also unanticipated disease and environmental destruction.

PHOTOGRAPHING THE NORTH

At the same time as Gilbert LaBine's Eldorado radium mine became big news across the continent, the RCAF's northern photo surveying really kicked off.[1] By 1932 the RCAF had flown almost sixteen thousand hours and photographed roughly 750,000 square kilometres of the country, including parts of the North. Historian Peter Kikkert notes that General Andrew McNaughton pushed the photo survey work as a means to train RCAF pilots and create a new role for that branch of the military. Competing sovereignty claims and the North's mineral wealth were also good motivation.

In July 1930 two crews were dispatched from Ottawa to the Northwest Territories with a single-engined bush plane, Fairchild 71 (G-CYVX), and a Vickers Vedette flying boat (G-CYWS) to inspect fuel caches and explore the territory's main water and air routes. The pilots — F.J. Mawdesley and Harry Winny — were given strip maps "of little-known air routes" around the Mackenzie Basin as well as Great Slave and Great Bear Lakes, and Corporal S.C. Dearaway took 3,100 photographs from the Vedette to help fill in the blanks and look for future RCAF base sites. During the course of their two-month trip across the Northwest Territories from Aklavik to Chesterfield Inlet, the crews flew approximately 21,000 kilometres.

At the same time, the RCAF dispatched No. 9 Photographic Detachment to the Northwest Territories to establish its first northern base of operations. The officer in charge, C.R. Slemon, selected a site on Ryan Island in the Slave River and rented a small house in nearby Fort Fitzgerald, Alberta, to serve as an officers' mess; the airmen camped in tents. On days when weather and visibility allowed, the crews

LAC/ PA-062588

Fairchild 71B, G-CYVX, upon its return to Rockcliffe base near Ottawa on October 1, 1930. The crew, made up of A/Sgt. S.C. Dearaway, F/L F.J. Mawdesley, F/Sgt. H.J. Winny and C.S. Macdonald, DLS, had just flown 'CYVX and a Vickers Vedette, G-CYWS on an epic flight through the North. Although fog had prevented them from reaching Herschel Island, and at one point the Fairchild had forced landed for emergency fuel, overall it was a very successful trip.

conducted photographic flights between Great Slave Lake and Lake Athabaska. There were inevitable hiccups, and winter set in before they could build a permanent base, but according to historian S. Bernard Shaw, these first forays "tested the reliability of equipment and the viability of detached, northern operations." They also taught the RCAF a valuable lesson: in the Northwest Territories, October 1 was the cut-off date for float-flying.

In July 1931 the RCAF once again sent two crews on photographic operations. This time, float-equipped Bellanca Pacemakers headed to the west coast of Hudson Bay. They photographed over 1,900 kilometres during their two months

of operations and pioneered the use of right angle oblique air photography (at 1,500 metres) with excellent results. They also did, in the words of Flight Lieutenant E.P. Wood, "the usual assortment of odd jobs which always fall to the lot of anyone with an aeroplane in such regions," including flying freight from Baker Lake to the new post at Beverley Lake for the Northwest Territories Department, and flying the first official airmail flight from Chesterfield Inlet to Fort Churchill on August 5, 1931.

For the most part things went smoothly, but abandoned plane wrecks were a constant reminder to be cautious. On one photographic flight, Officer Cox was forced to land when his engine died, likely because of carburetor icing. On another occasion, the flight crews discovered that a Barren Lands survey party was a week overdue. One of the Bellancas quickly took off with Inuit observers aboard, and the crew undertook a two-day search. Wood recalled this was "rendered none the pleasanter by numerous forced landings on glassy water caused by overheating of the Wright J6 engines, which had not been fitted with oil coolers. Then, when the survey party was finally located, its members were highly insulted by the fact that anyone had so much as dared to consider them lost!"

The region's active mining claims spurred on the work of mapping the region. In the spring of 1934, for example, a detachment was sent to survey the area around Cameron Bay, Great Bear Lake, and Yellowknife River to find a land route for Eldorado Mines to bypass the rapids in the Great Bear River. From there, Flight Lieutenant C.L. Trecarten noted, they used a "surprisingly accurate" sketch map "prepared from information procured from Indians, trappers, and the odd government party" to find their way to Dead Man's Valley along the South Nahanni River, the purported site of a lost mine.

"In about 1932," Trecarten later wrote, "considerable interest was revived in that area by certain prospectors who had been in there and returned with samples of gold and stories of the possibility of untold wealth." While they never found the mine, Trecarten did not come away empty handed: he "panned for gold on non-photographic days — and actually succeeded in obtaining a fair showing." The detachment also took many vertical and oblique photographs and Eric Fry, a representative of the Lands and Mines Department, took star observations. Later,

the Topographic Survey would be able to use the plotted photos to create an accurate map to record future mineral claims.

For the rest of the decade work proceeded along similar lines: detachments from Ottawa would start in southern areas as ice went off waterways — generally in May — and move north. These detachments normally consisted of two aircraft (usually on floats), two pilots, two camera operators/aircraft mechanics, and a fifth man who remained at the base to service the planes and cook for the Detachment. A Department of Lands and Mines representative would also be part of the crew. While the RCAF personnel had not known what to expect, Flight Lieutenant Wood noted "the men supplied by the Department for this type of work were rugged individuals. They enjoyed their work, seemed to have a great capacity for living among mosquitoes, and ate and slept comparatively little."

The RCAF stopped photo operations in the Northwest Territory in 1939 with the outbreak of the Second World War. In the decade of operations in unfamiliar and often unforgiving conditions, there had luckily — perhaps surprisingly — been no fatalities or aircraft write-offs. But there had certainly been some close calls and lessons learned. After a costly month-long search for a missing Fairchild 71 and its crew in August 1936, for example, it became clear that bases and aircraft needed radios. Beginning in 1938, Group Captain Ralph C. Davis noted, "all pilots were given a short astro-navigation course at Trenton and each was given a good watch and a crude sextant." If they got lost on operations after that, he wrote "it was a simple matter to land on one of the countless lakes, set up camp, deploy our aircraft trailing aerial, and report our position" using a radio.

WINGED MOUNTIES

The RCAF also gained northern experience in the 1930s by partnering with the RCMP.[2] The Mounties had shown hints of air-mindedness since the Great War: in 1918 RCMP Commissioner A. Bowen-Perry advocated buying war surplus aircraft, saying, "I think possibly the service could be extended into the far north and speedy communications could be had, if required, even with points on the Arctic Coast at no very great expenditure of money." Much to Bowen-Perry's disappointment, the Force did not purchase the airplanes and held off on any official flying activities until the 1930s.

In 1931 a new Commissioner, Sir James MacBrien, was appointed. MacBrien was the former head of the Canadian Flying Clubs Association and Director of Canadian Airways. He had a clear vision of "Winged Mounties," which began with a partnership between the RCMP and the RCAF to apprehend rum-runners off Canada's east and west coasts. MacBrien also saw the value of aircraft for visiting northern detachments, and flew several inspection tours of RCMP posts aboard RCAF aircraft during this time. In July 1936, for example, he flew 17,700 kilometres in an RCAF Fairchild 71 on floats in a month-long tour that included more than a dozen stops in the Northwest Territories and Yukon.[3]

Air Commodore Gordon was pilot and navigator on this trip. "I was still using the 35-mile-to-the-inch map of the Territories," he noted later. "Plus some strip maps taken in previous years by the RCAF."[4] These maps did not extend far, and from Fort Reliance east to Chesterfield Inlet "once we got off the strip map, navigation was somewhat confusing on account of the great

number of unmapped lakes and other waterways." Landmarks were very important in this kind of dead-reckoning navigation, and he got nervous if they did not appear when the map indicated they should. He also encountered some nerve-wracking weather during the trip — especially near Hell's Gate in the Nahanni region. "Our flight along the canyon under low clouds was in pretty rough air," Gordon recalled. They also hit a severe rain and snow storm in the Mackenzie Valley and landed on the Liard River to wait it out. When they had reached the Arctic coast, they ran into fog around Coppermine and had to fly above it "on a magnetic course" for about 110 kilometres. When the fog cleared he discovered the ice had not yet broken up in Coronation Gulf. Floatplanes were not designed to land on solid ice, and this could have meant disaster if they had been forced down. Luckily, they reached Cambridge Bay, where there was just enough open water to land.

In 1937, despite their successful partnership, the RCAF severed ties with the Mounties due to budget constraints and departmental shifts. At a conference in Halifax, the RCMP decided it was time to manage its own aviation affairs, and on April 1, 1937, the RCMP Air Section was created. It quickly purchased four D.H.90 Dragonflies (CF-MPA, MPB, MPC, MPD) and drew eight qualified pilots from its ranks. Soon, the Air Section added a Noorduyn Norseman, CF-MPE (later re-registered CF-MPF) and added more pilots. The *Falcon*, as the Norseman was nicknamed, would become a regular sight across the North.

When Canada declared war on Germany in September 1939, the RCAF and RCMP worked together again — if only temporarily. The Dragonflies were quickly pressed into

Claude Tidd, YA/008253

Left to right: Chief Peter Moses from Old Crow, Claude Tidd, and RCMP Commissioner Stuart Wood pose with other men in front of RCMP Air Services' Grumman Goose, CF-MPG in July 1946 at Fort Yukon. The RCMP bought it as war surplus from the RCAF and used it for long distance inspection trips. In 1951 it flew from Newfoundland to Herschel Island at the far point of Canada's Western Arctic, as well as up to Cambridge Bay and Iqaluit. It was finally retired in 1994 and donated to the Canada Aviation and Space Museum.

service and nine of the ten RCMP pilots joined the RCAF.[5] As Larry Milberry notes, the RCAF was desperate for these men and machines as the force had shrunk to 4,200 people and only had 270 aircraft, and its transports mostly consisted of "antique" Bellancas, Fairchilds, and Vedettes.[6] The RCMP Norseman also helped in the war effort: in 1940 RCAF crews flew it along the Hudson Bay and Arctic coasts to destroy emergency fuel caches to keep them out of German hands. There were fears U-boats, aircraft, or even German missionaries-turned-spies might use them. Once the fuel-cache run was complete, the Norseman spent the rest of the war based out of Edmonton for use in the North.

Another northern institution — the Hudson's Bay Company — also lost a number of its personnel and pilots to the RCAF, but kept the twin-engined Beech 18, CF-BMI, it had bought in 1939.[7] Beginning in February 1940, pilot Paul Davoud and pilot/engineer Duncan McLaren flew HBC executives on aerial inspection tours of British Columbia and the Yukon.[8] Although there were weather and mechanical delays, the aerial tour was faster than a recent three-month inspection of the same posts by dog team. This was good news for headquarters, but as author Peter C. Newman notes, often an "unwelcome surprise [to] local store managers, used to getting warnings of visits by Company brass via the staff moccasin telegraph."[9]

Paul Davoud, Hudson Bay Company Archives/ N17329

Hudson's Bay Company Beech 18, CF-BMI, beside an Inuit camp at Bathurst Inlet, Northwest Territories, c. 1941. A few months later it was damaged while landing at Richmond Gulf. Then, after repairs had been completed, a eighty-kilometre-an-hour gale whipped up overnight and it was blown onto its side and eventually sank. The HBC replaced 'BMI with a sister ship, CF-BVM, in November of that year.

In May 1940 the HBC doubled its fleet when McLaren went to Montreal to take delivery of the company's new inspection aircraft, a single-engined Beech E-17B, CF-BHA.[10] Over the course of the year, the HBC increased its aerial operations and personnel, but as the Allies began mounting major offensives in Europe, it lost several pilots to the war effort. Harry Winny, for example, who had been involved in the RCAF photo surveying during the interwar years, rejoined the Air Force and became an instructor on Vancouver Island. In 1941 Paul Davoud followed suit: he went overseas to lead a squadron of night-fighters and shot down a Dornier 217 bomber into the Atlantic. Even with the world threat-ened by war and the loss of key personnel, the editor of the company's magazine, *The Beaver*, maintained a perspective hard-won over the HBC's 270-year history: "To this old Company, a state of war is, unfortunately, nothing new." It was committed to fighting Nazi Germany on all fronts and confident that it could once again ride out the storm.

NORTHERNERS IN THE RCAF

While they were far removed from the battlefields of Europe, northerners were keen to "do their bit" for the war effort. The North's population was small at the time

— about five thousand in the Yukon and nine thousand in the Northwest Territories — but there were still men and women who wanted to enlist.[11] They did so out of patriotism, a sense of family tradition, a desire to travel, or to make their way in the world. According to Gordon McIntyre of Whitehorse, however, getting to recruiting centres "required considerable time and money" and it could be for nothing if they were turned down because of age, medical concerns, or other reasons. So while some did venture south on their own, McIntyre noted "the rest of us waited around for something to happen, for some recruiting officer to appear on the scene."[12]

When a recruiter finally came to Dawson City in 1940, Norm Hartnell was there to join up.[13] "I had an application in for the RCAF but couldn't wait for their answer so joined the Army in Dawson," he notes. Hartnell, Chickadee MacDonald, Len Nelson, and the other "boys" from the Yukon headed to Vancouver that year by river steamer, train, and ship. After nine months in the Army, his Air Force acceptance arrived and he was shipped off to the Toronto manning depot. He ended up a wireless air gunner, and after his training was complete he sailed for Great Britain. John Gould also began his military service in the Army, although he knew from the start he wanted to be in the RCAF. In 1928 he had seen his first airplane. It was on the beach at Dawson, and the seven-year-old boy was enthralled. "We went down to have a look at it and could have had a ride if we had five dollars," he said. "But that was a day's pay so Dad could not afford it." In November 1942 he began his RCAF training for the chance to finally fly his own plane, first in Edmonton and then Ontario.

In 1944 he was attached to the Royal Air Force in Great Britain as a fighter pilot and flew Hawker Hurricanes, Miles Masters, and P-51 Mustangs overseas.

Northern women also went into the armed forces once it was open to them, but information is very sparse on their experiences. Elsie Nightingale of Dawson City joined the Women's Division of the RCAF in 1942, and likely others left the territories to join up.[14] RCAF WD members from Outside (as well as American Women's Army Corps members) also served at Whitehorse during the war years. There is no record of First Nations or Inuit women from north of 60 in the RCAF WD. As historian Grace Poulin notes, they came up against a double barrier: there was no active recruiting of women until after 1941, and then, recruiting propaganda was only aimed at white, middle-class women. Even so, a 1950 government memorandum indicates seventy-two Status Indian women served overseas during the war and hundreds more in Canada as drivers, clerical workers, cooks, or other important non-combat roles.

Despite their physical and cultural distance from the war, First Nations and Inuit men in the North also joined up, but not in the Air Force.[15] In addition to the difficulty of reaching recruiters and getting Outside, indigenous people were also initially barred from the RCAF. Even once those official restrictions were lifted in November 1939, they continued to face barriers of health, education, and unofficial racism. There were higher levels of tuberculosis and trachoma among indigenous peoples, for example, and there were several recorded cases of recruiters who "dissuaded or even denied Natives the privilege of submitting an application."

William L. Drury fonds, YA/82_333_113

A group of nurses, school teachers, and bank tellers in front of the Teslin, Yukon, RCAF building, c. 1945. They had been bussed in from Whitehorse to attend a dance to help keep the morale up of southern servicemen far away from friends and family.

Even so, a few dozen First Nations individuals from southern Canada entered the RCAF and, according to historian Whitney P. Lackenbauer, "flew with bomber and fighter crews around the world." For both indigenous men and women, once they were in the military, accounts suggest they were, in historian R. Scott Sheffield's words, "treated as equals by their peers in a way they had never been before or since."

NORTHWEST STAGING ROUTE AND THE MILLION DOLLAR VALLEY

The majority of northerners — indigenous and otherwise — "did their bit" in other ways. Women worked as communications personnel, nursing staff, or in aircraft fac-

tories.[16] Yukon towns held friendly competitions that resulted in the purchase of hundreds of thousands of dollars' worth of victory bonds. Chief Peter Moses was so moved by the plight of war orphans in England, he and the people of Old Crow "collected a sizeable donation" for their care — an act for which he later received a British Empire medal. Northerners also worked to support the war effort — and their families — on the massive joint defence projects in the territories, or by providing services to the forty thousand people who streamed into the region at the time.

The first project to get underway was the Northwest Staging Route. In 1941 the U.S., which was still officially neutral, passed the Lend-Lease Act to supply aircraft and munitions first with Britain and then the

YA/81_21_445

Single-seat P-39 Airacobra fighter planes and A-20 medium bombers at Whitehorse Airport in 1944. Pilots ferried these types of planes from American aircraft factories, through Canada, and into Alaska along the Northwest Staging Route. Russian pilots then flew them across the Bering Strait for use on the Eastern front. Smaller bush planes, like the one seen tucked further back in the line, were used by the RCAF and U.S. Army Air Force locally for communications and transportation.

U.S.S.R.[17] The airplanes to Britain — and many destined for Russia — went via eastern routes across the Atlantic, but a sizeable number were to be delivered to Alaska, where Russian ferry pilots would take them across the Bering Strait to Siberia. They used the inland route pioneered by Yukon Southern Air Transport, which comprised more than a dozen airfields carved out of the wilderness east of the Rockies.[18] The 3,057 kilometre route eventually stretched from Great Falls, Montana to Fairbanks, Alaska. While the airway saw its first few Lend-Lease aircraft by early September

1941, it was not until after the Japanese attacked Pearl Harbour in December that the wisdom of choosing this route became apparent.[19] As the editor of *Canadian Aviation* wrote, instead of taking six to seven days to move troops by ships along a threatened coastline, "within 24 hours, a powerful striking force of men and aircraft could be mustered from all over the North American continent and swiftly transported to the defense of Alaska."[20] At least in theory; in reality, it could take as long as sixteen days because of bad weather, mechanical difficulties, and limited daylight in winter.

The inland route had two stops in the Yukon: Whitehorse and Watson Lake. Due to local efforts, landing facilities in the territory had improved since the long-distance flyers of the 1920s, but they still needed work to handle the demands of wartime aircraft and personnel numbers. Whitehorse, for example, had a "crude airstrip" already in place and was easily expanded and resurfaced to meet military and Department of Transport (DOT) requirements. It was more difficult to provide accommodations for the RCAF and U.S. Army Air Force. As Blake Smith notes in *Warplanes to Alaska*, when the Americans arrived in town on July 21, 1942, "they found no barracks, tents, warehouses, mess hall or hangars. They pitched tents for living quarters and mess hall.... Water and wood hauling by the one available truck became a never-ending chore." The forty-three RCAF members faced this living situation until October, relying on the Americans for meals and even briefly for mail runs. By April 1943 it was "considered the best Unit on the NWSR."[21]

The Watson Lake airfield was even less developed, but ideally located — at least for air traffic. It was mostly level, sat on a large peninsula that jutted out into the lake, and contractors could use local gravel as a base for the runways. Despite Yukon Southern's attempts to clear landing fields at Watson Lake, however, when survey crews arrived they found large tree stumps in the way. It was also incredibly difficult and time-consuming to reach: the first 725 metric tons of building supplies were first shipped from Vancouver, British Columbia, to Wrangel, Alaska, then freighted over rivers and trucked overland, often using nothing more than bush trails, for another five hundred kilometres.[22]

The deadline for completion of the runways and military buildings was supposed to be August 31, but when they fell behind schedule, U.S. Army General Gaffney, nicknamed the "Screaming Eagle of the Yukon," threatened to send in American recruits to finish the job. In the end, a compromise was reached and U.S. Army engineers worked on the airfield while Canadian civilian contractors worked on the twenty-three log buildings. Soon the barracks were ready for American personnel at Watson Lake but the Canadians were not so lucky. As the Yukon descended into the coldest winter in half a century, the RCAF still did not have adequate temporary duty pay, proper accommodations, meals, or gear. In the fall of 1942, the personnel at Watson Lake were "often forced to eat their emergency rations for want of supplies" and had to borrow from the USAAF, much to their embarrassment. Squadron Leader Du Temple and his airmen even built a boat with a washing-machine engine to go out to catch fish to supplement their diet.[23] The RCAF's daily diary noted that Fort St. John, British Columbia, was the first unit to officially start "eating" on February 11, 1943, and that Watson Lake was the last on March 10. By this time food staples had been flown in and stored, but refrigeration was still an issue, and units still found themselves "dangerously low" on supplies when RCAF planes were unavailable or could not be sent due to flying conditions or unserviceability. The frustration is apparent in the daily diary's messing appendix: "Surely commodities obtainable to DOT and Civilian Contractors are not to be denied us?!! All our Northern personnel know the situation, and it is not a good one." Even once the messing situation had been sorted out, there were times during the NWSR's life when weather prevented the regular transports from leaving Edmonton for northern bases.[24]

As 1942 drew to a close, the RCAF still had no winter clothing. When the personnel at Whitehorse opened the Christmas load, they "received it with much enthusiasm" — until they discovered the cartons that were supposed to contain winter clothing was just battle dress.[25] It would be several months, during which the temperature hovered around -52°C for weeks, before the necessary gear would arrive. Hangar facilities were not available at Staging Units at the beginning of the war either, and work done on the RCAF's three Norseman, Avro Anson, two Lockheed 10s, and Beech 18 "Expeditor" was in the open with bare hands. Luckily the USAAF generously lent several of its Jeep heaters, which could be used in conjunction with engine tents to keep the RCAF from freezing while doing repairs.

By the fall of 1944, when the RCAF's Northwest Air Command officially took over control of the NWSR, Watson Lake and Whitehorse's buildings were still unfinished. In fact, the only thing at 100 percent completion at that point was the teletype-telephone system.[26] At least by then a stove had been installed at the partially completed barracks, and the health and morale at the Yukon bases were considered "satisfactory," even though radio reception was usually poor and daily papers were out of date by the time they reached them.

Travelling priests from different denominations looked after the spiritual welfare of personnel throughout the war, sometimes combining services. At Whitehorse the personnel enjoyed a variety of recreational activities, including: a travelling library; hobby and photography clubs; welding, mechanics, and taxidermy classes; skating and skiing in winter; four movies each week; beer available three nights a week; and an airman's dance at regular intervals. Friendly competitive leagues pitted Canadians versus Americans in hockey, softball, and baseball.[27] Personnel also took part in the tradition of doing a lottery to predict the breakup of ice on the Yukon River at Dawson City. Many threw in a few dollars and made their best guess, but could not beat local expertise to snag the five-thousand-dollar pot.

Personnel were also treated to concert parties from time to time. During the early war years these were put on by the Americans, so in April 1943 when the RCAF was able to put on a "Joint Forces Smoker" with entertainment and two thousand cans of beer at Watson Lake — the first time beer had "been in evidence at the base" — they were quite proud. The men were also desperate to blow off some steam as it had been four months since they had had a party. Later in the war, the RCAF brought in troupes of civilian entertainers — often women — from Calgary, Edmonton, and other southern locales. The Victory Variety Players and Gloom Chasers, for example, toured the NWSR bases in 1945 "and were enthusiastically received at every point."[28]

Even with recreation and entertainment, Gordon Toole, who was posted to Watson Lake in 1942 with the RCAF, remembers "some guys went round the bend" because of the isolation.[29] Joseph A. Berger noted one of the ground personnel there got drunk one night and "decided to go AWOL — as if there were any place to go, surrounded by wilderness. He got a large bag of onions, potatoes … a butcher knife, crawled into a rowboat and started rowing out into the lake. In the morning he was discovered passed out in the boat, floating in the center of Watson Lake."[30]

Toole thrived in remote conditions and in November 1943 transferred from Watson Lake to even more isolated Snag, where another airstrip was just being built. "I offered to go," he recalls. But getting there proved to be tricky: the Air Force flew him to Whitehorse where he was stuck for three weeks because the road did not reach to Snag yet. "They were hoping to get in with an RCAF Norseman," Gordon says, "but that didn't work out. Instead, they drove me up the Alaska Highway, which was just a narrow trail through the bush with 8 to 12 inches of fresh snow on it." He arrived at Snag in the middle of the night: "There were no buildings — just tents, powerhouse, and generators. I stayed in the kitchen tent overnight. Soon, though, I was assigned a tent — with my bunkmates Gerry and Jerry — and issued my two army blankets. I remember we had a barrel stove in the corner going 24 hours a day."

The cold was also hard on the roughly eight thousand airplanes ferried to Alaska for the Soviet air forces during the war. As Smith notes, "an airplane shrank, part by part, at different rates, depending on whether it was steel, aluminum or rubber.... Tires froze with a flat spot on the bottom, nearly shaking the instruments out of the panel during the takeoff roll. Occasionally tires would even explode when heated by the friction of high-speed rolling after being subjected to severe cold. Ice tires were used, some with metal studs embedded into the tread, but these often sent ice-chips flying in their wake, pitting the leading edges of the tail." The Bell P-39 Airacobra, a single-engined fighter and the most numerous aircraft type to travel

the NWSR, turned out to have some serious issues in the cold, reaching "excessive coolant temperatures ... even during brief engine run ups." This problem was eventually fixed in the design, but not before it was nicknamed the "iron dog" and became "possibly the most maligned U.S. fighter of the war." The cockpit was also small, which became a potential hazard during winter when pilots were bundled in layers of clothing "including a bulky parka, parachute and three-inch-thick emergency survival seat pack" and had to shoehorn themselves in. Pilots with larger frames were often reassigned to other units during winter because it was feared they would be unable to bail out in emergency.

The Yukon's cold winters and isolated conditions proved to be more dangerous than any foreign enemy on the northern front. In December 1940 *Canadian Aviation* published a list of tips from bush pilots at Canadian Airways for RCAF personnel in the North "to many of whom winter operation will be a novelty."[31] They cautioned RCAF pilots to heat the engine and oil properly before trying to start an aircraft up in frigid weather, to "take-off as quickly as conditions permit," and "always land as slowly as possible" — especially if there was fresh snow that could mask dangerous drifts. Of course, many of the USAAF ferry pilots were even less prepared for the North. Pilot Jack Greger said, "During the first few months of ferrying airplanes to the Russians, we didn't give much thought to what would happen if we went down in that wilderness. Even when the weather turned cold in autumn, we continued to wear uninsulated leather flying jackets, light pants and shirts, as well as low-cut, standard issue shoes.... When it became very cold we wore so many layers of clothing you couldn't tell anyone's rank." This ignorance nearly killed Lt. Pennington when he forced-landed his Curtiss P-36 Hawk fighter plane en route to Whitehorse: he spent two days in the bitter cold before rescuers found him and airlifted him to Edmonton. Luckily he only lost his toes, but he became a cautionary tale in a new USAAF film, *Land and Live in the Arctic*, which ended with a close-up of Pennington's blackened feet — minus the toes.[32]

After Pearl Harbor, winter conditions combined with the rush to get planes to Alaska to fend off imminent Japanese attack resulted in several large crashes.[33] The most famous of these occurred in January 1943, when the USAAF sent thirteen Martin B-26 Marauder bombers north as reinforcements. After being held up at Edmonton because of bad weather, the last ten were cleared to go north on January 16. According to tradition, they split off into smaller groups en route. Between Fort Nelson and Watson Lake one of these groups lost contact with the radio beams that helped them zero in on airfields and got lost. When their fuel was almost out, the pilot of the lead plane forced-landed in a "broad snow-covered valley" that turned out to be the Upper Grayling River, about 179 kilometres southeast of Watson Lake. As the bush pilots had warned, the fresh snow hid the uneven terrain, and when the pilot set down with the landing gear extended, it was torn away, and the nose and cockpit were crushed. The captain and co-pilot were injured, but, incredibly, the rest of the crew just suffered cuts and bruises. The other two pilots elected to do belly landings after seeing this turn of events, and their crews were completely unhurt. Even so, waist-deep snow separated the aircraft, and the twenty-four crew members with their inadequate gear "shivered through their first night."[34] It could have been worse: apparently a warm Chinook happened to be blowing.

Jack Baker, who worked the radio in Watson Lake, had been expecting the planes and sent word to the military when they were overdue. The next day a Curtiss P-40 Warhawk spotted them and buzzed the crew to let them know they had been seen; soon another plane dropped off supplies along with an RCMP constable with northern bush skills. Russ Baker, who was in charge of Canadian Pacific Airlines' Whitehorse base at the time, returned with his single-engined Junkers W-34 on skis and flew out the most injured while the rest of the USAAF crews cleared a rough runway nearby so they could be evacuated over the next few days.[35] The aircraft were never removed, and to this day it is known as the Million Dollar Valley.

After this series of events, the USAAF decided it would be a good idea to hand ferry aircraft over to pilots familiar with the northern part of the route, but pilots continued to lack instrument ratings or proper weather information. The weather data from U.S. Navy ships off the west coast was the most accurate, but the U.S. Army was not given decoding keys. Author Blake Smith notes it is unclear "whether it was because of interservice rivalry, the red tape of protocol or overcaution," but it cost thirteen lives on February 6, 1943. That day, Colonel Mensinger, a former airline pilot with more than ten thousand flying hours, took off from Watson Lake in a Dakota in marginal weather. There were eleven men on board, likely ferry pilots returning to the continental U.S. They lost contact en route and while searchers scoured the region around Fort St. John for two months, they never spotted them. The wreckage was finally found in September 1948 by hunters northwest of Fort St. John. The Dakota had hit Mount Mary Henry and all aboard had immediately died.

Also on February 6, 1943, a twin-engined USAAF Douglas C-47 transport plane went down near Watson Lake.[36] A snowstorm whipped up with little warning and the pilot, Johnny Hart, was unable to find the runway. Hart tried to land but "missed and pulled up for a go around." Running low on fuel, he forced-landed on a deserted bridge about six kilometres from the airfield; the impact killed him and his co-pilot. The other two crew members each broke a leg, and sat at the wreckage for eleven days, surviving on emergency rations while they watched in frustration as over one thousand takeoffs and landings took place nearby and search aircraft overflew them. On February 23, nineteen days after it had disappeared, the C-47 was finally spotted by chance, but it would take rescuers another day to reach the site because of deep snow and dense bush. When they arrived, the survivors were gone but an RCMP constable proficient at tracking was called in and they picked up the trail. The survivors had finally decided to leave the crash site and make their way to help. They were so close to the Watson Lake airfield they could hear the planes warming up their engines, but with their broken legs and weakened states, it felt like an insurmountable distance. For a week they crawled through the deep snow and tried not to freeze to death as the mercury plummeted from -28°C to -37°C every night. They were about to succumb to their pain and weariness when the trackers finally found them.

This and similar instances spurred the training of para-rescue crews for northern operations. Lieutenant French wrote that No. 2 Air Observer School in Edmonton "constantly received calls to search for lost crews, men who were not trained to take care of themselves in the wilderness."[37] Former bush pilot Wop May, who headed the school, knew all too well the northern bush was not a forgiving place to crash. While May initially formed a team of civilian para-rescue volunteers, it soon became apparent it was a job better suited to trained RCAF personnel with proper equipment. Once the Northwest Air Command was created in 1944, "a training syllabus was developed emphasizing parachute jumping, bush lore, survival skills, and mountain climbing, as well as medical training and maintenance of specialized equipment.[38] Soon "Para docs" — flight surgeons who could jump in to a site — were available, and later "Para-pups," K-9 paratroopers, were used at Fort Nelson, British Columbia and other locations to drop medical supplies.

ALASKA HIGHWAY AND CANOL PIPELINE

There were two other major wartime projects in the North at the same time as the NWSR: the Alaska Highway and Canol Pipeline.[39] Both were ostensibly started in response to the Japanese threat, although there were suggestions at the time (and have been since) that commercial and sovereignty interests were also at play. In May 1942 a Japanese attack force of transport ships, carriers, and cruisers did head for the Aleutian Islands in the Bering Sea, where American long-range bombers were patrolling in anticipation. Then, on June 3 and 4, the Japanese

Navy began bombing Dutch Harbour, a small outpost on one of the Islands. Z. Lewis Leigh, an RCAF pilot stationed in Alaska was part of the sixteen-month Aleutian campaign, certainly recalled that everyone worried about a Japanese invasion.

This sense of imminent danger spurred the rapid building of the Alaska Highway — or Alcan as it was often known — from northern British Columbia through the Yukon to Alaska. The initial road hacked through the bush was completed in eight months by the U.S. Army Corps of Engineers between March and November 1942. As those involved in the planning had very little knowledge of the region, aerial photography — even with a few miscalculations and underpowered aircraft —meant that they picked a route more quickly than would have otherwise been possible.[40]

The U.S. Army did not have airplanes of its own in the region, though, and the RCAF's small NWSR fleet was either in use for the Canadian war effort or down for maintenance.[41] To get the work done as efficiently as possible, it hired bush pilots such as Les Cook and George "Dal" Dalziel to scout locations using their aircraft. General Bill Hoge of the Public Roads Administration came along at times, even sitting on a gasoline drum instead of a passenger seat the first time Cook took him up in his Norseman. "Cook was just a crackerjack," Hoge would recall later. "He's the one that showed me the route to follow."

Headaches — and a lot of unnecessary work — would have been avoided had aircraft been used from the beginning. Chester Russell was one of the "grunts" working on the pioneer road toward Whitehorse with the U.S. Combat Engineers.[42] In his memoirs, he recalls how his detachment cleared a twenty-two-metre wide right-of-way — first using only hand tools and then Caterpillar tractors in northern British Columbia. In late 1942 they got to work on the Winter Trail from Fort Nelson to Fort Simpson, ostensibly to establish ground access to the Army Air Corps base there. "Whether our project was a rescue mission to evacuate stranded personnel," he writes, "or simply the next step to transform an air base hastily built in 1941 as part of the Northwest Staging Route into a more fully equipped and permanent operation, the enlisted men in our Company didn't really know." In a last-ditch effort to find a route, the U.S. Army hired a civilian bush pilot — possibly Cook or Dalziel — to take up an officer for a look. "They saw on the Liard River the enormous ice jam (which would be treacherous and impassable for our heavy equipment) that had stymied the trailblazers," notes Russell. "Somehow we needed to cross over the river before we could complete the last segment leading into Fort Simpson, but no one (even with air surveillance) could find an appropriate place to cross." In early January 1943, after months of grueling labour, the road was abandoned.

The Alaska Highway, according to historian William Morrison, was built "without much concern for engineering principles" and "much of it had to be rebuilt when bridges and rights of way washed out in the spring of 1943."[43] The road repairs fell to civilian contractors under the direction of the U.S. Public Roads Administration. In mid-1943 one of these contractors moved more than a thousand workers north from Edmonton on special charter trips using CP Air's Lockheed Lodestars. Because it was so much quicker to fly them up than go overland, according to the editor of *Canadian Aviation*, an estimated 114,000 staff hours were saved.[44]

YA/79_27_48

After the war, the U.S. and Canadian militaries simply walked away from Canol Pipeline camps like this one. Local residents hoped that heavy equipment and canned goods would be left for them to take, or at least sold to them for a few cents on the dollar. Instead, the military's policy was to destroy leftover supplies — but many residents "liberated" useful goods before this could happen.

Despite not living up to boosters' promises of troop and supply transport to military bases, the Alaska Highway did link the NWSR airfields and became a navigational aid for ferry pilots. On some occasions during the war, it also became an emergency landing strip. In November 1942, for example, Les Cook helped save the life of Sergeant James West, a U.S. soldier. Cook flew two Army medical officers from the Northwest Service Command base hospital to the remote Donjek River Crossing camp. West's appendix had ruptured and he was too ill to move. According to the

Whitehorse Star, "After a two-and-a-half-hour battle with storm and darkness" Cook landed at an emergency roadside strip along the Alaska Highway with "five army trucks forming an 'L' and illuming a roadside strip with their headlights." The medical officers "hastened to an improvised operating room in the end of a rough barracks and performed a successful operation."[45]

Scholars such as Morris Zaslow say "[the Alaska Highway] was an ill-coordinated series of projects conceived in haste and panic, with little attention to fiscal sanity, local conditions, or even America's long-term needs."[46] Even so, once the war was over, the Yukon segment of the Alaska Highway reverted to Canadians and it has remained an important transportation route. Over the decades it has also saved the life of several pilots who have had to set down on it.

History has been even less kind to the Canol Project.[47] The pipeline was meant to send petroleum from Fort Norman in the Northwest Territories, to a refinery at Whitehorse, and then on to the American military in Alaska, whose supply from the Lower Forty-eight could not safely be shipped by sea because of Japanese ships and aircraft in the Aleutian Islands. Looking back, however, historian William Morrison argues that by the time construction started in 1943, "there was no real threat to the supply of oil to Alaska by sea." On top of that, Canol cost the American government $140 million — the same price as the Alaska Highway, but it never operated fully. In 1946 the Whitehorse refinery was dismantled, the pipe was taken apart, and everything was carted away. North American taxpayers were dismayed, but northerners were perhaps the most disappointed as they had hoped it would give them a cheaper source of local fuel.

One positive outcome was the "Mackenzie route," a series of airfields that provided landing sites for aircraft working on the Canol Project. Conceived by northern aviation giant Grant McConachie and overseen by bush pilot Matt Berry, these airstrips, from Edmonton through the Mackenzie Valley, were transformed postwar. According to Arctic expert and northern pipeline booster Richard Finnie in 1980, they "remain in constant use, now paved and enlarged as full-fledged airports," and were used for oil exploration in the area.

HOPE AND HEARTACHE

Projects such as the Alaska Highway and Canol Pipeline meant tens of thousands of military personnel and civilians poured into the territories, many of them American.[48] "Even in the case of the friendliest occupations," historians Ken Coates and William Morrison note, "there is always a certain amount of tension between host and occupier." On the national level, many were concerned that Canadian sovereignty in the region was threatened, and the government was already thinking ahead to the postwar situation: by reimbursing the Americans for wartime expenditures on Canadian soil — to the tune of roughly $123.5 million — and engaging in negotiations for proposed fuel reserves for future defence, it hoped to "re-Canadianize" these projects.

The impact on local people and resources was also significant, if not always clear-cut. Many had positive experiences. Sue Van Bibber, for example, who was a young widow with seven children, remembers the soldiers at the camp in Champagne, Yukon, coming to her assistance on a cold winter's day when she had run out of gas while driving with three of her little ones. "One of the soldiers came by and helped me.

RIGHT, ABOVE: Kaska trappers trading winter furs with U.S. Army servicemen at Watson Lake during the war. Many First Nations men also worked on the Alaska Highway Project doing slashing, general construction work, or guiding, and women took in laundry, cleaned maintenance camps, and sold handmade fur mitts, gloves, mukluks, and slippers to the underequipped servicemen.

RIGHT, BELOW: A group of Tlingit, U.S. Army doctors and personnel, and Roman Catholic missionaries at Teslin during the war. Indigenous communities along the Alaska Highway were badly hit by epidemics such as diphtheria. Teslin, however, had an Army hospital and locals were immunized against the disease.

Richard Finnie, YA/81_21_649

YA/82_428_3

YA/82_458_27

Black soldiers made up nearly 10 percent of U.S. service personnel during the war. They were, however, generally barred from combat service, and were often assigned to construction units. In the Northwest Service Command, black soldiers made up 25 percent of the total number of personnel.

He got us some gas and made sure the kids were warm."[49] Many also associated the newcomers with the increased availability of work, goods, and entertainment.

Van Bibber also remembers the soldiers unknowingly brought disease with them: "It wiped out two families I know from Champagne. A lot of the old people died, too." First Nations communities near the Alaska Highway, in particular, were overwhelmed by measles, pneumonia, influenza, chicken pox, mumps, whooping cough, meningitis, jaundice, and dysentery. Venereal diseases also reached epidemic proportions despite attempts to stop their spread.

Operating during a time of crisis and considerably less environmental awareness than today, the military also did not evaluate the impact its activities would have on the land. Trees were cleared for the Alaska Highway, and also cut down for bridge and culvert construction and to provide heat for buildings. The air forces at Whitehorse alone burned an astonishing ten thousand cords, or roughly thirty-six thousand cubic meters, during the frigid winter of 1942–43. Many waterways were ruined or temporarily fished out, game was largely depleted near towns or construction sites, and, as Morrison notes, forest fires were "touched off by careless smokers, by poor storage of petroleum products, by the huge piles of brush left by the bulldozers, and by the smoky fires built to keep mosquitoes at bay." The military engineers did not have much information about construction in permafrost zones, either, and the Canol Pipeline was, according to Morrison, "built in a manner that guaranteed environmental damage. Stripping off the shrubs and turf and laying the pipe directly on the ground ensured that the permafrost would thaw, the ground would subside, and the pipeline would break, pouring out oil."[50]

The quintessential example of how wartime projects and aviation brought both hope and heartache to the North is the Eldorado mine of Great Slave Lake, Northwest Territories.[51] In the 1930s it had meant the promise of profits and cancer-healing treatments, but radium's darker side came out during the war. After it was reopened in 1942 as a Crown corporation, the Canadian and American governments began extracting uranium instead of radium from the pitchblende. Under the veil of complete secrecy, the uranium was then sent south along the Mackenzie River on barges or flown out from the nearby American air base, Bennett Field. It was destined for Los Alamos, New Mexico, where the U.S. military's Manhattan Project was constructing and testing the first atomic bomb.

The bomb all this uranium helped make — code-named Fat Man — would end the war, but with incredible human cost. On August 6, 1945, the *Enola Gay,* an American Boeing B-29 Superfortress bomber, dropped it on Hiroshima. Immediately, 343,000 people were killed. Tens of thousands died of radiation poisoning in the months afterward. A world away, Allied workers were also suffering negative effects from toiling in the radioactive dust. While Ottawa mining officials knew this dust was toxic, they did not alert the local Dene workers or their families: women used discarded sacks to repair their canvas tents, and children played with the ore. In the years after the war, the Dene community near the mine became known as the "village of widows," because so many of the men died of cancer.

ON MAY 8, 1945, A BBC RADIO BROADCAST proclaimed peace in Europe. The *Whitehorse Star* reported "the town was gaily decorated for the occasion" with flags from the Soviet Union, Great Britain, and the U.S., and two thousand people gathered at the baseball park.[52] Under blue skies, they listened as representatives from the military services and the RCMP delivered speeches from the raised platform, and choirs sang hymns and the Allied nations' anthems.

The tone was bittersweet for some, as they thought of the Yukoners and ferry pilots who had been killed while serving at home and abroad, or the lives lost through epidemics and accidents. It was also optimistic. Northerners had proven their resilience and innovation. A new war was beginning, however, and soon the very Russian allies who had received thousands of airplanes over the NWSR would become adversaries in a standoff that would centre on the Arctic.

CHAPTER 5

Arctic Threats

Once the Second World War was over, relations between the Allied powers and the Soviet Union collapsed. As the Iron Curtain came down between the communist east and the democratic west, the Korean War and Cuban Missile Crisis unfolded in the media. Afraid of nuclear annihilation, Canadians and Americans once again joined forces for continental defence. More than ever, it seemed, the Arctic was both a potential theatre of war and route of attack, but the real threat to northerners at this time turned out to be tuberculosis, the "White Plague."

THEATRE OF WAR

To keep the upper hand in what became known as the Cold War, Canada and the U.S. needed to quickly understand what conflict would look like in the Arctic.[1] Beginning in February 1946, the Canadian Forces undertook a series of important operations to study northern conditions in the air and water, and on the ground. It began with smaller operations — Eskimo, Polar Bear, and Lemming — and culminated in Operation Muskox, which involved forty-eight army personnel trekking almost five thousand kilometres from Churchill to Edmonton via Victoria Island and Fort Norman in the Northwest Territories using cabbed snowmobiles called "Penguins." They did not arrive until May 6, having had to leave behind several snowmobiles because of the amount of fuel they consumed. During the trek, No. 1 Air Supply Unit Dakotas and Norsemen established caches and para-dropped roughly ninety-one thousand kilograms of material, much of it forty-five-gallon drums of fuel for the Penguins. They faced extreme cold and hardship, but Muskox proved to Canada it could conduct military operations in the Arctic, if needed.

Over the next decade, the RCAF would complete exercises as part of the Mobile Striking Force, such as Operation Sweetbriar, as well as other realistic "war games" with Allies, Aggressors, and Umpires. In these operations they used Canadian North Stars and de Havilland Vampires, as well as American F-80 Shooting Stars, B-45 Tornados, and F-82 Twin Mustangs "painted black for use as night fighters, which gives them an appearance of deadly efficiency."[2] They painted field guns white to camouflage them, wore white coveralls and hoods, and even

YA/91_37_54

RCAF Dakotas over Whitehorse. The RCAF continued to operate out of the Yukon until 1968, and civilians in town generally had good relationships with them. Stories abound of people enjoying the band, drama club, and Sunday movies and parties on base. Cadets and Girl Guides also enjoyed unsanctioned flights to Edmonton aboard the air force "sked."

dropped propaganda leaflets and took prisoners. As one sergeant on exercise was told, "the only thing lacking should be the 'smell of blood and the screams of the wounded.'"

The two nations also worked on overcoming navigation challenges in the Arctic, where magnetic compasses proved unreliable and, at the North Pole at least, all directions point south.[3] To this end, three B-29 bombers with long-range fuel tanks (and no armaments) along with a Douglas C-47 Skytrain flew patrols in addition to the government's ground monitoring program, and a Douglas DC-4 operated out of Edmonton for special flight testing.[4] These were all American aircraft, as Canada did

not have the necessary planes. The "junior partner" was, however, able to contribute ground facilities, information, and talented personnel such as Keith Greenaway, who was honoured on both sides of the border for his work in navigation techniques and technologies that got around the unreliability of the magnetic compass in the Arctic.

Testing communications technologies such as the Low Frequency Long Range Navigation (LORAN) and Short Range Navigation (SHORAN) systems became a priority at this time as well. The joint forces installed what was called the Beetle Chain of LORAN stations in 1947, which required an airlift of four hundred metric tons of material to an ice strip at Cambridge Bay that spring — primarily using American resources. By mid-1948 there were three high-latitude LORAN stations in Alaska and the Northwest Territories, and the RCAF tried to maintain control by insisting that the commanding officer and at least half of the personnel at the stations were Canadian. These stations, in Peter Kikkert's words, "acted as a series of interdependent 'light-houses' that ships or aircraft could use to pinpoint their position through triangulation."[5] Unfortunately, Arctic atmospheric conditions stymied these efforts as well: it turned out the stations could not send strong enough signals to determine the exact position of aircraft, and they were largely abandoned by the end of 1948. The RCAF Station at Whitehorse continued to research long-range radio communication at northern latitudes until 1968, when the Air Force left the Yukon. Meanwhile, locals like Rusty Erlam, who rubbed shoulders with the personnel at social and sports events, half-jokingly "speculated about all kinds of plots taking place against the Russians."[6]

RCAF Whitehorse was also the launching point for photo-survey operations meant to create accurate maps of the Arctic, which were still sorely lacking.[7] In May 1949 RCAF Lancaster bomber FM 211, nicknamed "Zenith," was equipped with long-range tanks and eighteen hours of fuel. It left Whitehorse headed for the geographic North Pole (becoming the first Canadian aircraft to reach the Pole), with a stop at the Kittigazuit ice strip; from there, they made a fourteen-hour non-stop, round-trip flight. They cruised at 2,750 metres (9,000 feet) and in the unpressurized Lanc, as in other high-altitude aircraft of the era, that meant

the crew had to wear oxygen masks and be constantly on the lookout for signs of oxygen deprivation or "the bends."

Fred Aldworth, who was a navigator on the 408 Squadron Lancasters between 1955 and 1957, remembers those flights well. "The squadron flew out of Whitehorse and every time it flew, the direction was north into what I felt was the never-never land of the High Arctic," he notes. "My duty was directing the aircraft to a point in the Arctic, halfway between two SHORAN radar sites and take the readings required by the scientists back at Whitehorse from Mines & Surveys to derive accurate distances. Then [these] were applied to photos of the landscape taken by the photo Lancs. From all this data, maps were made back in Ottawa." These flights continued eastward from Churchill and finally Thule, Greenland. Canada was still concerned about its sovereignty over the area, and so Americans were not included in this activity; in fact, they were barred from conducting aerial photography or RECON in the region.[8]

Other RCAF aircraft were also used for these photo surveys. George Theriault, of the 408 Squadron at Rockcliffe, Ontario, recalls in his memoir how his group pushed north in four RCAF float-equipped Norsemen as the lakes melted in the Northwest Territories during the summer of 1949 — and even August in the case of Great Bear Lake, the latest in its history. Maintenance staff and ground personnel were flown in on Dakotas. "Our entire team included a detachment of DC-3 photo aircraft plus a crew of thirty men with the four Norseman seaplanes and two Consolidated PBY-5 Canso flying boats," he notes. Over the next two summers, he and his crews set up geodetic sites, flew in personnel and materials to construct Distant Early Warning (DEW) Line sites, and flew skeds (scheduled runs) on Dakotas with wheel-skis from Goose Bay, Labrador, or Edmonton to Iqaluit (Frobisher Bay), and other northern settlements. Dakotas also resupplied the Lancaster photo-survey crews out of Edmonton with fuel, personnel, and other necessities. "We were kept busy flying film, fresh rations, mail and oxygen bottles," flight engineer Geoff Brogden recalls. And Aldworth remembers "the Dakotas carried teams of radar technicians into remote sites all over the place where they set up SHORAN radar equipment and later fired them up any time the Lancs were airborne out of Whitehorse, Resolute Bay, and Norman Wells."[9]

In the years after the war, another Lancaster FM148 — like its sister ship Zenith — became an important part of research and development with the Winter Experimental Establishment (WEE). WEE tested equipment and trained personnel in extreme cold, not just for the RCAF but for the Royal Canadian Navy, Royal Navy, and several British aircraft firms. First based at Gimli, Manitoba, it then moved to Edmonton. When winter there proved too mild, it was shifted to Churchill and Watson Lake, which was consistently -58°C during the winter of 1946. The crews tested emergency equipment, survival kits, toboggans, and cold-weather clothing, and WEE (and its later incarnation, CEPE Climatic) became the global authority on aircraft and equipment operation in cold weather. Unfortunately, accidents and fatal crashes did occur during this time, and remains from several of these can still be found in the water at Watson Lake and the surrounding area.[10]

The RCAF also expanded its wartime Survival Training School in Fort Nelson to a second location at Cambridge Bay.[11] Bryce Chase was a pilot with the RCAF at the time and recalls flying students there in the mid-1950s. "I was an outdoorsy type so that was fun, and it was a very valuable course," he notes. "The first five nights it got down from -55°F to -60°F — it was fresh!" He also remembers that some of the students, who came from different military branches from the Canadian, American, and British forces, were not exactly suited for outdoor survival. "I had a guy who was doing the course for the second time," he says. "He was from Toronto and had a degree in engineering — terribly bright but when it came to common sense ..."

Luckily Canada also had people adept at bush living — and spotting potential threats — on its side. In 1947 the military created a nationwide reservist force called the Canadian Rangers, and many northern indigenous people joined up to keep an eye out for enemy ships or aircraft north of 60. In December 1956 there were 2,725 Rangers in Canada and on several occasions, historian Whitney Lackenbauer notes, they reported "submarine and ship sightings, suspicious individuals, even unexplained bombing activity on Northern Baffin Island, "producing bits of bombs as evidence."

ROUTE OF ATTACK

In addition to a possible theatre of war, Canadian and American militaries saw the Arctic as airspace a Soviet bomber or missile might simply pass through on its way to a final southern destination. During the Second World War, the Joint Board of

Don MacNeil

HMCS *Labrador*, an icebreaker with the Royal Canadian Navy, was commissioned in 1954 and became the first ship to circumnavigate North America east to west via the Northwest Passage. It was equipped with Helicopter Utility Squadron 21, two Bell HTL-4 light observation helicopters for ice reconnaissance, and a Piasecki HUP-3 tandem rotor helicopter, which had a rescue winch.

Defence had built a series of what were called Crystal Stations along the Crimson Staging Route. These were meant to provide weather reports to the Allies and refuelling stops for Allied fighter planes between aircraft factories in the western U.S. and Scotland. Larger fuel tanks meant the stations were no longer needed for war by the time they were constructed, but it meant there were airfields in the Arctic when it came time to consider continental defence options.[12]

In 1947 the Americans still operated three of these wartime airfields in Canada, including Frobisher Bay, where they returned with four hundred personnel to ensure runway No. 1 was functional. As Kikkert notes, they also had plans to improve the runways at Eureka Sound and Resolute. While it seemed unlikely that the Soviet Union would (or could) launch a "round-trip bombing mission to the United States," writes Kikkert. "American military strategists and the press still obsessed over the idea of enemy planes coming over the Pole to launch raids on the continent's industrial heartland."[13] Any incoming aerial attack would likely come over the North Pole, making use of Spitsbergen, Greenland, and Canada's Arctic islands as stepping-stones to the continent. Frobisher became a base for Strategic Air Command (SAC), and Boeing B-52 Stratofortress bombers carrying nuclear bombs flew between Frobisher and similar bases in the United States twenty-four hours a day, ready to deliver "massive retaliation" in the event of attack.[14] All this unsupervised American activity in the North made Canadian officials nervous, and they soon decided to step into the fray. The only problem was the RCAF did not have aircraft capable of trans-

porting the big, heavy loads into the Arctic sites. This made the Canadians completely reliant upon the Americans for construction and supply missions for several years. In 1950 the RCAF took over at Resolute and Frobisher, and, with newly acquired planes for the job, could now complete the semi-annual supply service for the sites. It was also able to haul construction materials to the new Alert Wireless Station — which continues to be the most northern permanently inhabited settlement in the world at roughly 82.5° N latitude (the Geographic North Pole is at 90° N).[15]

In 1954 the RCAF announced a call for bids from civilian contractors to undertake massive airlifts for the construction of DEW Line sites, and over the coming years companies such as Spartan Air Services, Pacific Western Airlines (PWA), Transair, Nordair, and Bradley Air Services would secure major contracts. Pierre Berton was a young journalist beginning his career when he did a tour of the North in 1954 and 1955 for *Maclean's* magazine. Even with his purple prose, his descriptions of the diversity of men and machines and the hectic nature of the airlifts ring true. In April 1955 he wrote that the DEW Line sites were "little more than scratches on the white surface of the Arctic.... [A] handful of construction workers on the scene had scarcely had time to level out runways for the big planes bringing in supplies, oil, food, and equipment, to build each station." When he landed at Frobisher in an Avro York with a heavy load, there were twenty-one aircraft parked, including other Yorks, Dakotas on skis, Canso flying boats, Curtiss C-46 Commandos, Flying Boxcars, and Globemasters. "Planes seemed to be arriving by the minute now," he wrote, "each trying to get one last cargo before the light failed." Early the next morning the pilots readied to complete two more trips "up-island" before returning to Mont-Joli, Quebec, for another load.[16]

The forty-one DEW sites in Canada were completed in 1957, the same year the North American Aerospace Defense Command (NORAD) was created.[17] NORAD evolved over the coming years to incorporate detection and interception of not just manned bombers from the U.S.S.R., but intercontinental ballistic missiles and "orbiting space vehicles" as they were called in the September 1963 issue of *The Roundel*. In addition to the DEW Line, other acronyms began to appear: SAGE (Semi-Automatic Ground Environment), BMEWS (Ballistic Missile Early Warning System, and SPADATS (Space Detection and Tracking System). These spoke to the obsolescence of the radar facilities as the new weapons could cross the Arctic in minutes instead of hours, and satellites could instantly detect when a missile launched.

Even so, the DEW Line sites continued to be staffed and operated for another decade before they were slowly decommissioned. This meant ongoing supply missions for the RCAF transport squadrons. "Resolute Bay was the hub of our spring and fall resupplies," says Bryce Chase, who in addition to training military personnel to survive in the Arctic, piloted a Flying Boxcar with 435 Squadron.[18] "We flew out from Resolute Bay to Mould Bay to weather stations, Eureka, and to Thule in Greenland. We also did shuttles from Thule to Alert after the ships dropped supplies there." He recalls that the resupply missions took about two weeks in the spring, and the pilots, ground crew, and support

staff connected to four aircraft from 435 and 436 Squadrons would stay onsite during that time. He also remembered the close calls on these flights, including a near miss with a Lancaster on a covert operation and a hairy landing or two. "I was coming in to Cambridge Bay one night and the wind was blowing 40 knots across the runway, blowing snow up to 800 feet," he says. "I let down into that crud and tried to find the runway. I got down on the sixth trip with the port engine dying and it's a good thing I got in because it was a long way back to Yellowknife on one engine."

In addition to the resupplies, part of Chase's work in the Arctic was playing Santa. Each year during the early Cold War era, the RCAF undertook Operation Santa Claus in concert with the Canadian federal government and civilian operators to bring Christmas cheer to those at northern stations — including Inuit, who travelled to town after they heard the airdrop schedules on the radio. "Santas" like Chase dropped Christmas trees and panniers (wicker baskets) attached to parachutes from their Flying Boxcars to the Arctic outposts. "It was great fun," Chase recalls. "Of course it was dark, but it was moonlit and there are not a lot of clouds in the Arctic so the visibility was great. The most interesting one was to Alexandria Fiord on Ellesmere in 1958. We had to drop to the Mountie station — there were two Mounties and two Inuit there. We went to the top of the glacier, put the wheels and flaps down and just stayed off the glacier and then we had to do a smart turnout." Sometimes they picked up cheap bottles of rye — and other "extra goodies" — at the USAF station at Thule, Greenland, and snuck them into the panniers.

Don MacNeil

TransAir's Avro York, CF-HFQ, after it ran off the runway at the FOX-Main DEW Line Station at Hall Beach, Northwest Territories in September 1956. It was damaged beyond repair. Companies like TransAir, Spartan Air Services, Nordair, Hollinger-Ungava Transport, and Pacific Western Airlines all had big contracts hauling people and goods into the Arctic during the this frenetic period of Cold War construction.

Frobisher Bay and Resolute became military hubs for postwar defence activities across the Eastern Arctic. Frobisher had an airfield as well as weather and radar stations; what it did not have was enough people to keep services running on base. According to estimates, larger stations required roughly forty personnel, while smaller ones were staffed by five to twenty-five people.[19]

The USAAF and RCAF needed a local labour force, and Inuit needed wages to replace the Arctic fox fur revenues they had lost when the price dove from thirty-five dollars a pelt to just three after the war. When the resource economy tanked and the cost of trade goods skyrocketed across the North, Inuit found they could no longer afford southern food staples like sugar, rice, and

flour. They also could not buy ammunition and modern hunting equipment. At the same time, they discovered the game had been depleted around the posts — or hunting was restricted by new game laws. Inuit life around the bases shifted: they began incorporating wage labour into cycles of subsistence hunting and fishing combined with trapping. They began to work for the bases, driving tractors and trucks, pumping out and distributing oil to station personnel by truck, and operating the local laundry. When supply ships came in the summer, they unloaded the cargo.

They also quickly realized the *qallunaat* (non-natives) valued their artwork and handicrafts. Even before Toronto artist and government agent James Houston worked with the Cape Dorset Inuit to

Don MacNeil

Hudson Bay clerk, John MacNeil, and Sub. Lt. Fitzgerald examining Inuit carvings and dolls at a post in the Arctic in 1956. Servicemen during this time purchased a large number of these types of work and helped popularize them for southern collectors.

produce unique block printing, sealskin stencil printing, and soapstone carvings in the 1950s, Inuit sold their furs and crafts. Bush pilot Ernie Boffa, for example, brought out soapstone carvings and polar bear skins to sell on the Inuit's behalf, and RCAF personnel regularly purchased artwork. As Peter C. Newman notes, the artwork especially soon became internationally renowned, and by 1960 the HBC bought forty tons of carvings each year for resale in southern Canada. Considerable sums of money were then sent back to the carvers.[20]

Despite their mutual co-operation and interests, the government and RCAF brass tried to keep Inuit and military personnel apart as much as possible. An RCAF Station Standing Order placed the Inuit village near Resolute out of bounds "to all personnel except on business"— and "between 2:00 and 4:00 p.m. Sunday afternoon for taking pictures."[21] Inuit were kept out of the stations as well. Tomassie Naglingniq remembers when he and some other teenagers got too close to the upper base while out hunting. The armed American military personnel took the ptarmigans they had shot and called the RCMP to escort them home. "The next day," he notes, "they did not return the ptarmigans, but they gave us pop and

Don MacNeil

Charlie Sagiaktuk at the Frobisher Bay military base in 1955. Inuit were critical to the successful functioning of military bases and DEW sites, but opportunities for employment were often limited.

chocolate in return. That was a scary experience … they just told us not to go up there again." There were negative experiences, as historian Whitney Lackenbauer writes, but several Inuit "remembered how service personnel 'would pile up food, such as a hundred pounds of flour, or a hundred pounds of sugar,' where they knew Inuit visited." And even Naglingniq recalls with fondness the new food, cigarettes, mechanized vehicles, and movies (usually westerns) available at the RCAF/USAF Frobisher station in the postwar years.[22]

There was some waged labour available to Inuit outside of military bases as well. Southern workers were usually ready to give it their best shot, but some decided it was not for them after they landed in darkness, blowing snow, and freezing temperatures in winter — or a cloud of mosquitoes in summer. As author Frances Jewel Dickson notes, one man stepped off the plane at the Hall Beach DEW Line site, FOX-MAIN, "took a look around and blurted out, 'What the hell am I doing here?' He resigned on the spot and boarded the same aircraft back to Winnipeg."[23] Still, for the one thousand southern workers employed by DEW Line sites, contractors only hired about one hundred Inuit. As Edward Nazon of Arctic Red River told Northern Affairs Minister Jean Lesage in 1954, the mines, oil companies, airlines, and transportation companies did not want to hire indigenous peoples. "All these firms," writes Pierre Berton, "at great cost and trouble, coping with high turnover and premium wages, were importing reluctant white workers from the Outside."[24]

When they could find work, Inuit were not always happy with the way they were treated by non-indigenous co-workers or managers. Minnie Aodla Freeman, an Inuk from Cape Hope Island, worked as a translator in the late 1950s at Frobisher. "I lived with a *qallunaaq* woman," she says. "The *qallunaat* with whom I worked accepted me from 9:00 a.m. to 5:00 p.m.; socially, I did not exist."[25] Anthony Apakark Thrasher, who had spent most of his childhood in the residential school at Aklavik, began working at various DEW Line sites when he was eighteen years old.[26] He once had a foreman turn a hose on him in -60°C weather, and was soured by southern business practices: "They tell us to get jobs, yet there are few jobs. When we do get hired, it is often for not longer than two months and twenty-nine days. We are laid off then because, after three months, we would have to be regarded as permanent workers entitled to benefits like northern allowance and isolation pay." He also could not believe how his monthly pay dropped after he joined the Canadian Government Manpower Training Course that sent him and thirty other Inuit to Edmonton aboard a C-46 transport plane for a six-week, government-run driving course. Before, he had made twelve hundred dollars a month, but driving the water hauling truck at a DEW Line site only netted him two hundred dollars.

THE WHITE PLAGUE

While military strategists were paranoid about a Soviet invasion coming over the North Pole, local residents faced a real and present danger: tuberculosis. TB, as it is commonly known, has existed in most societies since antiquity, and among North American indigenous populations for at least three hundred years. In the first half of the twentieth century, it found a particularly fertile ground in Canada's residential schools and indigenous communities. Sometimes called the "White Plague" because of an infected person's pallor, or "Consumption" because of how patients seemed to waste away, most people are familiar with its most visible symptom: coughing up blood. But as scholar Laurie Meijer Drees notes, "[it] can also attack the bones, including the spine, as well as a person's internal organs and glands."[27]

For most of the disease's history, there was no cure, only treatment, and many died from it. When TB took hold of Arctic communities after the war — some estimates from the mid-1950s reported that one-third of Inuit were infected with active or inactive forms of the disease — it understandably alarmed southern public health officials.[28] Unfortunately, these officials did not know what today's research has taught us, that "TB cannot survive in adequately ventilated environments ... [and that] stress, malnutrition, and other illnesses play a large role in exacerbating the disease." So when non-indigenous people had encouraged Inuit to congregate in settlements — the HBC for the fur trade; missionaries for gaining converts and ministering to their flocks; the military as a source of labour; and the government for administration purposes — they had been courting disaster.

For their part, Inuit agreed to move to these communities in large numbers between 1945 and 1960 to be closer to children attending residential schools, and to access housing and social assistance when the fur trade collapsed. These sites, though, were often overcrowded and unsanitary, and nutritious country food was not always available. In the case of Simonie Michael, who wanted to work at the Frobisher Bay military base, it meant setting up camp on a nearby island called Ukalirtulik which he found "'impossible to live in,' with no water, harbour, or easy access to work on the mainland. They gathered scrap packing material and boxes to make houses, which were not insulated and only warmed by makeshift heaters furnished out of powdered milk tins."

"There are all kinds of ways of dying out there," Thrasher wrote about life in the Arctic, but TB was as formidable as whiteouts, polar bears, or rotten ice.[29] Inuit had strategies to survive the inherent dangers of the North, and traditional medicine to deal with many ailments, but TB was different. Many saw it as a *qallunaat* disease that required outside treatments, and as historian Mary Ellen Kelm argues, "By offering therapy for the new ailments, Euro-Canadians seemed to be recognizing their culpability for the diseases, and this fit nicely into Aboriginal notions of causality." The problem was the availability of non-native medicine in the North at this time was basic at best. For example, Biddy Worsley, who was a nurse at the Aklavik Anglican Hospital, says "We had the basics but there was no water supply or sewage system. There were about one hundred beds, and most were filled with long-term tuberculosis patients."

And Aklavik was considered a major centre at the time. Most of the Arctic's population relied on the rudimentary medical training RCMP officers, missionaries, and HBC post managers like Ernie

Lyall received.[30] Lyall was representative of these essential, but unofficial, practitioners: he was given a medical kit and a manual on how to use the items and what different symptoms meant. He also took a course from St. John Ambulance. "Not too much [training], but it helped," he recalls. "Unfortunately we've had people die in our kitchen because we didn't know enough ... or have the right medicine, or we didn't get to them in time."

Soon Lyall would be part of a widespread campaign to eradicate the White Plague once and for all. In 1947 an annual TB vaccination and X-ray program was launched. Their first routes were along the Alaska Highway in the Yukon, and in the Arctic, medical teams were sent as part of the Eastern Arctic Patrol using icebreakers like the *Nascopie* and *C.D. Howe*. To reach distant camps and settlements with no roads or harbours, the government relied on planes. In 1949 the government hired Associated Airways out of Yellowknife to conduct a tour and sent word to Lyall ahead of time asking him to try and gather people at Spence Bay at the appointed time. In May, before spring breakup, pilot Ernie Boffa arrived in his Norseman along with a doctor, dentist, and two X-ray technicians from the new Charles Camsell Indian Hospital in Edmonton. Lyall recalled that people camped in igloos around the partially built HBC post and for four days, they filed into the stove-warmed kitchen. "The people would stand up against this X-ray screen," he says. "The people didn't mind being X-rayed, they went along with that, but of course this was the first time that anyone was going to be shipped out for this disease."

An Inuit woman and her child in front of an Associated Airways Norseman and its crew, c. 1950. Associated Airways was based out of Edmonton and flew tuberculosis X-ray tours around the Arctic to Inuit communities. If individuals were found to be infected, they were often transported to the Camsell Hospital in Edmonton for a "rest cure" that could last years.

First X-ray tour experiences did not go so smoothly in other parts of the Arctic. Apphia Agalakti Awa was alone at her camp with her five children at Upirngivik during the summer of 1955 when an airplane landed nearby.[31] She and her children went down to meet it. "When we got to the beach, a man came out of the plane and started talking to us," she says. "He was making airplane noises with his mouth. He was making signs with his arms and talking in a language that didn't make any sense at all. Since I didn't know what he was doing, I just watched him ...

suddenly the man pick him [her son, Simon] up and put him on the plane. I yelled at him, 'That is my child! Don't take my child!' I was scared. He was trying to get us to follow Simon into the plane."

She was worried about leaving her untended sealskins in the tent near the dogs, and not being able to leave word for her husband who was out on the land, but her concern over Simon won out. She and her four other children boarded the plane, where the anonymous pilot had pulled Simon on to his lap to play with the plane's controls. When

Awa's eyes adjusted, she saw that her older sister, her brother-in-law, and their five children were also on board. It was a short flight to Ikpiarjuk, but in the packed plane, Awa — made ill by turbulence and fear — vomited. When they landed, a Catholic priest came over to explain that they were going to be X-rayed; this was a foreign concept to her, but she had heard of surgery, and was afraid they were going to cut into her chest. The priest reassured her, interpreted for her throughout the procedure, and afterward gave her and the other Inuit tea, flour, sugar, and similar staples. Then the pilot flew them back to their camps. "It was not as bad as the first flight," Awa noted, "we were not vomiting any more. We had drunk tea and eaten Qallunaat biscuits, so we were all very cheerful."

Once the X-ray film was processed in Edmonton, individuals like Awa realized the tours were just the first step. "An awful lot were found with TB," Lyall remembers. "Later they sent planes around to pick up those that had to go out to hospital." Boffa returned with his Norseman and delivered the first ten patients to Cambridge Bay, where they boarded bigger planes, such as four-engined C-130 Hercules cargo aircraft, bound for Edmonton. There were those like Joe Teemotee who enjoyed the trip from Iqaluit (Frobisher Bay) to Mountain Sanatorium in Hamilton, Ontario. The seven-year-old boy flew by DC-3 to Moose Factory, Ontario, in 1958 before he transferred to a train; he was "very excited the whole time. This was so different from the dog teams his father had." But Lyall remembers others — especially after the first round of patients did not return immediately — who protested the move south. "There was an awful lot of fuss kicked up," he says. "A lot of weeping and whatnot going on, and saying they wouldn't go, they'd rather

commit suicide first…. I can remember two or three times when people that had to go out for TB treatment even tried to run away so they wouldn't have to go out."[32]

These strong reactions are not surprising. In the 1950s, reports estimated that one-sixth of Inuit were in southern sanatoria — sometimes for years.[33] Indian Health Services, under the direction of Dr. Percy Moore, prioritized these facilities over setting up local health stations and hospitals. As in other instances of federal government "Indian policy" at the time, it is possible that Moore and others like him had good intentions with bad outcomes; many suggest racism led to darker motives. While most treatment protocols were the same in segregated Indian Hospitals as elsewhere, as Drees notes, "at times Canada's Aboriginal population was used as a 'test' population for new drugs or TB interventions."

Sometimes a person would be evacuated from their northern camp very quickly, without being able to tell their family where they were going. To compound this, Indian Hospitals would often return school-aged children to residential schools "with or without parental knowledge or consent." Patients could also be there for years, as the only known treatment at the time was what was called a "rest cure." The majority of patients at the hospital made a partial, if not full, recovery. Not all survived, however, and while the government paid to have patients flown to Edmonton for treatment from distant parts of the North, they would only send bodies as far as the rail extended unless the deceased's family paid for it. Sometimes no one even notified their families. This meant that many northern indigenous people who died while at the Charles Camsell Hospital were buried in Edmonton.

Don Hamilton and a Fairchild 82A, CF-AXL, which he used for his charter and cargo transport business out of Edmonton, c. 1960. This aircraft is now only one of two remaining in the world and is housed at the Reserve Hangar at the Canada Aviation and Space Museum in Ottawa.

Patients also lost loved ones while they were away. Anthony Manernaluk, who was adopted by an Oblate missionary at the age of fifteen and became his companion and guide, was sent to a sanatorium at Brandon, Manitoba, in 1956. "I tried to tell the doctor that I didn't want to go," he says. "I knew that Father Buliard won't make it on his own and I wanted to be with him." Buliard, who had already been airlifted once to save his hand after falling through the ice, was not adept at Arctic life; without Manernaluk's help, he soon disappeared while checking his fishing nets and was never heard from again.[34]

The pilots who transported X-ray teams and patients saw these jobs as both important

for public health, and an important source of revenue. Pilot Don Hamilton began flying the annual X-ray tours in March 1959 using one of Pacific Western Airways' single-engined Otter bush planes, and Ernie Lyall often went along as interpreter and guide.[35] From his base at Cambridge Bay, Hamilton would fly ten hours a day for roughly two hundred hours on each survey, bringing the medical team to DEW Line sites, and flying Inuit in from outlying camps. He noted that one person would always stay behind to feed the dogs, and "I would have to fly another trip to have him X-rayed. It was essential not a single person be missed, as they could be

Gerry Rivest

Callison Flying Service's Stinson 108 Voyager, CF-EZQ, in the late 1940s at Thistle Creek, near Dawson City, Yukon. Pat Callison had a long career in the Yukon, spanning several companies that he founded, including Klondike Helicopters.

a TB carrier. This was great, as it added more hours to an already lucrative contract." By this time the technicians could develop the X-ray film on-site or even in the aircraft while flying, so they would immediately indicate who needed to be evacuated for treatment. The rest would be returned to their camps.

These "Easter tours," as Hamilton called them, were not easy on the pilots and aircraft. Although it was spring, he notes it could be -55°C, so he would go out to start the Otter's engine periodically while the technicians worked. Pilots also exposed themselves to disease. Pat Callison, who was a pilot in the Yukon in the late 1940s, transported hundreds of people — indigenous and other — infected with polio, meningitis, and TB, from their communities to Whitehorse.

From there, an RCAF aircraft would fly them to Edmonton. "CP Air found that their passengers objected to having patients on the regular carriers," he wrote in his memoir. "I realise now I never gave a thought to the risks of my own health when I would be enclosed for 2 or 3 hours in a small, practically airless aircraft cabin."[36] Hamilton actually contracted polio while transporting patients and was hospitalized for several weeks in the 1950s.[37]

Much of the history of northern disease reverberates with heartache and suffering, but there were bright spots too.[38] Many patients at Edmonton's Charles Camsell Indian Hospital made deep and lasting friendships and communicated with each other through an in-house newsletter, the *Camsell Arrow*. Some "broadcast tapes of themselves singing or sending messages" to their families at home through a radio program set up by a Catholic priest at the hospital. Schoolwork also provided a distraction and some enjoyed learning new skills like playing the guitar. Many also enjoyed the occupational therapy programs where they could make artwork, handicrafts, or carvings. They would then sell these in the gift shop to make money. What is ironic, considering TB often attacks the lungs, is the most popular item patients bought at the hospital canteen was cigarettes, which they smoked freely. Finally, some went on to rewarding medical careers, or took advantage of the Hospital's rehabilitation and job placement program in other trades.

In 1960, Ernie Lyall remembers, the people of Spence Bay had a new association with airplanes: a huge Hercules transport, likely from the RCAF, flew in with the "beginnings of a nursing station," which "the people were very pleased about" because they would not have to be sent out for treatment as much.[39] By this time, doctors had found actual cures for tuberculosis using new antibiotics that people could take at home, and "sanatoria had practically vanished from the landscape of TB treatments."[40]

In the 1970s the Indian Hospital system was gradually dismantled as indigenous communities began agitating for administration of these health services.[41] The legacy of the TB X-ray tours — like the experiences of patients at the sanatoria — is mixed. "Many of us believe that if we weren't treated for TB in southern hospitals there would be a lot fewer Inuit," says Eemeelayo Annie Nataq,

who served on the Baffin Health Board for several years. "TB was so rampant, contagious and we had no way to treat it up North, so our gratitude is huge." Nevertheless, there were gaps in communication and consent, and Nataq became involved in health services to ensure they "were adequate and relevant to our people."[42]

As HISTORIAN WILLIAM MORRISON NOTES, the "basic premise of the post-war world was that life should be better for everyone."[43] Government policy-makers may very well have been acting in this spirit with TB X-ray and evacuation programs, but they were often products of their time: colonially minded and culturally ignorant. Unfortunately, the same can be said of many of the pilots involved during this period. What the RCAF, government agents, and others tasked with solving the "Inuit problem" mostly ignored was the agency and adaptability of the North's indigenous peoples.

At the same time as Canada fought TB in the North, it positioned itself as the defender of Arctic skies and the expert in cold-weather warfare. It may have been a balancing act, but Canada and the U.S. largely worked well together on joint continental defence, with the smaller nation taking advantage of American technical expertise and superior equipment, while at the same time retaining sovereignty over the region. The two nations certainly made important technological gains with wide-ranging applications for northern aviation in all its forms.

CHAPTER 6

New Horizons

By the 1950s the stereotypical bush pilot in movies and books was a man's man flying the Great White North, but that image was slowly giving way to a new reality. Women, people of colour, and indigenous aviators were pursuing their passion for flight and adventure however they could, and serving remote communities in the process. Northern indigenous towns and settlements lobbied for air service and airports as well, finding airplanes increasingly useful for passenger, cargo, and medevac flights. "Flying school buses," however, which brought children to distant residential schools, were much less popular with families and, often, with the pilots flying them.

A NORTHERN BOY

When Métis pilot Fred Carmichael began flying in the 1950s, it showed how things were changing. Within a generation of the first aerial forays into the Northwest Territories, the region was producing its own pilots — and indigenous ones at that. Southern media may still have been alternately romanticizing and bemoaning the North and its "natives," but Carmichael showed homegrown skill in the hangar, skies, and the office, and made a lifelong career for himself, inspiring others along the way.[1]

"It was quite a struggle," Carmichael says of his path. "I come from a trapline. I drove a dog team and the next thing was an airplane — even before a vehicle. We were called 'half-breeds' — we didn't fit in as Indians or as whites so we learned to be independent. I'm Métis, that's what I am. My mom was Gwich'in and my dad was

Irish-Canadian." It was when Carmichael's family was living on the trapline outside of Aklavik, Northwest Territories, that he saw his first airplane: his mother had chartered it to fly supplies back to camp. "When I saw that Stinson come in, that's when I caught the bug. I was twelve years old." Four years later, he got his first ride from Don Violette, a Protestant missionary who had come to the area after the war. The airstrip in Aklavik was right next to the baseball field where Carmichael and his friends played, and one day when Violette was doing the inspection on his Stinson Voyager, he asked Carmichael to help him put the cowling on. "Then he asked if I wanted to go up for a test flight. Man, I jumped at that!"

Violette saw how interested Carmichael was in flying, and he lined him up with an Air Force colleague who was the instructor for Gateway Aviation in Edmonton. To make enough money for lessons, Carmichael

NWT Archives/Dept. of Public Works and Services/G-1995-001-4511

Fred Carmichael was the first indigenous person in the Northwest Territories to receive his private and commercial licenses. Antler Aviation was just one of the companies he founded during his long career, and it operated several Cessna 185s like this one (likely CF-TTJ) in the mid-1980s. Carmichael went on to receive the Order of Canada for his contributions to aviation and the North as well as his many air rescues.

worked as a "ramp rat" for Mike Zubko at Aklavik Flying Services and as a mechanic's helper on the local DEW Line sites. "In the fall of 1954 I caught a ride down with Mike who was going to do a changeover on his Aeronca Champion," he says. The next year, after flying evenings and weekends while attending Bible College, he got his private licence — the first indigenous person in the North to do so — and headed back to Aklavik to save enough money to buy his first airplane. After working another six months on the DEW Line he paid $2,600 to Don Hamilton in Edmonton for a Stinson Voyager of his own, CF-EYB. "I flew that back North and built up enough hours to get my commercial," he says.

After he received his commercial licence — again the first indigenous person in the Northwest Territories to do so — he went looking for a job. "I remember writing to Wardair and they told me I needed 2,500 hours and I probably had 250." Unable to find flying jobs, the nineteen-year-old worked for the government at Reindeer Station as operations manager. It was there he saw his opportunity to get a foothold. "I saw a need — there was only one flying service in Aklavik and the people at Reindeer Station had to wait a long time to get an airplane. They would call to bring supplies out to the four reindeer herding camps and fly around and keep track of the reindeer. So I applied for a licence — Class 7 specialty aerial patrol and inspection."

Carmichael was not approved, and his appeal was also rejected. "I even appealed to the Minister — I'm not a quitter!" He was finally granted his licence after a friendly encounter with a government official at Reindeer Station and he built a radio station and two-hundred-metre airstrip.

In 1959 Carmichael decided to apply for a full charter licence for the company, called Reindeer Air Service. Like his mentor, Mike Zubko, who had started Aklavik Air Service with RCMP officer Stan Byer in 1947, Carmichael brought in partner and friend Lyle Trimble, an RCMP Constable in Aklavik who also had a Stinson. "He was a good writer so he did all the applications," Carmichael notes. By that time, most people had left Aklavik for the newly-constructed town of Inuvik, so the pair applied for Reindeer Station and Aklavik, knowing it was an easier sell. "We operated out of there for six months or so and then applied to transfer base to Inuvik," says Carmichael. "I quit my job with the government because it was boring as hell compared to flying and I moved into Inuvik in 1960."

It was a busy time for Reindeer and the other two operators in Inuvik. "There was lots of work for everyone — it was a good time," Carmichael recalls. "There were thirteen or fourteen communities to service and a lot of trappers them days living on the land. There were scientists around, and a little bit of exploration." Reindeer changed its aircraft from the Stinson to a Cessna 180 on skis and floats since there were no airstrips, and Carmichael flew it constantly. "There was no limit on the hours of flying like there is today. We'd fly around the clock in the summertime. I ate a lot of chocolate bars and drank

a lot of Coke some days. But honest to God, the best days of my life were flying the Cessna 180 servicing the little camps. People really appreciated it — it was just like a big family out there."

They especially appreciated the air evacuations from the communities to the new hospital in Inuvik.[2] "Didn't matter, day or night, we were flying medevacs — stormy weather, didn't matter. We flew in tough, rough conditions without the kind of navaids they have today," he says. Often he flew women who were in labour, and on at least two occasions the baby made an early arrival. One time, he picked up a mother-to-be with her medical escort, as well as four off-duty doctors and nurses in a Beech 18 at Holman Island, 650 kilometres away from Inuvik. "Somewhere over the Arctic Ocean she delivered premature. We had a battery-operated incubator on board and we fired it up and put the baby in there, but the battery was dead. Luckily Verne Oppal, the maintenance guy from the hospital, was riding up front with me, and we took the cover off the light, shut off the switch to the light, cut the cord on the incubator and tied it in to aircraft power supply." Thanks to their quick thinking, baby and mother were fine.

Carmichael also rescued a lot of people who had gone missing. "If you're in somebody's backyard, ask him to come as a spotter," he notes. "So I would bring people along that knew the area." This helped him find two Inuvik residents who decided to go to Tuktoyaktuk one summer day in a power boat and took a wrong turn. "They wound up tangled up along the Arctic coast," he says. "Air Force SAR came up, but after ten days they couldn't find them. As soon as they left town I could go searching in my

AAM

Pilot Cedric "Ced" Mah standing with the Super Beech 18 he flew for Gateway Aviation in 1969. Mah was famous for dumping forty million USD over the Himalayan Mountains during the Second World War to avoid crashing. The money was never found and the U.S. Internal Revenue Agency continued to keep a close eye on the popular bush pilot's spending until his death in 2011. 'GNR is now operated by Vancouver Island Air.

Cessna 180. So I got two of the herders from Reindeer Station and we found them in one and a half hours just by eliminating all the possible turn-offs. Those herders knew every nook and cranny."

In the late 1960s Reindeer Air built the first real commercial hangar in Inuvik and a three-thousand-foot airstrip at the west end of town. "It was a real pain for the trappers to haul their fish and meat through the terminal building," he says. "There were a lot of private pilots here at the time, so everybody chipped in — we had crews down picking up driftwood and chopping willows, so it didn't take too long." The company also got into the "heavies," like DC-3s and C-46s, and applied for a licence in 1970 to operate a scheduled service

down the Mackenzie Valley to Yellowknife. "We wound up in a public hearing against Wardair and CPA," Carmichael recalls. "Everybody and their dog intervened — even from Saskatchewan and Manitoba. All these high-priced lawyers came up to fight this little guy from the Arctic." In the end, unbeknownst to him, Carmichael was represented by one of Canada's top lawyers, Richard Rohmer, for the price of an airline ticket. He just thought Rohmer was a nice reserve Air Force pilot he had flown from Tuk to Inuvik. "I let him fly and we became very good friends," he says.

With fifteen aircraft, including four Dakotas, a C-46, a Beech 18, and Cessna 180, Carmichael relied on his staff of pilots, engineers, and ground crew that included legendary pilots like Cedric "Ced" Mah who had flown many missions — and dumped forty million USD — over the Burma Hump during the Second World War. "We were part of a family," Carmichael remembers. Which is why, when Dakota CF-TQW was overdue on December 1, 1972, with Carmichael's good friend George Landry at the controls, he went into high alert. "We had been hauling fuel from Norman Wells into the Mackenzie Mountains," he remembers. "I was on one ship and we were going round the clock — twelve-hour shifts. At 3:00 a.m. I get a call from flight services saying my DC-3 was overdue. It was storming like hell but I got in an Aztec to fly over the route. We searched for ten days until finally the weather kicked up a bit and someone spotted the wreckage."[3]

A freak storm had blown them thirty kilometres off course into the mountains and the Dakota had crashed only sixty metres below the summit of a nearly two-kilometre-high hill. "This was George, my buddy," Carmichael notes sadly. "George had three children, and the other guy had two. That was one of the toughest things for me." Later that year he was approached by Gateway Aviation to buy the company but was swayed by local friends to sell to them instead: "They said, 'Freddie, you know, you're a northern boy and Reindeer's a northern company, kind of a shame to let it go to a southern company.' These guys didn't have much money but they had a plan." Carmichael sold Reindeer Air in 1974, but as he notes, he was not a quitter, and would soon return to flying.

FLYING THROUGH GLASS CEILINGS

Fred Carmichael, George Landry, and Ced Mah were part of the new generation of bush pilots working for companies based in, or flying into, the North, like Wardair, Gateway, Pacific Western Airways, and Canadian Pacific Airlines.[4] They shared the skies with other resourceful people determined to make a go of it despite the long hours, hard work, and — at times — brick walls. Women, for example, were told after the Second World War to return to the home, but some wanted to fly out of northern towns or outposts in the Arctic. Gertrude De La Vergne, Canada's third licensed woman pilot, had wanted to fly the airmail run from Edmonton to Aklavik in the late 1920s, but "they told me a woman would not be suitable," she says. "The commercial licence was too expensive to take without the assurance of finding work so I regrettably gave up flying about a year later."[5]

In 1932 Eliane Roberge Schlachter approached Grant McConachie of Yukon Southern Air Transport for a job after she received her commercial rating — but as a secretary.[6] Soon, however, she "convinced him to check her out on all of Yukon Southern's aircraft and to let her fly the right seat as required." Officially, she was the secretary and dispatcher; unofficially she served as co-pilot or spotter for search and rescue and firefighting missions, but Eliane's flying activities were a well-kept secret. As author Shirley Render notes, "Raised in the north and able to handle herself in the wilderness, Eliane was not lightweight, physically or mentally. A strapping woman with a friendly no-nonsense manner, she was perfectly capable of moving freight, spending the night in the bush, or throwing a drunk off a plane."

Northwest Territorial Airways's DC-3, CF-BZI, on a Northwest Territories government charter flight for members of the Legislative Assembly, c. 1967. The Yellowknife-based company founded by Robert "Bob" Engle, had a fleet of five DC-3s in the 1960s on scheduled services throughout territories, as well as Beavers, Beech 18s, and eventually two Lockheed Hercules aircraft based out of Calgary.

One way for women to get into aviation was by becoming an air hostess or stewardess, which mainstream society saw as an extension of their "natural" nurturing role. A February 1940 article in *Canadian Aviation* announced that Trans-Canada Air Lines had been "snowed under with more than 1,000 applications for positions as air hostesses" after they announced a new training school in Winnipeg.[7] The editor tried to normalize their ambitions by calling them "homemakers in the sky," but let slip their real mission: they were "anxious" to "get a foothold in flying," whether as aeronautical engineers like Elsie MacGill, aircraft assemblers, or base managers. Some reached their goals. In the Yukon, for example, Jessie MacLean had supervised air traffic for Yukon Southern out of Whitehorse beginning in 1939. "Yukon Jess," the editor noted, had started as a stenographer in Yukon Southern's Edmonton office, became "their first and only stewardess" on the Barkley-Grow airliner out of Edmonton, and then took on the agent job in Whitehorse. There, she was in charge of getting weather reports, watching the skies, and persuading people "that the only way to travel is to fly."

Dick de Blicquy

Bradley Air Services' Super Cub on Bathurst Island in 1959. It was the first year of the thirty-six-inch tundra tires, made by Goodrich Tire to Weldy Phipps's specification, using a mould from the early Lockheed Electra. They were very successful: five Cubs flew about fifteen hundred hours and made hundreds of "off strip" landings during that three-month season.

In 1942 Grant McConachie, who had by then moved to CP Air, hired two young nurses, Jewel Butler and Melba Tamney, to be stewardesses on the Lockheed Lodestars into Whitehorse from Edmonton and Vancouver. "The early days were very exciting and adventurous," said Butler in an article in *CP Air News* forty years later, "especially for a girl who had led a very sheltered life until that time. I was so nervous I don't remember much about my first flight north." They usually looked after twelve to fourteen passengers, often business flyers or pregnant women going south to deliver. On one flight that was delayed at Watson Lake for five days, Butler "served as surrogate mother to a

group of nine unaccompanied children passengers."[8] Another way in was to help out with a husband's flying operations. Watson Lake Air Services was started after the war by Jim Close, Stan Bridcutt, and Gordon Toole, who was still with the weather service, but now had his commercial licence. The base was by the Toole house, and Gordon's wife, Rose, had her radio operator's licence and would work the radio to manage their forestry flights and supply trips for Canada Tungsten (Cantung).[9] Frances Coolin, who became Fran Phipps after she met and married Welland "Weldy" Phipps, had wanted to get her licence but decided flying with the "goddamndest pilot the Arctic's ever

113

known" (as one prospector put it) and raising their nine children, was enough adventure for her. She kept the home fires burning, though, first in Ottawa when Weldy worked at Spartan and Bradley Air Services, then in Resolute in 1962, when Weldy started Atlas Aviation. "It looked like it would be a good future," Fran says. "He really wanted the family up there — he had a lot of free time. We found a school for the children, and there were other families moving up there. And we had good Inuit friends."[10]

Most women flyers in the North found work — at least initially — because they came as part of a husband-and-wife team. Betty Campbell (née Booth) and her first husband, Jack Fleming, flew special photography missions for Spartan Air Services in the far north, after the Air Force had relinquished this work to commercial operators.[11] Campbell was a pilot as well as a scientist with the Research Council of Canada when she signed on with Spartan as a photographer. "There were virtually no maps, no services," she remembers. "Maintenance, weather reporting, fuel all had to be organized by the companies doing the work. Spartan even built an airstrip at Pelly Lake so that they could complete the photography of the central Arctic." By the late 1940s companies like Spartan, Kenting Aviation, and Aero Surveys Limited began filling in the "blank spots" using war-surplus aircraft capable of flying at high altitudes such as Avro Ansons, P-38 Lightnings, B-17 bombers, and de Havilland Mosquitoes.

In 1954 PWA hired Dawn Connelly to manage the Yukon Flying School at Whitehorse and fly the odd charter on its Beaver and Junkers W-34, CF-ATF;

her husband, Ron Connelly, would fly the scheduled flights. "I was given a seniority number and I wore their bush issue: leather jacket, tan shirt, and green slacks," she notes. "When one of the presidents of an oil company found out that I was going to be his charter pilot he was not too happy. However, after an engine failure and a safe return he was only too happy to fly with me again. And once they had flown with a woman pilot they would take great delight in saying their pilot was female."[12] After four and a half years, PWA withdrew her seniority number when it began negotiating to join the Canadian Air Line Pilots Association. "PWA was not strong enough to withstand pressure from the powerful Association and it did not want to fight one woman's battle," she notes.

She was not defeated — far from it. Dawn and Ron moved to Dawson in November 1959, bought Callison Flying Service's fixed-wing operations, and went into business as Connelly-Dawson Airways. The company had two Beavers and two Cessna 180s, which it used for two sked runs as well as charters for oil and mining companies. Ron primarily flew and managed operations, while Dawn did the books, dispatching and the odd charter. In 1960 they added a DC-3. "We were the first company in western Canada to use a DC-3 as a bush aircraft," she says. "We flew it like the Beaver.... We used the DC-3 primarily for fuel caching during the winter, for the summer geological camps and their helicopters." They continued this partnership until 1962, when the couple split up and Dawn went to work for Cassidair out of Watson Lake, flying charters and running its flying school.

Stuart Russell

A camp shack is loaded into a Pacific Western Airlines Lockheed Hercules L-100 air freighter, CF-PWO, at Yellowknife in 1968. In 1967 PWA became the first commercial air carrier in Canada to operate the civilian version of the Hercules C130 military cargo plane, doing everything from hauling loads to build the school in Old Crow to moving oil rigs for Panarctic Oil. PWA crews had nicknames for each of the six Hercs the company operated: 'PWO was called "Oscar."

By the next year, Dawn had married her former beau and fellow pilot Gordon Bartsch. "We started our married life by flying fish hauls in a DC-3 in the Territories that winter," she says. They moved to Calgary and established Range Airways, which mostly worked out of the northern areas of the provinces. In 1966 they mended fences with Ron Connelly and created Great Northern Airways (GNA) by combining Yukon Flying Services, Connelly-Dawson, and Range Airways. GNA connected Dawson, Old Crow, Inuvik, Sachs Harbour, and points in the Arctic islands, then took

over CPA's Yukon skeds, flying DC-3s between Whitehorse, Mayo, and Dawson. At its peak it had one hundred employees, and twenty-four aircraft, including Twin Otters, Fairchild F-27s, and a Douglas DC-4. In 1969 it also started a Whitehorse–Inuvik sked service called the Arctic Trader Service, and ran it until GNA folded in 1971 after a "run of bad luck and heavy losses." Dawn split her time between Calgary and the North, and worked as operations manager, traffic manager, executive assistant to the president, and "hauled everything from fish to oil rig equipment" in Beavers, Otters and DC-3s.

Atlas Aviation's Otter, CF-RWU, in typical spring weather at Disraeli Fiord on the north coast of Ellesmere Island. Atlas was working with the Defense Research Board on Hydrographic studies of floating ice sheets and shelf ice.

Other women started as "package deals" with their husbands. Molly and Jack Reilly began flying for Peter Bawden Drilling Services of Calgary, Alberta, in 1959. They both flew DC-3s in extensive periods of darkness and extreme weather conditions, often without radio communications or navigation aids. In the 1960s, Lorna de Blicquy and her husband, Dick, split their time between New Zealand and the Arctic. Then, in the summer of 1967, Weldy Phipps convinced the couple to relocate to Resolute to work for Atlas Aviation.[13] With the promise of a family trailer and time on a new Twin Otter, they flew a twin-engine Piper Apache up — with their infant along for the ride. On one memorable occasion, Lorna rescued Dick and his five passengers when his Twin Otter lost an engine and they were forced to land on Ellesmere Island, sixteen hundred metres up on a glacier. "I'd done all of three circuits in the Beaver and thought, no problem," she says. "So I volunteered for the rescue mission. I was brave but stupid. I had some instrument training and the forecast called for improvement within the hour, so I barreled off from foggy Resolute and into cloud." Two hours later, she realized she was lost. "A search for a man down in the Arctic was bad enough; a search for a female would be a blow for women pilots everywhere. I wanted to pass on a decent record to the next girl. Making a fool of myself five hundred miles from the North Pole wasn't the way to do it."

The weather cleared enough for her to pinpoint her position and an hour later she touched down at Eureka. Lorna spent two summers in the High Arctic flying Beavers

Elaine de Blicquy

Lorna V. de Blicquy at the controls of a Beaver in 1967 at Resolute, Northwest Territories. In addition to her pioneering work in the air, the "Fiord Flying Mama," as she was affectionately known, became the first woman civil aviation inspector in Canada in 1977.

and Apaches, flying right seat with her husband, Dick de Blicquy, in the Twin Otter, and "spent a summer flying the Beaver as air support for the Department of National Defence Research Board's scientific program on Ellesmere Island." In 1968 Lorna took Spartan's conversion course on helicopters and received her commercial rotary licence on a Bell 17.

OUR AIRPLANES

Commercial air services did an amazing array of jobs using a variety of equipment. Merlyn and Jean Carter set up Carter Air Services in Hay River, Northwest Territories, in 1962, with Merlyn as pilot and Jean running the business side of things. They catered to prospectors, trappers, and hunters, and they flew fish and freighting.[14] Over his career, pilot Ernie Boffa did everything from freight fish from Great Bear Lake, to DEW Line work, to helping map migration routes of ducks, geese, and caribou, to flying for a fishing lodge on Great Bear Lake, servicing the camp, and connecting guests from airlines in Yellowknife.[15] Don Hamilton also started flying supply for DEW Line sites with Bradley Air Services in the 1950s. Then he moved on to Pacific Western Airlines where he flew medevacs in an Otter, aerial reconnaissance, and wolf baiting trips (though, he was "never comfortable setting out the poison baits, [so] losing this work did not particularly hurt my feelings."). He even transported a ten-month-old polar bear cub, secured in a forty-five-gallon barrel, from Holman to Yellowknife, from where it left for the Alberta Game Farm in Edmonton.[16] Other pilots have chronicled

similarly varied and colourful experiences flying in the North.[17] When it came down to it, northern bush operators could not afford to specialize too much.

Aircraft also increasingly brought northern indigenous peoples into contact with the Canadian government for administration. This included the notorious identification numbers given to Inuit in the 1940s, worn like military dog tags around their necks, and "Project Surname," which took place between 1968 and 1971, recording Inuit's preferences for last names.[18] Commercial pilots also regularly flew Indian Agents to communities for treaty payment gatherings, and when the circuit court system was put in place, companies such as Great Northern Airways flew justices of the peace to places like Old Crow.[19]

Indigenous peoples' encounters with the justice system, however, were fraught with cultural misunderstandings. Ernie Lyall, who lived in the North from his teens on and married an Inuk, notes: "In those days the [Inuit] didn't really understand that they were Canadians, what that meant, or what the law was." In his memoir he describes a flight where he went along as interpreter with the RCMP, who were investigating the suspected murder of a woman in Aveetochak, halfway between Thom Bay and Fort Ross in the Northwest Territories. It turned out the woman had been old and asked her son to help her die. The RCMP kept the son, his wife, and the man who had helped them at Spence Bay for several months until a Canso came in to take them to Cambridge Bay for the inquest. There a doctor confirmed her advanced illness, but the son was still convicted of "aiding in the commission of a suicide" and sentenced to one year. "When we arrested this boy, we'd explained to him what

Dick de Blicquy

Pilot Bob O'Connor checks out a Northward Aviation Dornier DO28 that found a soft spot on a strip on Melville Island in the Northwest Territories, c. 1964. The strip was in regular use by Beavers and Otters on tundra tires but the Dornier did not fare as well on this occasion.

the law was and what he had done wrong and why we had to take him out," Lyall says. "I don't think he was worried about being arrested, or resented it, or even felt guilty, because what he'd done was a thing that they used to do from years and years back ... this wasn't murder in their minds."

Air services relied on local residents to act as on-the-ground agents. In Old Crow, the Yukon's only fly-in community, Stephen Frost Sr. has been there for almost every aircraft landing. "I was maybe seventeen years old, they had a little Stinson aircraft used to fly in here from Fairbanks, Alaska," he says. "They had the contract for mail — came in once a month. I remember meeting the plane. There'd be three to four sacks of mail — no passengers. And should the weather be bad, it's cancelled 'til next month."

In the 1950s Connelly-Dawson began delivering the mail on the second Wednesday of every month. Frost Sr. and Charlie Thomas recalled when the company came in with their Beavers, Beech 18, and DC-3 on wheels before the airport was built, landing on the frozen river in winter and sand bars in summer. At first the company only handled freight, but when they began carrying passengers, "It was fifty dollars to Dawson, no ticket, just hand him fifty dollar bill," Thomas recalled. The town stayed in contact with the air services through the RCMP's daily radio contact with Dawson and Aklavik.

As air traffic increased in the region, Frost Sr. found himself in demand as a helper. The first contract he had was when Ron Connelly hired him and his brother at ten dollars a day to carve out a landing strip next to a damaged PWA aircraft. They took a boat up the Porcupine River, hiked thirty kilometres in, and then lived in the bush for a month while they built an airstrip and waited for enough snow cover for Connelly to fly in mechanics in his Beaver. "Kind of crazy when you think of it," the seventy-seven-year-old chuckles. He would also stake out the landing strips on the river in winter and radio local conditions to pilots, using the hill behind Old Crow as his two-thousand-foot indicator. In summer, he would take his boat to scout sandbars on the river, and call pilots with the information. "Some of those strips were supposed to be two thousand steps for DC-3 but it was quite a bit shorter than that," he says. "And we'd have to go on there and throw bigger rocks off. Some of us called it the international airport."

Over the next decade, he looked after the airplanes — "we called them our airplanes" — and passengers, while his wife was the local ticket agent. There was no mechanic in town, so he helped patch a Beech 18 with "strong plaster"; he helped change a piston on a DC-3, and finished it off when the mechanic was called away; he squired people to and from the airport once it was built in the late 1960s, and he comforted passengers who were nervous about flying. "I had lots of fun," he remembers. "Most people in our community did it without pay."[20]

By the 1960s, famous Gwich'in "Here are the News" columnist Edith Josie faithfully reported the comings and goings of aircraft to and from Old Crow in her signature style. Connelly-Dawson figured prominently in her columns, bringing the mail, freight, police, and doctor into town, even the odd journalist or tourist, returning patients home after surgery or giving birth, or flying out Old Crow's famous cross-country skiers

to compete in Inuvik and Fairbanks in 1968. She also expressed the town's disappointment when planes could not get in. On January 16, 1965, she wrote: "Connelly Dawson airways DC 3 will arrive Old Crow with mail and everyone expect aircraft so bad. When we see aircraft sure make us feel different. When no plane sure look lonesome town. Every day they expect Connelly Dawson aircraft from Dawson but never see nothing. For about couple days the weather are bad sometime ice fog and it is not clear. So no plane for long time."[21]

Josie also reported on their efforts to secure an airport at this time. On September 5, 1965, she wrote, "Airport is the most important thing for the aircraft to land on. When River is raise high and no place to land because no sand bar show." By 1968 residents had electric lights in their homes, but still no airport, and she called on Yukon premier Erik Nielsen, a pilot himself, to help the community build one. It would take the beginnings of oil exploration in the region and visits by VIPs, like Indian Affairs Minister Jean Chretien and the Governor General of Canada in 1970, however, to finally get one built.[22]

FLYING SCHOOL BUSES

Missionaries also found airplanes useful for spreading the gospel around the North.[23] The bishops of both the Anglican and Catholic churches flew as passengers in commercial planes to visit the distant reaches of their districts, and in 1937 the Catholic Bishop G. Breynat bought a single-engined Waco biplane, CF-BDY — though the septuagenarian decided to leave the flying up to pilot Louis Bisson of Hull, Quebec.

NWT Archives/June Helm fonds/N-2004-020-0250

The Oblates of Mary Immaculate operated this Beaver, CF-OMI, from 1957 until its northern missionary pilot, William Leising, retired in 1965. Famed bush pilot Punch Dickins had given the Oblate Bishop his first plane ride in the North, and he convinced them to buy a Beaver when it was time to trade in their old Norseman.

It was a Protestant flying missionary, Don Violette, who gave Fred Carmichael his first airplane ride when he was sixteen years old, and several other priests became pilots in this period. None embraced aviation as enthusiastically as Father William "Bill" Leising of the Oblates of Mary Immaculate (OMI). In September 1940 Leising flew to Edmonton and traveled north to Fort Smith, Northwest Territories, overland. For the next seventeen years he worked as a secretary, pilot, and then air engineer under Bishop Joseph Marie Trocellier. In 1945 he had learned the importance of aviation in a personal way: while building a church in Yellowknife, he was airlifted to the hospital at Fort Resolution after he cut his index finger off with a power saw.[24]

In 1951 an Ohio couple donated their red four-place Aeronca Sedan to the Oblates after one of Leising's successful fundraising tours, where he showed films of his northern travels. With his new private licence, he flew the Sedan, CF-GMC, to the mission home at Fort Smith. Two years later, he also received his aeronautical engineering degree, and began envisioning a fleet of Oblate aircraft flying northern skies. This fleet never materialized, but over the next decade and a half, Leising visited missions, flew Oblates to their northern assignments, and did mercy flights first in the Aeronca, and then in bigger bush planes such as the Norseman (CF-GTM) and Beaver (CF-OMI).[25] One of Leising's main aerial responsibilities, though, was to shuttle indigenous children

Noorduyn Norseman, CF-EIH, flies over Yellowknife, c. 1946 when it was operated by McDonald Aviation. It crashed shortly afterward in Allan Lake, Northwest Territories, and was submerged for forty-six years before being salvaged in 1993. Once it was restored, it was donated to the Alberta Aviation Museum in Edmonton, where it is currently mounted on a pedestal outside.

to and from the North's residential schools. He often called his plane the "Flying School Bus," as he and an Oblate Brother or the Bishop picked children up from settlements and flew them to distant schools at Chesterfield Inlet, Aklavik, and Churchill, Manitoba.[26]

Northern Affairs also hired bush companies to do this work. Lamb Airways' pilots Keith Olson and Jack Lamb recalled moving Inuit children to and from school to villages like Repulse Bay, Gjoa Haven, and Pelly Bay during the period in the company's Beaver and Norseman.[27] Olson remembered taking the kids away was "really hard." Long-time northerner Ernie Lyall wrote in his memoir that one of the pilots he knew "took to calling himself 'the chief kidnapper.'" The description would

have felt apt to Lyall, who worked for the HBC and federal government out of Spence Bay and married an Inuk, Nipisha. His children went to the Anglican school at Aklavik, sixteen hundred kilometres away, and he recalled it was "five years before any of mine came back; I never saw them once, not even in the summers ... when my kids came home they didn't think of us as their parents."

The Anglican and Catholic schools tried to get children home for Christmas and summers, but Leising acknowledged it depended entirely on weather conditions — and if he could find the parents. "Sometimes the parents would move from, say, Sachs Harbour on Banks Island over to Minto Inlet, three hundred miles away, to find good fishing and sealing," he said.

"If we couldn't find them, we'd bring the child back to school. Some were sad not to have found their parents. They'd go and sit in the airplane. 'Maybe my father die?'"

Often children were unable to contact their parents at all during their time at school because of lack of phone or mail services. With these long absences and silences, it is no wonder many indigenous parents resisted sending their children to school. They had other good reasons too: children were abused, forced to abandon their native languages, and split-up families strained to make a living and get enough to eat. In some extreme examples, children died while away at school.

Lyall knew first-hand how hard it was on families, but still worked with Northern Affairs, RCMP, and flying companies from the mid-1950s to the 1960s to collect children from settlements and bring them to school. He needed the work, so did his best to follow instructions, telling the parents "how things were going to change in the north, and if their kids went to school and got an education, they could get a job."

"Sometimes the parents would want to go with the kids," Lyall notes. "Lots of the parents cried."

Lyall often flew as interpreter with Don Hamilton transporting children from Arctic settlements to the Catholic and Protestant residential schools in Inuvik. In August 1960 they loaded twenty-eight children into a PWA twelve-seater bush plane to meet one of the company's DC-3s at the Gladman Point DEW Line station on King William Island. Hamilton recalled that first year, "this was accomplished easily, as all the kids wanted to take an airplane ride. The Eskimo parents let the kids make the decision, which is usually

their way. Neither the kids nor their parents realized they would not see each other again for at least nine months.... In subsequent years, it was difficult to get the students to sign up for Inuvik."[28]

With the sheer number of flights undertaken in challenging northern conditions, it is a miracle none of the children were ever hurt — and a testament to the skills of pilots like Leising and Hamilton.[29] They both had close calls, however. Leising had a forced landing with four children from Holman Island and Coppermine en route to school at Aklavik, but luckily everyone was fine. In June 1965 Hamilton smashed an engine while coming in for a shore landing at camp near Thom Bay, Northwest Territories while ferrying six children home from the school in Inuvik. Luckily no one was injured and they were able to radio for help. Within a day residents of Spence Bay came to their rescue on snowmobiles and dogsleds.

Many parents did release their children to the schools. When Anthony Apakark Thrasher was six years old his father, who worked at the Catholic mission in Tuktoyaktuk, sent him to residential school in Aklavik: "Perhaps he didn't want to send me away but the priests at the Church had told him I needed an education, needed to learn of the ways of civilization down South."[30] Many parents wanted their children to receive instruction in *qallunaat* ways, but wanted them nearby, safe, and to retain traditional knowledge. They also felt pressured by the "law of the teachers" and the federal government. Once the Family Allowance was introduced across Canada after the war, the government had a bigger stick to enforce compliance: it would withhold this small but significant in-kind payment from families unless they sent their children to school. The Awas experienced this first-hand. When Apphia's husband decided to keep one of his sons home to help him feed the family — and learn how to live on the land — the teacher at Pond Inlet threatened "they would cut off the family allowance that we were getting for him. My husband said that was okay, and that is what the government did. They cut off our family allowance."

Leising extolled the educational benefits of residential schools, and they did, in the words of historian William Morrison, "produce a growing educated elite" who in many cases advocated for indigenous rights in boardrooms, courts, and different levels of government.[31] Leising also believed there was no lasting damage wrought by the extended absences and separation from family and culture. Residential school survivors and scholars like Morrison, however, clearly show that it resulted in "mission school syndrome" whereby individuals felt alienated from their home communities as well as non-native ones. For children like Anthony Apakark Thrasher, along with learning how to read and write and perform *qallunaat* jobs, he suffered from the types of trauma, addiction, violence, and other personal problems common to those sent to residential schools.

By the late 1960s the government had taken over administration of the schools from the churches. Residential schools in the Yukon were phased out and schools in the Arctic had largely shifted to a secularized,

racially-integrated day school model.[32] Many Inuit moved off the land into towns like Inuvik, Iqaluit, and Rankin Inlet, and they sent their children to the community schools. Due to pressure from parents like Ernie Lyall, schools also began hiring Inuit teachers and aides, adapted the curriculum to make it relevant locally, and taught mostly in the local language while integrating English slowly. Because of these changes, by 1968 almost all school-aged, indigenous children were regularly attending school — up from half a decade earlier.

AFTER THE SECOND WORLD WAR, CIVIL AVIATION in the North took off. Cheap war-surplus aircraft and out-of-work RCAF pilots along with a booming resource economy, government program expansions, and contracts for DEW Line construction and supply, meant if you had an airplane and a licence, you could probably find enough work to keep flying. There were as many pilots and companies as there were types of work and, as in other eras and places, the frontier was less socially conservative than the centre, and "rules" could be bent or broken as necessary. These pioneering individuals faced discrimination at times, but like the first bush pilots in the North, they persevered with characteristic resourcefulness, and a wry sense of humour. And residents appreciated them. "I always give credit to those long ago flyers," says Old Crow's Stephen Frost Sr. "They all did good and tried to serve the north."

CHAPTER 7

Miracles, Tragedies, and Just Plain Luck

From the first time aircraft flew above the skies of the Yukon and Northwest Territories, there were crashes, searches, deaths, and dramatic rescues. There were also more than a few mysterious disappearances in the "Watson Lake Triangle" and the Barren Lands. By the middle of the twentieth century, the amount of air traffic rapidly increased in the 3.9 million square kilometres north of 60, and navigation aids and regulations struggled to keep pace. That would change — some bush pilots might say for the worse — when a series of high-profile cases hit the global media.

SEARCHES AND RESCUES

Accidents affected all sorts of aviators in the territories — civilian, military, RCMP — and all levels of experience. There was the USAF C-54 Skymaster carrying forty-four people, including a civilian woman and her infant son, that disappeared on January 26, 1950, after making contact with the Snag airstrip. Despite the launch of "Operation Mike" involving seven thousand Canadian and American personnel, eighty-five search aircraft, and one million dollars, to this day the wreck of USAF #2469 and the remains of its crew and passengers have gone undiscovered.[1] In 1951 ex-RCAF pilot Johnny Bourassa went missing in his Yellowknife Airways Beaver on his way back from Bathurst Inlet. Four months after his May 18 disappearance, the plane was located 560 kilometres south-east of Yellowknife, but Johnny was never found despite a massive air search as well as a ground search by local indigenous reservists, the Canadian Rangers. He left behind his wife and two children and an enduring mystery.[2]

Sometimes even the rescuers needed rescuing. This was the case when eleven Canadian Forces personnel were stranded south of Watson Lake in October 1968. The 442 Squadron Grumman Albatross was dispatched after two American hunters crashed their small floatplane, but then the amphibious aircraft had a mechanical issue on take-off, so a twin-engined, tandem-rotor Labrador helicopter was sent in with a new propeller. Then it suddenly lost power and crashed. When another Labrador was finally dispatched to bring the SAR techs and accident investigators out, its engine caught fire, the cabin filled with smoke, and the pilot was forced to "ski" down the mountain into the river valley. Luckily no one was injured.[3]

Cases like these could be puzzling or tragic, but they did not attract the same kind of national and international attention as a series of high-profile crashes and survival stories from the 1960s and 1970s. Each seemed more sensational than the last, and the public eagerly followed them, partly out of voyeurism, and partly, perhaps, because they could see themselves more readily in the survivors' shoes. Commercial and private air travel had jumped in popularity, and as people read their newspapers or watched the news on their television sets they asked themselves, "Could I do it? Could I make it out alive?"

R.J. Mokler was assistant searchmaster at the Rescue Coordination Centre in Edmonton in the early 1960s and mostly dealt with small, civilian planes that went AWOL.[4] In 1968 he detailed several SAR operations in the North in a memoir. He recalled the challenges of finding mining charters out of Yellowknife as pilots would often leave notes with their wives rather than spill the beans on prospectors' flight plans. He also wrote, "The policy of the picturesque mining town seemed to be, 'If I'm missing, one of my friends will find me.'" They might know their friends'

LEFT, ABOVE: CH-113 Labrador Helicopter that crashed on October 24, 1968, in northern British Columbia while delivering a new propeller to the downed Canadian Forces Albatross. George Popadynec, an aerospace engineer who was part of the two-person board of inquiry, dubbed the ensuing series of events the "Cold Fish Lake Caper."

LEFT, BELOW: Three of the Royal Canadian Air Force's Grumman Albatrosses from 442 Search and Rescue Squadron out of Comox, British Columbia. In mid-October 1968, one was dispatched to Cold Fish Lake, B.C. to recover the bodies of two American hunters who had died when their small float plane crashed. The Albatross suffered a serious propeller-pitch control problem, however, and the rescuers soon needed rescuing themselves.

flying habits and the country, but in the years before civilian SAR organizations like Civil Air Search and Rescue Association (CASARA) and Civil Air Rescue Emergency Services Alberta (CARES Alberta), the Air Force was called in — and was in charge.

In 1961 alone, Mokler was involved in several large-scale Air Force searches north of 60 for downed aircraft. Two involved the same single-engined, four-seat Mooney M20A, in the same area of Southampton Island (but with different pilots). The first time the plane went missing was in June. It had carburetor troubles on a flight from Churchill to Coral Harbour. The pilot had a radio compass and radios, but no emergency transmitter; even so, a USAF Douglas SC-54 Skymaster search aircraft sent up from Goose Bay, Labrador, with VHF homing equipment quickly picked up its signals. "It was located in a hilly area and could be seen only from the west side of a ridge, which would have made a visual find just plain lucky," Mokler wrote. An RCAF Otter brought containers of fuel and two aircraft technicians to do an on-site repair, but after trying to take off, the Mooney lost all power and crashed, damaging the nose and propeller. They left the small plane in place and flew the Mooney's pilot out in the Otter to safety.

In October a pilot-mechanic went up to fix the damaged Mooney and was in the process of flying it back to Churchill via Rankin Inlet when he lost radio contact. When he did not arrive at Rankin, an Otter and Dakota were deployed on an expanding track crawl, but had to stop periodically as blizzards blew up. A few days later, the pilot arrived in Chesterfield Inlet and told the SAR team that he had been "forced down by poor weather and landed on glare ice on a lake 185 miles north of Chesterfield

Inlet.... he then built an igloo, where he remained comfortably through the storm that followed." Luckily the pilot had a sleeping bag, rifle, ammunition, and rations — and knowledge of how to survive on the land. This was not always the case with northern flyers, as Mokler would discover in the biggest SAR operation of his career.

MIRACLES HAPPEN

On March 26, 1963, a Canadian Pacific Airlines plane landed at Whitehorse on a special trip from Watson Lake. On board were two people long given up for dead by all but their families. But while they were gaunt and injured, Helen Klaben and Ralph Flores were miraculously alive after crashing their small plane and spending almost fifty days in the bush in freezing temperatures without training or supplies.[5]

The saga had begun in early February when Klaben had answered Flores's ad to share fuel costs on a flight from Fairbanks, Alaska, to California. Flores was a forty-three-year-old father of six, who had been working as an electrician on the DEW Line for eighteen months; he was heading home in his Howard DGA-15P (N5886), a five-seat airplane built in 1941, to see his family. Klaben, twenty-one, was originally from Brooklyn, New York, and had set off for Alaska the year before with a friend to explore the world and find her place in it. After working at the Bureau of Land Management in Fairbanks, she was ready to move on to the next phase of her adventure, and California in February sounded appealing.

Klaben was originally going to fly south with an airline, but getting there in a small plane was even more exciting. She had

only been in a small aircraft once before, and never on a long-distance cross-country flight in winter. They left Fairbanks without mishap, but after landing at Whitehorse the weather closed in and the temperature dropped to a bitter -41°C. They finally took off at 11:00 a.m. on February 4, and headed toward Fort St. John, British Columbia, using what local pilots dubbed the "Trench Route." It was to be a three-hour flight, but seasoned bush pilots like Jack McCallum "knew that the route was notorious for high winds and few safe places to land. In a storm it could be very unforgiving."[6] Sure enough, the Howard soon encountered a blizzard. "For the next two hours we flew constantly in and out of bad weather," Klaben wrote in her memoir. "Then we ran into storm clouds closer and closer together so that, at last, they seemed to have closed in all around us." While the Howard should have had double the needed fuel for the flight, the engine died mid-flight and the airplane crashed nose-down into a thickly-forested area on the side of a mountain sixty-four kilometres south of Watson Lake.[7]

Klaben blacked out. When she came to in the steeply angled cabin, she looked for Flores. She saw that their baggage had struck the back of his seat, "breaking it loose and pushing him into the sharp edges of the instrument panel. The panel was covered with blood." They would soon learn that, along with the lacerations on his face, he had broken his jaw and several ribs. Klaben had not fared well either: she had a broken arm and a split chin, and her foot had been crushed. But they were alive. Before shock and the cold could immobilize them, Flores crawled out through the broken windshield to build a fire; he then made a splint for Klaben's arm and dressed her foot, collected up as much warm clothing from their baggage as possible, and the two spent the night in the plane. They draped the engine cover over the hole in the windshield as best they could to keep out the howling wind.

When the Howard failed to arrive in Fort St. John, the authorities were alerted. This included R.J. Mokler, the RCAF SAR flying officer and assistant searchmaster who worked at the Edmonton Rescue Coordination Centre. That night a Fairchild C-119 Flying Boxcar departed 435 Transport Squadron at Edmonton to do a track crawl from Fort St. John to Whitehorse, following the flight path the Howard was supposed to have taken. When morning broke, several local pilots — many of whom had had their own close calls — volunteered to search the area, including Lloyd Romfo, Pat Callison, Lloyd Ryder, Maurice "Moe" Grant, and Bob Campbell. Jack Chapman flew an RCMP Beaver on skis to Watson Lake, then took the Alaska Highway route back to its Whitehorse base, hoping to catch a glimpse of the downed plane. But the Howard was painted white and cream, so it blended into the several feet of snow already on the ground and as well as the new accumulation, which covered broken branches or any other potential evidence of a crash. "The trees were laden with snow," noted Mokler. "So burdened that they leaned over in whatever direction, and could easily camouflage a downed aircraft from view within fifty feet of the roadway."

Even with another SAR operation underway near Winnipeg, more military aircraft were sent, including two amphibious Albatross from Vancouver, an Otter from the Air Force Auxiliary Squadron at Calgary, and Dakotas from Edmonton and Cold Lake.

They were needed. As Mokler wrote, with a six-hour fuel tank, the Howard "could have been well out in the Pacific to the west, Alaska to the northwest or the Arctic to the north ... in the Rocky Mountains to the south, as far as the states of Washington and Montana." For the first week, however, following SAR protocols, the military pilots and civilian volunteers focused their attention within a 120-kilometre radius of Whitehorse. That weekend, bolstered by a whole squadron of auxiliary RCAF planes brought from Edmonton, they expanded their parameters to the most likely zone: it still covered almost one thousand kilometres.

Throughout this period, the RCMP Beaver was used to follow up on hundreds of tips from trappers, local indigenous people, or other pilots. But none panned out and the RCAF called off the search March 1. By that time, thirty-five RCAF planes had flown 825 hours and covered almost a quarter of a million square kilometres. Its pilots had worked an average of fourteen-hour days, flying in fog, freezing rain, and light snow; they had received extensions on scheduled inspections and commercial airlines had flown in spare parts. These herculean efforts had cost the RCAF one million dollars. As Mokler noted, without survival gear, provisions, or bush experience, "the odds during the bitter cold ... swung heavily against the survival possibility. Further, if the missing plane's occupants had landed safely, surely they would have alerted passing aircraft by means of a fire or some sort of message on the ground."

It turned out Flores and Klaben *had* tried to signal to the search planes, but to no avail. Flores had immediately set to work fixing the plane's radio after the crash, but could not repair the distress frequency.

He also cut down trees with a hammer and chisel — he had no hatchet or axe aboard the Howard — and dragged them into the fire. When the radio did not seem to work, they used mirrors, painted a red SOS on part of the fuselage with oil paints, and Flores wrote the plane's registration on fabric and climbed a tree to hoist it like flag. Three weeks after the crash they heard and saw a Cessna. "It flew down so low over our little clearing we were sure it had spotted us," Klaben wrote. "We were so excited. We screamed and yelled and danced around, waving and hugging each other."

The plane did not return, dashing their hopes of rescue. By this time, they had been without food for eleven days. Klaben had decided the trip was a good opportunity to go on a diet, so had packed only some fruit and Tang drink crystals. They had also expected to eat at refuelling stops at Fort St. John and other points on the way to California. Flores had a few cans of sardines, tuna, and fruit salad, along with saltine crackers and five small pieces of chocolate. Thinking they would be rescued quickly, they had eaten it all during the first ten days. When it became clear this would not be the case, Flores tried to catch rabbits using a homemade slingshot, snare, and spear, but had no luck. Then they began a morning routine of melting snow and eating toothpaste, and pretended it was milk, tea, or soup.

At this point, even with his pain and weakness, Flores hiked through deep snow for four days toward the sound of a distant chainsaw to find help. Later he would learn the chainsaw was being used at a trapper's cabin only sixteen kilometres away from the crash site on Airplane Lake. But at the time, Flores only made it halfway to the cabin. Klaben, who could not stand the pain of walking on her frostbitten feet, stayed behind, not knowing if she would survive on her own or ever see her companion again. She stayed in the wreck for over a week until Flores came back, and it was the closest she came to giving up: on her seventh day alone, she stopped tending the fire or melting snow to drink. Luckily Flores returned, restarted the fire, got her water, and told her his plan to move to a new site by a lake.

Common wisdom tells crash victims to always stay at the wreck, but after Klaben and Flores had spent over a month watching planes bypass them, they decided to move. Determined they would be more visible at a new site at the edge of a clearing, Flores made a toboggan out of part of the fuselage and a piece of spruce, and loaded Klaben — who by this point only weighed forty-five kilograms — and a few items onto it. Using her red oil paints, they wrote that they had gone three kilometres downhill with an arrow pointing in the direction and the date. The trek exhausted them.

Flores got Klaben settled at the new site and decided he would try to find the chainsaw sounds again. He tried to gather enough firewood to last his young companion two days, but the exertion was too much. "He was seized by violent attacks of abdominal cramps that left him doubled up in the snow," Klaben wrote. "I had never seen Ralph cry before, but now I watched him stop chiseling wood when the spasms attacked him, and stand there, his arms around his belly, tears streaking down through the dirt and stubble of his face ... I tried to think of something I could do for him. In the end, I started reading the Bible aloud to him."

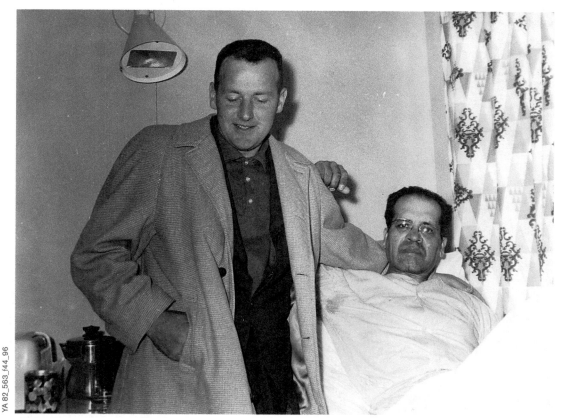

YA 82_563_f44_96

Ralph Flores, the pilot of the small Howard plane that crashed south of Watson Lake in 1963, with one of his rescuers, Chuck Hamilton, at the Whitehorse General Hospital. In 1998 Flores's children hired Trans North Turbo Air out of Whitehorse to fly them to the crash site. They found Flores's tool box, empty food tins, and even the SOS sign Flores had tied in a tree. His son, Frank, took the pieces of his dad's plane home to Mississippi and is slowly rebuilding it. When he finishes, he plans to go to Fairbanks and fly the Howard along the trench route to California to finish his father's flight plan.

He managed the tortuous task and set off again on snowshoes. He hiked for six hours to an open space — which turned out to be a frozen beaver pond — and tramped out a twenty-two-metre high SOS in the snow and a long arrow pointing back to where their camp was. Then he boiled some snow to drink, made camp on a bed of spruce boughs, and slept fitfully in preparation for the next day's long walk toward what he hoped would be their salvation. He even climbed a twenty-two metre tree to try and get his bearings on the way, a feat that left him so exhausted he slept for thirty-six hours.

Chuck Hamilton flew over Klaben's camp on March 24 in a BC-Yukon Air Services two-seater Piper Super Cub.[8] His passenger, Frank George, spotted the SOS Flores had made in the snow and smoke from the pine boughs Klaben piled into the fire.[9] "Chuck wigwagged his plane's wings at me," she remembered. Her relief at being spotted was immediate, but she would not be rescued until the next day. Hamilton had not been able to raise Watson Lake airport on his radio, so flew on toward a cabin on Airplane Lake, roughly twenty-two kilometres away from the crash site. Once he told

131

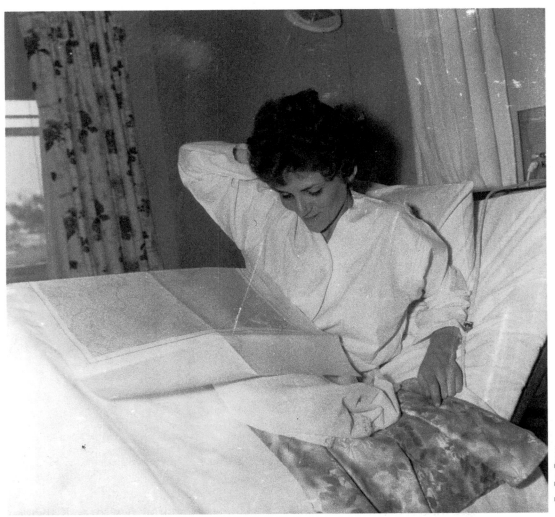

YA_82_563_f44_42

Helen Klaben at Whitehorse General Hospital after surviving in the bush south of Watson Lake for forty-nine days. The twenty-one-year-old Brooklyn, New York, native was flooded with offers for story rights, and a decade later the saga became a made-for-television movie starring Sally Struthers and Ed Asner. She and Ralph Flores played themselves in long-range shots and Klaben even re-enacted the scene where she desperately tried to flag down a plane flying overhead.

the trappers, Charlie Porter and Louis Boya, what he and George had seen, they went out by dogsled to find whomever had made the SOS and bring them in. Then Hamilton and George took off again for Watson Lake to notify the authorities.

Early the next morning, Klaben heard an aircraft again, and when she looked up, she saw the pilot reach out of his window and drop "a red balloon with a little package at the end of a string." The package had chocolate bars, chewing gum, and cigarettes, and a note to let her know two other planes were en route. Jack McCallum and passenger, Meteorological Technician Ed McNeill, had left Watson Lake Airport at first light to reassure Flores and Klaben help was on the way. McCallum had been told by Hamilton, who had only had his licence for a year, that there was no safe place to land near the crash site, but the older, more experienced pilot saw a spot to set down in the tamarack swamp.[10] Leaving McNeill with the plane, he snowshoed in to Klaben. "I grabbed him around the neck and hugged and kissed him," Klaben says. "I was crying, too, and I kept saying over and over again, 'Thank God, thank God, thank God.'"

An hour later, Chuck Hamilton arrived in his Super Cub. McCallum hauled out Klaben's luggage while Hamilton piggybacked her out on snowshoes to their two-seat plane. "It was a rough trail, crisscrossed with windfall logs," she later wrote. "Hamilton's snowshoes would drag and snag on the fallen branches, and he went down several times." After carefully placing her in the passenger seat and promising Frank George he would return for him shortly, Hamilton flew Klaben to the trapper's cabin on Airplane Lake. When they arrived, RCMP, a relieved Flores, and the trappers who had brought him in on dogsled, greeted her with moose steak, crackers, and hot tea. Then the two were flown to Watson Lake where a nurse and driver met the plane and took them to the First Aid Relief Station.[11] From there, they boarded a Canadian Pacific Airlines plane headed for the General Hospital in Whitehorse.

When they arrived at Whitehorse, the photographers were ready. As soon as news reached Outside that the pair had been found alive, media flocked to the territory. On April 1, Bob Grant of B.C.-Yukon Air Services and Chuck Ford of Klondike Helicopters flew two *Life* magazine staffers and a United Press reporter, as well as the Department of Transport inspectors, RCMP Constable George Leoppke, and hunting

outfitter Alex Van Bibber to the crash site.[12] In a new age of celebrity, Klaben especially garnered attention as a "pretty brunette," and while both insisted theirs was a father-daughter relationship, there was a whiff of sex and scandal that followed the story. According to Flores's grandson, even his grandmother had a moment of doubt, but was soon convinced of her husband's fidelity.[13] The two *did* take care of each other during this ordeal, however, and formed a close bond that may very well have saved their lives.

Chuck Ford told reporters the pair "had plenty of grit and determination and an exceptionally strong will to live to have survived through their ordeal on the mountain." They had not come out unscathed. At Whitehorse it was discovered Klaben had lost eighteen kilograms and Flores, twenty-six kilograms. Klaben's feet were severely frostbitten and gangrene had set in, but had luckily not spread; once she was safely back in New York, she would have several toes amputated.

The plane, however, was a total write-off. "Both wings are torn off, only one of which was found," Ford noted. "The engine is bent back underneath where it mowed the 40 to 60-foot spruce and jack-pine for 50 yards. The forward gas tank was crushed as was all the undercarriage."[14] The U.S. Federal Aviation Authority (FAA) investigation revealed that while descending, the engine failed because Flores had turned the fuel tank selector device onto an empty fuel tank. At that point, he was at such a low altitude that he was unable to restart it before it crashed.[15] They also determined he had violated more than a dozen rules, including: carrying insufficient provisions; taxiing to the Whitehorse runway without clearance; taking off after

YA 82_563_144_85

Local hunting outfitter Alex Van Bibber was brought in to the crash site after Flores and Klaben were rescued to give his professional opinion of the crash and camp. The pair had painted this sign to advise possible rescuers of their move to a new camp, and Van Bibber praised their ingenuity and ability to survive in the cold without much bush knowledge or rations.

admitting he did not understand the tower's information; and climbing under instrument conditions to 3,300 metres, even though he could only fly visual flight rules (VFR). In July 1963 Flores had his pilot's licence revoked for a year, but he resumed flying in 1966 and was later designated a hero by U.S. Congress.[16]

After the saga, many demanded that planes flying in the Yukon be forced to carry survival gear as well as ration and medical kits. A *Whitehorse Star* editorial also thought all light planes should have to use a homing device such as the emergency transmitter SARAH. "The cost of these items would be next to nothing compared to the hundreds of thousands of dollars spent — often to no avail — on the long air searches for missing planes," it argued.[17] But, as another pair of Yukon flyers would soon learn, SARAH (Search and rescue and Homing) could not guarantee discovery.

THE YELLOW PERIL

In November 1969 twenty-seven-year-old Edward Hadgkiss and his eighteen-year-old girlfriend, Kathy Rheaume, set off in his bright yellow single-engined Harvard from Whitehorse to visit California.[18] Hadgkiss

Jane Gaffin

Edward Hadgkiss bought this Harvard, CF-XEN, in late February 1968. It had been built in 1952 and was used for RCAF flight training at the school in Macdonald, Manitoba, until June 1960. In 1978, almost a decade after Hadgkiss crashed, his father issued salvage rights to Vic McMann of Delta, B.C. Eight years later, the wings were removed and the wreckage was slung by helicopter from Roderick Island to Shearwater, near Bella Bella, then dismantled and shipped by barge to Vancouver.

had worked his way north with the B.C. Highway Department in the mid-1960s, and had quickly fallen in love with the territory — and flying. In August 1965 he started work as a parts man with the aviation division of United Keno Hill Mines Ltd. and Cassiar Asbestos Corporation, and started taking flying lessons at Whitehorse airport. After he got his licence in 1965, he flew whenever he could, first in his small Cessna 120, CF-LRS, and then his Harvard. Over the next few years, he leased the Cessna out, did various charter work, and co-owned a Super Cub with Stan Reynolds, a local hunting outfitter. His journals reverberated with his passion for flight, even though the lessons and air time ate into his meagre wages.

Hadgkiss had run into mechanical issues — and bad weather — on cross-country flights before, and managed to land safely. And while he liked excitement and living fast, he generally respected the limits of his aircraft and skill and took necessary precautions. He bought a new battery and a SARAH beacon for the airplane, and, on the advice of a friend who was badly burned in a cockpit fire, he wore a nylon blue air force flying suit. Even so, as author and Hadgkiss's friend Jane Gaffin notes, "Operating and maintenance costs were done on a shoestring budget. Little things began to break down and go wrong."

Hadgkiss nicknamed the Harvard *The Yellow Peril* because of its canary colour and the fact it was such an expensive plane to maintain and fly. He felt safe in the sturdy ex-military trainer "built to crash." Perhaps too safe. In the past he had used the interior route through Fort Nelson, Fort St. John, and Prince George, but for the California trip, he decided to take the coastal route instead. It was known to be treacherous that time of year and Hadgkiss was only licensed to fly visual flight rules (VFR), that is, in clear conditions where a pilot can see where he or she is going. "This was the worst season for unsettled conditions," Gaffin writes. "Atmospheric disturbances created slate-gray, rolling clouds, low overcasts, thick walls of fog and bone-chilling, freezing rain."

The trip certainly got off to an ominous start: Hadgkiss and Rheaume were grounded for three days at Whitehorse until conditions improved. The skies finally cleared enough so they could take off at 10:00 a.m. November 10, 1969, but they hit bad weather between Prince Rupert and Port Hardy and crash-landed on a rocky ridge on Roderick Island off the coast of British Columbia. The aircraft was remarkably undamaged, and the couple were well equipped to survive in the wilderness until help arrived. In addition to rations and some fresh food, they had a Coleman stove, breakdown, fishing gear, flares, hatchet, handheld compass, mirror, first-aid kit, warm clothes, and Arctic-weight sleeping bags.

The Comox Air Force base on Vancouver Island was notified, but bad visibility and low clouds grounded 422 Squadron's planes at first. Finally they were able to send out three Albatross amphibious aircraft, two Voodoo jet fighters, two T-33 Silver Star jet trainers, two Labrador helicopters and a four-engined Argus patrol aircraft — in fact, "every squadron aircraft flew at some time

during the search" — and the Canadian Coast Guard ship *Skidegate* patrolled the coast. They flew track crawl then grid coverage but fog and turbulence hampered efforts, and ten radio distress signals that came through on emergency frequencies "teased and baffled" the searchers. Because of different tips and stories, and the fact no other planes were missing at the time, the aerial search went on for almost six weeks — four weeks longer than usual. Just days before Christmas in 1969, though, the military aerial search was officially called off.

Two months later, Don Hartt spotted the downed Harvard while flying a fishing charter from Bella Coola to Prince Rupert for Wilderness Airlines. When searchers made it to the site, they found the wreckage but no bodies — only Polaroids documenting their time at the crash site and a note on the last two pages of the Harvard's journey log inside the cockpit. The pair wrote that they had heard the fog horn from a lighthouse and when weather cleared could see a tugboat and the ocean, so had decided to hike down to water for better shelter, food sources, and a higher likelihood of being spotted by boats. They packed survival gear, provisions, and a few mementos and headed out.

With this new information and hope, search efforts resumed. Friends and family members scoured the area, as did the RCMP, which had launched a missing persons case. Search dogs and specialized dog masters were brought in, and the military continued to lend support with a helicopter and ground crew. No trace was found, however, and the searchers came to the sad conclusion the couple had likely fallen to their deaths and been buried in a rock slide or covered by the thick salal that blanketed the hillside. On Saturday June 20, 1970, the search officially ended.

Gar Lunney, LAC/ PA-176297

Yellowknife-based pilot Chuck McAvoy in July 1960. On June 9, 1964, McAvoy and his two passengers, geologists Douglas Torp and Albert Kunes, disappeared in their Fairchild 82, CF-MAK, en route to the Roberts Mining Company's gold claims. Despite a long search by the military and civilians, it would be nearly forty years before the wreck was spotted in 2003. The next year, Joe McBryan loaded his mentor's wreck into a Buffalo Airways' DC-3 and flew it back to the Yellowknife hangar for safekeeping and possible restoration.

"IF I EVER CRASH, THEY'LL NEVER FIND ME"

People could also disappear in the wide open spaces of the Barren Lands of the Northwest Territories. That was the case for Chuck McAvoy, his canvas-covered Fairchild 82 (CF-MAK), and his two geologist passengers, Douglas Torp and Albert Kunes.[19] On June 9, 1964, the men were flying to the

Roberts Mining Company's gold claims, 370 kilometres north of Yellowknife, when they hit bad weather. The thirty-one-year-old McAvoy had once said, "If I ever crash, they'll never find me," and it seemed this fly-by-the-seat-of-his-pants bush pilot was going to prove himself right. It wasn't until August 4, 2003, that Jeff Constable, a pilot with Great Slave Helicopters, spotted a burned out wreck just south of Bathurst Inlet. When they landed to inspect it, they found human remains and McAvoy's wallet. "The aircraft had landed short of a lake, hit hard on the boulder-strewn surface, and caught fire," writes author Shirlee Smith Matheson. Investigators confirmed that all likely died on impact.

Family members of the three men comforted each other as they were flown to the site aboard an Air Tindi Twin Otter. During a memorial service, they built an inukshuk at the crash site and placed a plaque commemorating the lost lives. Joe McBryan, owner of Buffalo Airways, had idolized McAvoy growing up in Yellowknife — the pilot had airlifted him to help after McBryan was hit by a truck as a child — and in 2004, he brought the wreckage back in pieces to Yellowknife aboard one of his DC-3s. Before he landed, he paid McAvoy one last tribute. "I just had to buzz over Chuck's old dock for him because I had his airplane on board and it was 40 years, two months and two weeks late," he said.

Bob Gauchie also went missing in the Barrens, but had a much happier end to his ordeal.[20] On February 2, 1967, he took off in his Beaver from Cambridge Bay bound for Yellowknife. Two hours later the thirty-nine-year-old pilot hit a snowstorm and discovered two of his instruments were not working, so he prudently set down. When he took off again the next day, he found his compass was not working. Then his SAR transmitter failed as well as his crash position indicator and radio. Lost and out of fuel, he force landed.

It was not his first time being stranded in the region. In 1962 he and two passengers had gone down in their Cessna 180 and it had taken two and a half days

to be rescued. But in 1967, temperatures dropped as low as -58°C, and because he had strayed off-course, searchers still had not found him after two weeks. By March, his wife, Fran, and three daughters in Fort Smith began preparing a memorial service. No one believed he could have survived. By March 31, he was not sure he would make it either, and wrote in his notebook that he thought he would only last another three days before succumbing to cold and starvation.

But fifty-eight days after he had gone down, he was spotted — alive — when Ron Sheardown and Glen Stevens flew overhead in a Turbo Beaver. When he heard the plane, Gauchie sent up one of his two flares and caught the pilot's attention. Sheardown had been flying the same route for five weeks en route to their base camp, and he later told reporters, "I know on occasion I must have flown right over top of him." Gauchie looked haggard, having lost twenty-three kilograms, and suffered from frostbite to his toes, but reportedly waited for them to land "calmly, with his suitcase packed." They loaded him into the airplane and flew to Kugluktuk (Coppermine) where a small child required evacuation, then brought them both to Yellowknife. His relieved family rushed to join him.

Luckily, Gauchie had had his sleeping bag as well as four others left behind by the government engineers he had just dropped off in Cambridge Bay. He also had a few boxes of frozen arctic char he had picked up for friends, well-stocked emergency rations and a survival kit. "I covered the airplane and made my bed in the airplane on the floor," he said in a CBC radio interview. "I talked to the wolves the first twenty-five days, and then they left me. And after that I just tried to survive."

"WELCOME TO THE CAMP OF A CANNIBAL"

Survival was Marten Hartwell's mantra as well after his twin-engined Beech 18, CF-RLD, went down north of Yellowknife November 8, 1972. "The Survivor," as he was dubbed by journalist Peter Tadman, was rescued thirty-one days after the crash. Unfortunately, his three passengers were not so lucky, and when SAR techs parachuted into the crash site, an injured and malnourished Hartwell greeted them. "Welcome to the camp of a Cannibal," he said.

At the same time as Hartwell's disappearance and rescue, the international media was focused on the story of forty-five people who had gone down October 13 aboard Uruguayan Air Force Flight 571. The plane, a Fairchild FH-227D, which carried a rugby team and their friends and family, had crashed in the Andes Mountains in Chile. One detail from both stories gripped the media and public: Hartwell and the Andes' survivors had both resorted to cannibalism to stay alive.[21]

Over the coming days, weeks, and months the full story would emerge.[22] Hartwell was flying for Gateway Aviation from Cambridge Bay to Yellowknife when he picked up an unexpected mercy flight.[23] In the late afternoon, he took off with Judy Hill, a young British nurse who had been at Taloyoak (Spence Bay) for a year; Neemee Nuliayok, an eight-month pregnant Inuk woman suffering from complications; and her nephew David Kootook, a fourteen-year-old Inuk, who was thought to have appendicitis.[24]

Forty-six-year-old Hartwell was originally from West Germany, and had been a pilot in the Luftwaffe during the Second World War, and gone on to secure his commercial licence before immigrating to Canada in 1967. Like many who move to the North, he wanted a fresh start: he changed his name (from Leopold Hermann) but followed his passion for flight, signing on with Gateway six months prior to the crash. When the accident took place, he had roughly two thousand hours flying time in his logbook, but only twenty-eight hours on the Beech 18. He also had only his day VFR rating, and so was prohibited from taking passengers up at night or in marginal conditions that might require instruments.[25] Still, it was an emergency case and he likely felt pressure to undertake the flight, even though he later wrote in his RCMP report that "he was not eager to go, and did not want to go" because of the conditions. It was not until an hour after takeoff that he would realize he had made a fatal decision.

The airplane was "a mess," SAR tech Harvie Copeland said. "It was completely broken apart."[26] Hartwell had gotten lost, and while trying to check his position, the plane's right wing had clipped the top of a tree, cartwheeling it into a hillside covered with nine-metre tall trees. "He got too damned low and just flew into the ground," Copeland noted.[27] Nurse Judy Hill died immediately, and Nuliayok was badly hurt. Kootook was relatively uninjured and "the boy went to work immediately moving the injured mother-to-be and making her comfortable," a newspaper reported at the time. Despite his best efforts, she died within hours.

Kootook would also take care of Hartwell, who had broken both ankles and fractured his knee in the crash. For the next ten days they ate emergency rations — corned beef, chicken noodle soup, rice, powdered potatoes, packs of raisins, glucose pills — then Kootook collected Caribou moss and made several aborted attempts to hike through hip-deep snow to a nearby lake to catch fish. The two even watched helplessly as a herd of caribou went by, but had nothing to hunt them with, as Hartwell had not brought a rifle. Kootook also chopped wood and tended the fire while Hartwell fended off the cold in a parka, several pairs of overalls, woollen underwear, and a heavy vest.

After three weeks, the 1.65-metre Kootook had shrunk to thirty-three kilograms. For the last few days of his life, he apparently lay on the ground, waiting to die. "After David was dead my will to live was reawakened," Hartwell wrote in his report to RCMP. It was then that Hartwell, a vegetarian, made the difficult decision to eat flesh from Judy Hill's body. After he was rescued he said, "I am still trying to forget this and probably will never succeed." He also defended his actions, telling reporters that people with enough food could not "understand the madness of starvation."

During his time at the crash site, Hartwell heard four planes fly over; each time he turned on his Dart Two, a hand-held distress beacon. But the massive search effort — by air and by Inuit ground parties — could not locate the silver-coloured Beech 18 hidden by trees and snow. Hartwell had been completely lost, 320 kilometres west of his flight path, so was outside their search parameters. He also had not checked in by radio when it was clear he was lost. It was not until a Canadian Forces Hercules on a sked flight from Inuvik to Yellowknife picked up his signal that he was found. He had turned on his Dart Two when he had heard an aircraft

overhead — likely Argus 10732 from 415 Squadron out looking for him — and left his shelter to try and flag down help.[28] After spotting him, an Air Force Voyageur helicopter piloted by Major A. H. Hayes then went in to pick him up. The remains of the three passengers were flown to Edmonton.

After Hartwell was rescued, the real media circus began. For the first forty-eight hours, he refused to speak to reporters, saying, "I don't want pictures. I don't want publicity. I'm the one who should be dead." He remained ambivalent about the media attention, especially when an inquest into the events was called at the Yellowknife Inn in February 1973 and he decided not to appear in person. Hartwell's lawyer, James "Red" Cavanaugh, had advised his client not to. "The press will crucify him," he said. But they did anyway, and the jury — which was mostly composed of northern bush pilots — felt he had a "moral obligation" to testify, not just provide a handwritten statement for the RCMP to read aloud.

Years after the incident, Hartwell told journalist Peter Tadman, "You can take any bush pilot's word and take my word and it will be the same. As a bush pilot you work twenty-four hours a day and get six or seven hours paid for, and once anyone has an accident you're condemned." Even so, the press and public wanted someone to pay for the tragic loss of life: Nuliayok and her unborn child — a girl, the autopsy confirmed — had died en route to help and left behind a loving family; the young British nurse, Judy Hill, became known as the "Angel in the Snow"; and everyone agreed David Kootook had been a hero (he was later awarded the Meritorious Service Cross).

Three different investigations and four government agencies tried to determine the chain of events and elicit recommendations in February 1973 so the tragedy would not be repeated. The inquiry found Hartwell and Gateway Aviation at the top of the list of those at fault, as did two private suits brought against them by Judy Hill's family and the Eskimo (Inuit) Brotherhood for negligence causing death. They both settled out of court with insurance companies for undisclosed amounts. The Department of Transport was also found at fault for not enforcing its regulations, and both it and the Northwest Territories Government scrambled to reassure the public it would create better transportation links and improve the communication and navigation infrastructure in the North.[29] On January 1, 1974, a new Air Navigation Order came into effect with "strict new standards for operation of small commercial aircraft" and training requirements for crews.

Two years after the crash, Hartwell returned to the Northwest Territories and to aviation. For twenty years he operated Ursus Aviation Ltd., a charter company based out of Fort Norman. While he had felt like an outcast Outside, where people seemed fixated on the cannibalism details, northerners were more pragmatic. "He survived and that is all there is to it," Yellowknife mayor Dave Lovell said. "They were more annoyed that he made the flight."[30] But the North had seen its fair share of foolhardy bush pilots, and even

loved and admired them, and local support grew over time. He had other close calls, but always walked away, and even learned to laugh along when friends good-naturedly told him they had extra snacks in case he got hungry.

EARLY SEARCHES FOR MISSING AVIATORS, LIKE the MacAlpine Expedition in 1929, no doubt enthralled radio listeners and newspaper readers, but by mid-century something had shifted. Air travel had grown so much among average citizens — it was not just the uber-wealthy or daredevils flying private planes or travelling aboard commercial jetliners. People from all walks of life were taking to the skies for work or pleasure and when planes crashed, increasingly the public could empathize. When they read stories of survival like those of Helen Klaben, Ralph Flores, or Marten Hartwell, they wondered — could they do it? Could they overcome cold, injury, and social taboos to stay alive?

For many pilots, it reinforced their fatalism. Sometimes there seemed to be no rhyme or reason: experienced, level-headed pilots would be caught in a freak downdraft and die, while foolhardy stuntmen would walk away from prang after prang. As some pilots continue to say, "When your number's up, it's up." Sometimes luck was the most important factor in survival. But preparation, proper supplies, and a good head on your shoulders could help.

CHAPTER 8

The Top of the World

As the North became more accessible and southerners' appetite for frontiers, wilderness, and adventure took off, so did air tourism in the Subarctic and Arctic. Unlike the Trail of '98 Klondike gold rushers who were motivated by greed, or nationalists searching for *terra incognito*, these expeditionists set out to break records and attempt new feats of endurance — or push the limits of science and human knowledge. And some simply wanted to enjoy the dramatic beauty of northern landscapes from the air.

"IT'S A LIFE OF HIGH ADVENTURE"

The Saint Elias Mountains in the south-west corner of the Yukon have drawn a lot of attention over the years from scientists and adventurers alike; however, the first ascent of Mount Logan, its highest peak and Canada's tallest mountain, did not take place until 1925.[1] It would be another decade before National Geographic led an expedition into the unmapped mountains and started exposing their mysteries and beauties to the outside world. Led by photographer and explorer Bradford Washburn, it was the first crossing of the Saint Elias Range from Canada into Alaska during the winter. National Geographic had contacted George Simmons, owner of Northern Airways Ltd. out of Carcross, to hire a ski-equipped Fokker Super Universal, CF-AAM. Robert "Bob" Randall was at the controls for photographic and supply

flights, and in the process, made the first airplane landing on a Yukon glacier.[2]

During the years after the Second World War, the Saint Elias Range largely faded from international view, but in 1962 scientists set up the Arctic Institute of North America's (AINA) Kluane Lake Research Station. The location was perfect for scientific research, as it afforded high altitude and polar-like conditions, yet was relatively close to population centres. The Institute, which had gotten its start in Washington, D.C. in 1945, set up first an Icefield Ranges Research Project (IRRP), and then its High Altitude Physiology Study (HAPS) in the early 1960s at the divide between Kaskawulsh and Hubbard Glaciers. Phil Upton, who provided most of their air support for over two decades, recalled standing on "Divide" (as it is known) with glaciologist and pilot Richard Ragle. "If we had an airplane with enough power, we

Joe Muff

Aircraft engineer and co-founder of Alkan Air, Joe Muff, with the company's Otter, C-FAYR, on wheel-skis in late spring, c. 1985.

could probably land and take off on that flat-looking area above sixteen thousand feet," Upton said.[3]

He had flown on submarine patrol during the war in Cansos and Beechcraft, but it was as a mountain and glacier pilot that Upton would really distinguish himself.[4] He decided a Helio Courier was the Institute's best bet and purchased one that could be modified with "turbochargers, installed oxygen equipment and a new high-frequency radio." As Joe Muff, an experienced aircraft engineer and Upton's friend and colleague notes, "It had a turbo-normalized engine, so he could bring it up to sea level pressure." He also notes that as

a true short-takeoff-and-landing (STOL) aircraft, it can fly at sixty kilometres an hour without stalling, and has the added advantage of being almost impossible to flip over.

After a year of preparation, Upton and two mountaineers attempted their first landing on Mount Logan on wheel-skis. "The surface looked good," he remembers, "the wind was calm, the day was bright and beautiful, and the altimeter read 18,000 [feet]." Upton found it difficult to judge distances with the "crystal-clear air" and the scale of the scenery, but with "the slope too steep to turn around or climb up," he was committed to land. They did this successfully, but once he was on the glacier, the engine quit.

They decided to get out and walk around to let things cool off, and Upton grabbed his portable oxygen. It was his "first time ever on a really big mountain" and he was not taking any chances.

With a pre-fab Helio Courier-sized building, freeze-dried food, and propane-fuelled generator and stove, a climbing party set out to ascend Mount Logan in June 1967 to ready the base camp and take part in the physiology program. "It presented a staggering challenge in logistics — all dependent on one small aircraft and a pilot," Upton notes. Upton ferried food caches ahead of the party, making a second landing about a week after his first. "While Barry [Bishop, of Mount Everest fame] unloaded, I sat still, breathing oxygen, and kept the engine running." On their third trip, the weather closed in just as the Courier's skis got stuck in four inches of new snow. "This episode didn't bother Barry — he was used to being in strange predicaments on mountains — but it gave me a lot of concern." Upton became even more nervous when they decided to fly three people to the upper campsite to set up and get back on schedule. With each landing, he noticed the three experienced members "were deteriorating fast. They were stumbling around the aircraft to the extent I was worried someone might be hit by the propeller," he noted. "They hardly spoke to each other or to me, and were taking longer to crawl out of their tent each time the aircraft landed." They brought in a "fresh" doctor to supervise two of the crew and air-lifted the third out immediately.

Over the next two decades, Upton and the Arctic Institute learned from these situations, and became more confident operating in the specialized — and changeable — conditions on Mount Logan. Even so, pilots in the Saint Elias Mountains had to keep close watch for oxygen deprivation and altitude sickness. As Muff notes, they had to be even more vigilant than the scientists or study volunteers because they did not have the time to slowly acclimatize. "The researchers were fine, because they would slowly work their way up," he says. But in the early years, Upton was flying without a net, so to speak, since there were no helicopters in the area in case of emergency. Upton had a few close calls: once he dug a wingtip and did about three thousand dollars worth of damage to the Courier, but was still able to fly it off Mount Logan. Another time he forgot to lean-out the burning mixture for take-off and almost killed the plane's small battery. "They only had one airplane," Muff says. "If they hadn't been able to start it they would have been both dead."

Muff was uncomfortable with this state of affairs, so he and his partner, Hugh Kitchen, at their charter firm, Alkan Air, leased an aircraft so the Arctic Institute would have two. "I didn't like them going up there with just one of aircraft," says Muff. "They had the two Helio Couriers, but could only afford to run one because they were a non-profit organization. We leased the other one for them and flew it commercially." This turned out to be a good plan, as Phil Upton did have to leave one of the Couriers behind one winter. "The engine failed," says Muff. "So he had to go and dig it out in the spring, change the engine, and haul it out on the ice. Only the yellow tip of a propeller was peeking through the snow. There was no GPS then, so he had to trig it from the mountain peaks. They barely found it."

In later years, Upton set up a commercial venture to fly into the Saint Elias range under Muff's company, and Alkan started advertising glacier flights. Aside from Helio Couriers, Alkan ran a turbo-charged Cessna 206 and single-engined Otter, CF-AYR, to get into high-altitude lakes in the area. "It had a 12:1 blower versus the standard 10:1," Muff recalls. "Because of this it was allowed to fly into Mount Logan. You had to treat it properly but at 8,500 feet it felt like you were at sea level."

During that period, Upton trained his protégé, Andy Williams, and they and a few select others became specialists at flying into Kluane at high altitudes. Williams was born and raised in Wales, then had worked in northern Quebec, British Columbia, and Antarctica when the logistics officer at Arctic Institute asked him to come up in 1973 to manage the Kluane Lake Research Station. He got his pilot training at the Whitehorse Flying School, and Upton hired him on as backup pilot with a second Helio Courier saying, "You know, we probably couldn't do any worse if you did this" — referring to a string of experienced pilots who had banged up the Courier during a season in the mountains. "Because Phil was doing it, I thought this was pretty normal," Williams notes. But as he and others have learned over the years, the Saint Elias Mountains are prone to fast-moving sea storms from the Gulf of Alaska that can rage for weeks and unpredictable winds. Williams has discovered the Saint Elias's capriciousness himself in the forty (and counting) years he has flown them, but he has risen to the challenge. "It's a life of high adventure," says Williams. "When I land up there at 18,000 to 19,500 feet, it's a legal high.

Then I get to take off on a dodgy downhill immediately over an icefield and glide down." He also has faith in his trusty Helio Courier: "It's safe and strong — a well-built structure, like a steel cage."

The Arctic Institute's High Altitude study ended in 1981, but Upton, Williams, and Alkan continued to have other interesting customers from the scientific world. "We supported some research projects up there," remembers Joe Muff. "One of the scientists drilled a one hundred metre ice core to preserve it and then send it out all over the globe to these laboratories for climatic studies." The power supply at Silver City, Yukon, was apparently unreliable, so the scientists had Williams fly the core (at high altitude to keep it frozen) so it could

Mike Waszkiewicz collection

Famed Yukon pilot Andy Williams at the controls of his Helio Courier above the Saint Elias Icefields. Williams has been flying researchers, skiers, climbers, and air tourists into the area for decades in his trusty flying "steel cage."

be stored at the Meterological office freezer at Whitehorse airport. "It was over Easter," Muff says. "Some enterprising person at the office decided to save on power over the long weekend and turned the switch off. So the next time Phil came in with a load there was a lot of water in the freezers and a few chunks of ice. Then we had to inform Jerry Holdsworth at the Institute, "You have to start all over again." The crew had spent over two weeks doing the work. "It was rotten weather," says Williams. "Some of them had gotten frostbite. And we had to tell them to start all over again."

MASSIFS, MOUNTAINS, AND GALLOPING GLACIERS

They also found a growing number of their passengers were skiers, climbers, and adventurers. Mount Logan had once again captured international attention in March 1965, when the Canadian government changed the name of East Hubbard to Mount Kennedy in honour of American President, John F. Kennedy, who had been assassinated two years earlier. His brother, U.S. Attorney General Robert Kennedy, was to be the first to climb the 4,200-metre mountain, except he had no experience. During the two-month expedition, Lloyd Ryder, co-owner of Yukon Airways, transported supplies and passengers to the base camp in a Beaver. It was not turbo-charged, but Ryder noted, "It would get up to about 12,000 feet. I could land at that altitude and get off again." Ryder mused later that "The advantage to glacier flying is having lots of runway before falling into a crevasse. So you didn't go in when the weather was milky."[5] Kennedy was airlifted by an RCAF

helicopter to a base camp at 2,750 metres, where two mountain climbers taught him basic mountain-climbing skills. The three made a successful ascent and Kennedy left a flag with the family's coat of arms, as well as Canadian and U.S. flags; he also left mementos belonging to JFK.[6]

In 1967 the Saint Elias range would also be in the media spotlight during Canada's centennial year. Yukoners such as Kurt Koken, along with climbing enthusiasts from around North America like Monty Alford, Craigh P. Hughes, and David Fisher, decided to pitch the idea of climbing a series of unclimbed peaks in the Range to the Centennial Commission.[7] The Yukon Alpine Centennial Expedition (YACE) would include twelve mountains — ten representing the provinces and two the territories — as well as a thirteenth in honour of Canada's and Alaska's centennials. The peaks were to be all over three thousand metres. With funding from the federal and territorial government, as well as grants from the provinces and private organizations, the plan went ahead.

In June 1967 experienced mountain climbers from Canada and the U.S. scaled a 4,500 metre mountain on the southern tip of the Yukon–Alaska border, which was called Good Neighbour Peak. The second phase of the expedition got underway in July when thirteen teams of four Canadian climbers arrived. Stan Rosenbaum was one of those climbers, and he recalls Great Northern Airways flew them and their gear from Kluane Lake to the Arctic Institute's IRRP base camp at Divide in a Beaver, CF-GYK. From there, Bullock Helicopters of Calgary ferried them in Bell 47 helicopters to high glacier bases in the centre, which had not been explored

Stan Rosenbaum

Mountain climber Klaus Boerger with Beaver, CF-GYK, in 1967 during the Centennial climbs in the Yukon. The plane was used to transport climbers and equipment to a mountain landing strip between two glaciers known simply as "Divide." 'GYK was first operated by Callison Flying Service out of Dawson, then went to a series of Yukon companies: Connelly-Dawson Airways, Great Northern Airways, and Trans North Turbo Air.

before. "Although these unclimbed peaks were set among the giants: Logan, St. Elias, Lucania, Steele, Walsh and Hubbard, all of which had been previously climbed, each team quickly discovered that their target was a substantial challenge," Rosenbaum notes. "Starting with skimpy information, the first step on arrival was to identify which peak or collection of related peaks was their assigned mountain. Then they had to conduct reconnaissance climbs to identify a feasible route to the highest point. After that they could plan and execute a summit attempt. All of this in just 2 weeks of changeable mountain weather, with fog, rain and snow." The climbers ascended the main summits of what was dubbed the Centennial Range, and named the peaks after provinces and territories. The highest

peak, which they called Centennial Peak "resisted three attempts, falling at the last just before the final helicopter lift," mountaineer and British army officer Lord John Hunt wrote later.

Lord Hunt and his wife both visited the Yukon during this time and made the first ascent of the three-thousand-metre Mount Oliver Wheeler on July 19, 1967. They stayed at the Alpine Club of Canada's annual summer camp, which the organization held in the Yukon to coincide with this expedition. The Club set up the camp next to Steele Glacier (named for the famous gold-rush era Mountie Sam Steele), which had become known as the "galloping glacier" when in the fall of 1966 it started to move two feet a day. In the lead-up to the camp's start, the Alpine Club set up tents

Stan Rosenbaum

A three-seat Bell 47G helicopter, CF-RLE, piloted by Jim Davies for Bullock Helicopters of Calgary as part of the Centennial climbs in 1967. Whitehorse-based Trans North also favoured these helicopters, and when it started in the early 1970s had four variations registered to it: 'ETR, 'RQM, 'VUB and 'VUE.

and organized food for the 100–200 people expected. Koken also built up a supply of avgas at the camp. One day a "frantic telephone call came in and one of the glaciers must have moved," he says. "The lake went up 32½ feet and since our barrels were only 20 [feet] above the lake all our barrels were floating in that lake. Nobody knew what to do. They were in there for months." Koken tried to find helicopters in the Yukon that could land on the lake, but came up empty-handed. Luckily a visiting officer from the British Army involved in surveying a road wanted to visit the famous glacier and asked Koken for permission to stay overnight at the camp. "I said, well, how about if we make a little deal," and he made the necessary arrangements in exchange for

fishing out the barrels using the officer's two pontoon-equipped helicopters.

In theory, the camp was easily accessible from the Alaska Highway, but when July rolled around heavy rain washed out the road along Kluane Lake as well as the Slims River Bridge. This was exactly when the Alpine Club's members began arriving in Whitehorse, and Koken received another panicked phone call: "For cripes sake please take care of these people," a colleague told him. "I was at the airport every time an airplane landed and all of a sudden we had piles and piles of people in the Vocational Training school. A few days later things started to settle down and they got the buses going again." Helicopters then transported the roughly one hundred people and their gear sixty-five kilometres over the Donjek River to the camp in what Lord Hunt called "non-stop shuttle sorties." After a fortnight, the first group left, but not without difficulty, and another took their place. When the expedition wrapped up in mid-August, nearly three hundred people had climbed, hiked, or worked for the project and it was a success, despite the best efforts of Mother Nature. As Hunt noted, "everything depended on the tenuous link provided by two small helicopters."

In the years since, the Saint Elias range has, in the words of mountaineer Monty Alford, "achieved recognition as one of the greatest expeditionary-mountaineering regions in the world." In the summer of 1980, when he and a team of ten others set off on skis from Alaska to Kluane Lake, he estimated there were thirty other expeditions. By that time it had been designated Kluane National Park and the glacier pilots, Andy Williams and Phil Upton, found themselves increasingly flying expedition-style ski and climbing parties between April and October.

"People have done remarkable climbs," Williams says. "Some are extremely dangerous, but they have to be well-prepared and well-equipped." Part of that preparation on Alkan's part was keeping track of their customers. "We had a schedule every morning and every evening to make sure everybody was fine," Joe Muff says. "We also made the climbers carry those 104-foot wire antenna radios all the way to the top and check in with us every day or else we'd go looking for them." Muff was interested in the welfare of his clients, but he also noted that "It's expensive and dangerous sometimes moving in there."

Once the area was named a national park, Parks Canada instituted a rescue service that went beyond Alkan's fixed-wing capabilities. They brought in a specially-trained Parks Canada Mountain Rescue team and set up agreements with Trans North Turbo Air to have a pneumatic hoist-equipped Alouette III helicopter on standby. These were put to life-saving use in the late 1970s and early 1980s when there was a spate of emergencies requiring the evacuation of climbers from Mount Logan. In June 1977 a man suffering acute altitude sickness and frostbite was put in an insulated body bag and "plucked from a knife-edge ridge at 14,000 feet" before being lowered down the mountain and rushed to hospital by a TNTA Jet Ranger helicopter. "The med people at Whitehorse told us that he would not have survived the day had he not been rescued," mission notes said.[8]

The next June climbers radioed the Arctic Institute for help when two members of the group were hit by falling rocks while ascending the massif. Andy Williams relayed the mayday to the Parks Canada office, which put its rescue team on standby along with TNTA pilots Ron Eland and Richard Warchoski. While it may have been summer in the rest of the territory, at four thousand metres on Mount Logan, it was -15°C with high winds and falling snow — and sharp downdrafts on the south face where the climbers were. It took three days for the conditions to improve enough for the helicopters and rescue team to airlift the four climbers to the base of the mountain. Even once they got in, the "two feet of freshly fallen snow resulted in some major problems due to the prop wash creating a blizzard effect," the Parks press release read. This severely compromised the pilots' and

Adam Morrison

Trans North's Bell 206B, C-FEXP, at Pinnacle Peak in the Saint Elias Mountains, likely piloted by Doug Makkonen. It was based in Haines Junction, approximately 160 kilometres west of Whitehorse. This helicopter was used primarily for moving people and equipment to base camps to start their climbs of Mount Logan and other peaks. On January 18, 1999, it was destroyed in Trans North's hangar fire.

rescue team's visibility during the six times the helicopter hovered to secure and release the climbers. In the end the climbers had to leave behind seventeen thousand dollars (in today's money) worth of gear. As the Parks warden noted in his report, it was "a good deterrent for other climbing groups wanting a free lift off the mountain when the going gets a little tough."

It could have been much more costly, however. Dr. Franz Mohling of the American Alpine Club and two of his friends, Stephen Jensen and Turan Barut, died in an avalanche on Mount Logan in June 1982. Alkan Air had flown the "Colorado Group" as they came to be known, in an Otter to the north side in late May. It was Mohling's third attempt on the

massif, and the group wanted to be the first to scale the north face.[9] "I was sitting in my tent and I never heard anything," said Doug Johnson, a member of the group. "It just collapsed on top of me." He and three others survived but were stranded in the -15°C weather for several days with no gloves or boots, and with wet sleeping bags. After digging out what supplies they could, uncovering two of their friends' bodies, and hiking one thousand metres to a base camp, they managed to radio for help. Food and other supplies were dropped to them by Eland in TNTA's Jet Ranger, but bad weather and the unavailability of the TNTA Alouette, which was scheduled to go to Alberta to fight wild fires, prevented their rescue for a few days. "If it [the Jet

Dick de Blicquy

Welland "Weldy" Phipps and Atlas Aviation's Piper Apache on a "natural" strip on Melville Island while supplying a BP camp, c. 1970. The intrepid aviator and inventor of "tundra tires" was well known around the Arctic, as was his Twin Otter, CF-WWP, known as Whisky Whisky Papa. On its door was the inscription: "The Alcoholic Twin Otter."

Ranger] had hovered, it could have crashed because atmospheric conditions at the time meant the machine was flying well above its altitude limit of 4,000 metres," newspaper reports said at the time.

Finally TNTA pilot Ron Eland and a rescue team went in with the Alouette, and airlifted the climbers to Haines Junction in two trips. From there, they were flown to Whitehorse, "exhausted, sunburnt and shoeless, with frostbitten toes wrapped in several pairs of socks." While Yukon Premier Erik Nielsen and others saw this as a reason to pay the extra quarter million dollars per year for the Alouette's stand-by fees (the service had been cancelled the year before), rescued climber Doug Johnson said, "Anyone that doesn't expect to get themselves out on their own has no right to be there."

ARCTIC AIR TOURISM

Interest in battling the elements to explore the North extended into the High Arctic as well. In one example, a party of filmmakers hired Atlas Aviation when they wanted to shoot a film for the Man and the Polar Regions pavilion at Canada's Expo '67. Atlas owner and pilot Weldy Phipps rigged a Piper Apache with two 35 mm cameras for the operation, then they waited for the fog to clear. During this time, a mayday call came in from an American pilot in a Beechcraft who was low on fuel and could not find the Resolute runway in the soup. Phipps went out to make a bonfire to clear a hole in the fog, but while they were setting up "the Beechcraft roared inches over their heads, sending all the spectators sprawling on the ground." The plane landed successfully, but even more amazingly, the crew had caught it on film.

The Canadian government awarded a contract to Gateway Aviation of Edmonton to provide services for the May 1967 Centennial flight to the North Pole. Pilots John Cameron and Harold Mordy, along with mechanic Andy Gleeson and Flight Engineer Ray Cox of Inuvik, flew two Otters (CF-MES and CF-LAP) with four scientists from Canada, the U.S., and Norway from Alert to the magnetic North Pole on May 13, 1967 – a distance of nine hundred kilometres. The flight crew – pictured here – then signed a flag in marker and planted it at the pole. This flag is now in storage at the Alberta Aviation Museum in Edmonton.

The next day one of Atlas's pilots, John Strickland, took the Apache up with the cameras and the crew, but the drag from the mounted cameras made it so the plane struggled through the air. When one engine went out, Strickland shouted to offload anything they could to stay aloft. "The crew grabbed everything they could get their hands on," author Norm Avery writes, "including valuable reels of exposed film, tape recorders, and ancillary equipment. One technician, an Austrian, even threw his passport out by mistake."[10]

Another group wanted to celebrate Canada's centennial — and the big Expo '67 party — in the northern skies. Ray Munro, a Spitfire pilot during the Second World War and owner of Munro Aviation in Lancaster, Ontario, and Ivan C. Christopher, a Toronto geophysicist, left Montreal, the site of Expo '67, on January 18, in their Cessna 180. The idea behind this twenty-six-day goodwill tour was that the pair of Polar Ambassadors would carry the Expo '67 message to remote areas and honour the bush pilots and prospectors of years past. They flew fourteen thousand kilometres without instruments and made more than a dozen stops in the Northwest Territories and Yukon including Yellowknife, Tuktoyaktuk, Inuvik, Dawson City, and Watson Lake, before heading down to Edmonton and making their way back across the Prairies.[11]

Dick de Blicquy

Atlas Aviation's Twin Otter, CF-WWP, after its first landing at Pangnirtung on Baffin Island, c. 1970. The strip was under construction, with only about ninety metres completed, when the community asked if the company could do a medevac. Pilot Dick de Blicquy recalls that it was an exciting trip and the Twin Otter's Short Takeoff and Landing (STOL) capabilities came in handy that day.

In the years after Canada's centennial celebrations, the Arctic also saw its fair share of VIPs. In the spring of 1969, the RCMP Air Division flew Canadian Prime Minister Pierre Trudeau on a tour of the Northwest Territories in its new Fort Smith-based Twin Otter, CF-MPB.[12] Weldy Phipps had the honour, however, of taking Trudeau for a memorable side trip to Grise Fiord in his Twin Otter, CF-WWP. Trudeau, who had been a private pilot himself, rode in the co-pilot's seat. Apparently he "grew increasingly apprehensive as the aircraft approached Grise directly towards the face of a cliff. By the time the aircraft landed, Trudeau had turned a couple of shades of white. When they rolled to a stop he caught his breath and said to Weldy that he wouldn't even try to park a Volkswagen

there."[13] Phipps and the RCMP also shared squiring duties when Queen Elizabeth II, Prince Philip, and a royal entourage visited the Arctic in July 1970 for the centennial of the Northwest Territories.[14] Apparently the flight from Inuvik to Tuk was particularly difficult because of bad weather, and the Queen signed Staff Sergeant George Filiatrault's logbook in recognition of the pilot's skill in getting them in safely.[15]

"A REFRESHINGLY MAD IDEA"

In the years since, the North has seen its fair share of tourists interested in "flight-seeing." Phipps first flew a Florida businessman to the North Pole in 1970 and word spread quickly. Soon, Atlas had dozens of inquiries about similar flights from across the U.S. and Phipps decided to pursue this potential venture further. He set a price of twenty-five hundred dollars for a round-trip flight from Montreal or Toronto to the Pole, and proposed to fly tourists from Resolute to Lake Hazen, where guests would stay in a military-issue Quonset hut. Landing was weather-dependent, but people would still be able to say they had flown over the Pole. As pilot Dick de Blicquy noted, this was really what they were after: "I've been to the Pole and there's not much there but a lot of ice and snow. Still, I can say I've been there, and I guess that's what these people want to say too." The Northwest Territories Commissioner saw the larger potential economic advantage of North Pole flights and hired Atlas to fly him and a reporter to the Pole. On April 5, 1971, Phipps, his wife Fran, and co-pilot Jack Austin flew to the Pole to make preparations — such as caching fuel and setting up a radio beacon. In the process, Fran became the first woman to land at the North Pole and was included in the Guinness Book of World Records — much to the chagrin of the Vancouver reporter, who had hoped it would be her.[16] In the end, weather prevented the reporter from landing regardless.

Tours to the North Pole never quite materialized for Phipps and Atlas Aviation — there simply were not that many people willing to spend the money, travel the distance, or chance the weather. But it remained a site of interest for the average traveller — at least to fly over in comfort. In the summer of 1969, Pan Am made its first passenger flight over the North Pole with Inertial Navigation System, a form of dead reckoning using early in-flight computer technology. It flew from London Heathrow Airport to Seattle with Captain Olaf Abrahamsen at the controls and passed roughly ten kilometres over the Pole in clear weather. In its promotional video of the occasion, the narrator said: "Once only believed accessible to a super explorer. For the Clipper's crew of ten, it will be just another waypoint."

Until Phipps sold the company to Kenting Aviation in the early 1970s, Atlas continued to provide support services for adventurers trekking across the ice to the North Pole on snowshoes, by bike, or snowmobile. It was even a destination for skydivers — two years after his stint as a Polar Ambassador for Expo '67, Ray Munro completed his five-hundredth jump by parachuting down to the Pole.[17]

Phipps may have simply been ahead of his time with regards to commercial Pole ventures. According to author and adventurer Lyn Hancock, "the great pole rush" really started in 1978.[18] She spoke with charter airlines based out of Resolute, including Kenn Borek Air, which said it had been "inundated by enquiries" from around the world. They had received requests for everything from someone wanting to stand there in a jacket and tie, to going on New Year's Day ("Rather difficult to find a landing spot in the middle of the six month's arctic night," one pilot apparently commented), or wanting to go "African Safari-style in a Hercules with a backup complement of tracked vehicle inside the plane." Several Japanese expeditionists went by dogsled or ice boat, a group of Canadian businessmen attempted to reach it from Alert with Twin Otters, and Jack Wheeler of Las Vegas flew a Playboy Tour to the Pole.

NWT Archives/Douglas Wilkinson fonds/N-1979-051-0267S

Fran Phipps and Mrs. Grosch at the North Pole in 1972. Phipps was married to famed bush pilot Weldy Phipps, whom she had met while hanging around the Ottawa airfield as a plane-crazy teenager. The year before, she had become the first woman in the world to land on the North Pole. The Mrs. Grosch pictured is likely one of early computer scientist Dr. Herbert R. Grosch's wives (he remarried several times); the former IBM and General Electric executive was adventurous and traveled extensively during this time.

What many of these people had in common was their completely unrealistic notions of what they would find at the Pole — and how they would manage the trip. One California man planned to ride his motorcycle and "expected no problems" since "there were roads and sled trails." As Hancock notes, yes, there were trails, but they had to be "hacked laboriously out of solid ice 40-foot high and then quickly obliterated by 90 mile an hour blizzards and fast-drifting ice floes." The man only made it out one mile before he had to turn back.

People loved to get behind these events, though. In the early 1980s the Trans Globe Expedition, which was the first to go longitudinally around the world by land, sea, and ice, even received royal sponsorship.

Prince Charles said it was a "refreshingly mad idea in the best tradition of British exploration." That particular crew actually succeeded, but many charter companies found themselves on rescue missions. Bradley Air Services and Kenn Borek were called in to rescue a British–Italian duo — and that was after the pair had been airlifted over the worst pressure ridges. "If you want the least trouble," Hancock wrote, "the safest way to get to the North Pole is by organized tour in a Twin Otter, preferably with another plane for refuelling and backup. Such expeditions are timed between mid-April and mid-May when the ice is hard enough to permit successful landings." These tours were offered by companies in Washington State and

Sue Bergre

One of Kenn Borek Air's Caribous, c. 1988. This aircraft is likely C-GVYZ, which was operated by Air North from 1986–88 before it was bought by Kenn Borek and flown for a year. It was later flown by Air Tindi of Yellowknife in the 1990s before it retired to Florida.

Vancouver, British Columbia, from the staging site Weldy Phipps had selected at Lake Hazen on Ellesmere Island. Landings — if attempted — were kept to half an hour "during which you lunch on smoked arctic char and champagne and stroll around" and could take photographs in Santa Claus costumes, T-shirts, or other outfits. On the way back to Resolute, the tours often stopped at Grise Fiord where local Inuit had opened a hotel and would take tourists for dogsled rides and show them how to build igloos, hunt, and fish. Back in Resolute, they would be presented with a membership in the "People Who Have Been to the Pole" club. The whole package would set a tourist back the equivalent of fifteen thousand dollars today, not including getting to Resolute from the continental U.S., Germany,

England, and Japan (the most popular originating countries).

In more recent years, people intent on reaching the Pole have had access to greater technology and information, but have still struggled to reach their goals — and to accept the limitations of local conditions. Aklak pilot Bob Heath dealt with this first-hand in Resolute while flying support for one expedition. "This woman was trying to be the first person to ever fly around the world in a helicopter from the North Pole to South Pole and North again," he remembers. "She had huge money and a beautiful Bell 407, with big fuel tanks installed in the back, high tech display — guidance material for the trip was there." When the weather got bad and she had to wait, she still wanted to press on. "She was not blessed with patience," Heath remembers. "She was bound and determined we were going and I was bound and determined we weren't. So I took her for a walk around the town of Resolute Bay and showed her the dead Avro York by the weather station, the dead DC-4 by the water source, the dead DC-3 by the sewage facility, and the dead F-27 — all because they tried to push the weather. It took seeing four spectacularly fatal crashes before I could convince her that maybe she could wait another day."[19]

As in the time of Amundsen and Andrée, not all expeditions to the North Pole ended successfully. Famed Japanese explorer Hyoichi Kohno died in May 1997 while trying to traverse the moving pack ice alone and on foot as part of his planned six-year journey from the North Pole to Japan. He was only two months in when he fell through the ice. First Air's Michael De Caria and Ross Michelin were dispatched to look for him when he failed to contact his expedition office. On May 19 they took off in a Twin Otter from Resolute. "We had satellite pictures of the leads, the thinner patches of ice where the ice had broken and refrozen," De Caria says. About an hour into the flight, they spotted something. "We found his sled, along with one ski and one pole. And it was just on the edge of some thin ice. There was no sign of him." The weather was not good enough to land that day, but when it cleared they took off with an RCMP officer, member of Kohno's support team, and two guides. They landed as close as they could, then took their on-board boat to investigate. "When we got to the sled, we slowly shovelled around it, and just below the ice, that's where Mr. Kohno's body

was found," De Caria notes. It was the first time the twenty-six-year-old pilot had had to recover and transport a body, and he hoped he would not have to do it again soon. Even so, he noted "It was important for the family that they had his body and it's closure for them."[20]

EVEN WITH THE DANGER — OR PERHAPS because of it — people have been increasingly drawn to visiting Canada's northern reaches. There are certainly some breathtaking scenes, and the difficulty in reaching them and the small local population makes for lots of space and potential wildlife encounters. Aklak Air pilot Bob Heath, who "came up north for a week twenty years ago," flew every type of job imaginable in the Western Arctic, but his experiences of "flightseeing" sum up what many pilots in the Arctic and Subarctic say. "We take mad scientists and geologists and explorers and adventure and adrenaline junkies who want to be the first to climb a mountain," he said. He also flew a lot of tourists, and had fun teasing the "one or two disgruntled ones I get back there in seat nineteen in the Twin Otter." He loved seeing people's reactions when he brought them to his favourite spot, Ivvavik National Park and the crystal-clear Firth River. "The people that you're flying there are mostly rafters from large American cities — sometimes Europe," he said. "When they're waiting to get in they're checking their cell phone reception and rustling their newspapers. But from the moment we take off until we get there, there is not a single sign of human habitation. And it never fails, when we land, they stop, look around, and burst into spontaneous applause."[21]

CHAPTER 9

The Old and the Bold

The last decades of the twentieth century saw some northern chapters come to a close — the Cold War ended, the last DEW Line sites were decommissioned, and residential schools were shut down — while others were just beginning. Many old patterns of northern aviation continued even as new technologies, regulations, and norms took hold. The boom-bust economy of the North saw to that, as did the ever-present challenges of weather and climate. Human nature also played its part. As people in the industry often say, there are old pilots and there are bold pilots; in the North, there were even some old, bold pilots who lived to tell their tales — and, unfortunately, cautious pilots who lost their lives far too soon.

"REMOTENESS AND MOUNTAINS AND WEATHER"

Don Bergren was an experienced and reputable Air North pilot when his Douglas DC-4, C-FGNI, crashed on August 14, 1996, about four hundred kilometres south of Whitehorse.[1] After the crew noticed electrical problems right after takeoff, one of the plane's four engines caught fire and fell off. Bergren, his co-pilot Dan Quaile, and the mechanic-engineer Stewart Clark realized they could not make it back to the airstrip so decided to try and land in the Iskut River, a tributary of the Stikine in northern British Columbia. Journalist Larry Pynn wrote that "With flames pouring from the wing, the crew members feared the aircraft would explode at any moment." They jumped in the frigid, fast-moving water and managed to make it to a submerged gravel bar, from where they tried to reach shore after the forty-two

kilometre an hour current swept them off. Unfortunately it turned out that Bergren could not swim.[2] Quaile and Clark were treated for hypothermia but were otherwise uninjured. "My husband was never seen again and was presumed drowned," says Sue Bergren, who was left to grieve with their eight-year-old daughter.

Bergren had been a commercial bush pilot for over fifteen years, twelve of those with Air North. Over his career he had amassed more than fourteen thousand hours on Beech 18s, DC-3s, and even a Kenn Borek Air twin-engine Caribou transport. This was an experienced pilot. On the trip he went down on he was flying twenty-five hundred kilogram loads of gold-ore concentrate aboard Air North's only DC-4 out of the busy Bronson Creek gravel airstrip at "Snip Mine" near the Iskut River. From there, they traveled eighty kilometers away to Wrangell, Alaska. He had flown

Sue Bergren

Don Bergren, pilot for Air North, with the company's Beech 18, in the Yukon, c. 1988. It is likely C-FRSX, one of only fifty-nine 3NM variants manufactured for navigational training purposes in the 1950s, and now on display at the Alberta Aviation Museum.

the DC-4, nicknamed the *Yukon Trader* as captain for three years, and had already flown the route twice the day of the crash. Joe Sparling, Air North's owner, praised Bergren's handling of the eighteen-tonne airplane. "It was a successful landing under dire circumstances," he said after visiting the crash site. "He did everything right." Sparling was just as puzzled at the turn of events as Bergren's family and coworkers. "The weather was good, the plane was running good," he said, and the plane had just been inspected.[3]

Too many pilots had died in the "Golden Triangle," as Pynn called it: nine chartered planes and helicopters had crashed in a decade, with eleven fatalities and twelve injured. Pynn wondered in his article what

was to blame. Was it the eccentricity or "macho attitude" of northern pilots? Pressure to fly in marginal conditions from airlines anxious to get the job done or miners eager to get out on leave? Overwork? The operators he interviewed lamented the accidents but could not — or would not — say why they occurred or how to prevent them. An air-accident investigator with the federal Transportation Safety Board, Gerry Binnema, said: "It's simply the way business is carried on up North because of the situation that they're in. We can't ban aircraft from flying up there.... We've got remoteness and mountains and weather. It all adds up, making a fairly difficult climate for aircraft."

Aklak pilot Bob Heath remembered some of his approach notes would say "'if

Nordair L-188 Electra, CF-NAX, coming in for a landing at the mine site as Asbestos Hill-Deception Bay on October 31, 1974. The Electra transported passengers – mostly miners – back and forth between the mine and headquarters at Dorval, Quebec, with the odd diversion to Iqaluit because of bad weather. To help the pilots find the airstrip in winter, those on the ground would use red dye.

you haven't been here during the day in nice weather, don't come.' Pangnirtung is one of those spots. We were in there about a dozen times doing medevacs when I was training about twenty years ago, and there's a cliff on one end of the runway and cemetery on the other."[4] Pilots like Heath were exceedingly careful, though. He would always carry an astro compass and know how to use it in case his instruments failed. "When I see my young co-pilots getting too reliant on GPS, I turn it off and make them navigate by watch, astro compass, and gyro," he noted. Heath once met the chief pilot for the Dornier aircraft company, who made a big impression on him. "He said, for the true

professional pilot, there are no war stories. Because you prepare and take steps to mitigate any errors you commit."

Heath also never expected, or wanted, to be a bush pilot. He actually got hired on at Aklak in 1990 while hanging around the dispatch office doing crosswords waiting for a business meeting. "The dispatcher was answering eight phone lines and three radio frequencies," he recalls. "Finally she said, 'It's too bad you're not a pilot, because we're just slammed here and could put you to work right away.'" When she found out he had his commercial and could fly Twin Otters he was hired on the spot. "Twelve hours later I crawled out of the airplane. In the first week I flew to

Greenland, Siberia, and took a little piece of an oil rig down to Vancouver. I flew the 99, Twin Otter, Navajo — just about anything I ever mentioned that I'd flown they strapped me into."

"I always thought they were underpaid jobs with under-maintained airplanes," he continued. "But you can eat off the hangar floor here and the airplanes belong to the engineers — we just get to fly them." Joe Muff agrees, noting that his first manager, Dawn Bartsch was "a tough, but fair, boss and instilled a serious commitment to safety and quality in me that guides my own aviation principles to this day." He also says that his old company, Alkan Air, has continued to be a "really safe and sound operation" under its current management, and that plenty of pilots he knows — his brother Win grudgingly included — were "prepared all the time, and never put a ding in an airplane."

But many pilots working for northern operators told stories of clients overloading the aircraft, and feeling pressure to push weather, and work long, hard hours to keep limited jobs in a competitive environment.[5] When Muff was working as an air engineer in the 1970s for Trans North, he says he would fly every trip, often up into the Arctic islands on medevacs to the oil camps. "That way you'd see what was going on and wouldn't have to start from scratch when you fixed the airplane," he notes. "Medevacs were not very formal; they would just call whoever had the twin-engined plane, which was Trans North in those days. You'd go into places with no lights in the middle of the night — just skidoo lights or RCMP pickup truck on the side of the strip. Dawson City used flare pots a lot — cans with

diesel fuel and a roll of toilet paper in them and set them on fire." He once flew for fifty-six hours straight, taking turns sleeping and handling the controls while the pilots napped. "Today you can't do that," he adds.[6]

PUSHING THE LIMITS

Many northern pilots were known to push the limits or ignore them altogether. According to veteran journalist Erik Watt, Jim McAvoy "knew exactly what payload any aircraft he flew could get off the ground, and that was often well above DOT's load limits." McAvoy was also known to drink and fight at the Gold Range bar in Yellowknife, fly under bridges, and buzz construction workers in his younger days. But mostly he was remembered for his uncanny ability to spot people who were lost or in distress, even if it meant breaking rules or searching "blind canyons too narrow to turn around in and too deep to climb out of." The many people he rescued were grateful, but he had a narrow escape or two.[7]

Willy Laserich, the owner first of Altair Leasing and then Adlair Aviation, was arrested by RCMP on at least one occasion, grounded several times, and racked up hundreds of charges from DOT. "Willy's Bandits" were the bane of Ottawa, but adored by the remote communities they served, flying in medevacs, supplies, and groceries, and flying out loads of Arctic char aboard the company's DC-4. It was with the support of those communities that he finally managed to secure a commercial licence in 1982, several years after he had begun the operation.[8]

Dan Reynolds checking traps on the south branch of the Tatonduk River in his Chinook ultralight with modifications. Reynolds has been flying these "Dan Specials" in the region since 1983.

Several northern flyers use homebuilt ultralight aircraft in creative ways. Dan Reynolds employs his modified "Dan Special" Citabrias and Chinooks in his guiding and outfitting business, which he took over from his dad, Stan Reynolds, in the 1990s. "My dad would do these landings — no strip, just natural ridges on the tops of mountains, where you'd only have about 150–200 feet," he says. He has adopted this technique, which allows him to get into every corner of the back country near Dawson City, Yukon where he lives. "Trapping would be impossible without planes," he says. "And in the winter time an ultralight on skis can handle waist-deep snow."[9]

This calculated daredevilry has not been limited to commercial flyers. Helmut Schoener, also of Dawson City, calls the Dempster Highway "one big airstrip" and he has made use of it, as well as the Alaska and Klondike Highways, since he started flying in the area in the early 1980s. "There were hardly any private planes at the time," he recalls. He started with a Cessna 172, CF-ADF, then moved on to a series of ultralights and homebuilts: a Chinook 82; a Clavair in 1988; a scaled-down version of a Second World War-era Fieselerstork; and finally a Skyfly 65 — a low winged all-wood aircraft with side-by-side seating. "I've had scary adventures — the weather changes so fast — but I like the adrenaline rush and love flying over the incredible beauty of the territory. It's a tough environment — you make a little mistake and you're done."[10]

John Faulkner

John Faulkner with his 1943 Beech Staggerwing, CF-BKQ, in Whitehorse, Yukon, c. 2009. John Faulkner, a local judge, used to fly around the territory on the court circuit in Twin Seneca, C-GZAQ, and then Cessna 185, C-FXZE. Now he flies 'BKQ mostly for fun.

Over the years there were many bizarre incidents and scandals involving northern aviators. John Faulkner, a judge and pilot in Whitehorse has followed some of these cases. Taku Air Transport of Atlin, British Columbia, which was owned by Dick and Theresa Bond, was involved in several crashes in the 1970s and 1980s. "After Dick got sick, his wife, Theresa, took over the flying but was involved in a very tragic crash in Dease Lake which killed a number of Atlin's leading citizens. Theresa was the only survivor," Faulkner says. The Beaver she was flying on September 27, 1986, apparently nosedived into the lake at full speed while coming in for a landing. After years of inquiries and few answers, Theresa

herself was killed when an airplane in which she was a passenger flew into the side of a mountain while en route to Dease Lake.[11]

John Rolls, the owner of Territorial Airways out of Ross River, also became infamous. "Terror-Air" as the company was known by some for its "hair-raising adventures and brushes with the Department of Transport," was only the beginning, according to Faulkner: "One day in September 1977, Al Kulan was holding a business meeting at the bar of the Welcome Inn in Ross River, when Rolls walked in and shot Kulan point-blank in the face with a .357 magnum revolver." Rolls was convicted of first-degree murder for killing the successful miner and former business associate; apparently

Adam Morrison with a Bell 47G3B2, C-FQJY, at the Trans North Turbo Air base at Dawson City in 1981. That summer Morrison was working with a geology crew at Clinton Creek, about eighty kilometres downstream from Dawson City. One evening two of his passengers were unloading their gear after they had landed, and one of the men threw his pick axe out and up into the main rotor blades – while they were still turning. The helicopter started "dancing" in the street, but luckily Morrison was at the controls and able to shut it down right away. Both main rotor blades were damaged beyond repair and they had to call in another helicopter to pick up the rest of the crews. The next day they had to fly in two new rotor blades aboard a Twin Otter, as well as engineers to replace the damaged ones.

alcohol abuse coupled with "mental instability" made him fixate on Kulan as the source of his misery.[12]

Adam Morrison, who was operations manager for Trans North Air out of Whitehorse, remembers one particularly unnerving incident in July 1989. "There was an American tourist, a vet from Vietnam," he says. "Around 7:00 p.m. the cook at Bonanza Creek called the RCMP because this guy was acting strange." Morrison, who has roughly thirteen thousand hours on helicopters, flew in with the Bell 206 to help locate the man at the request of the Dawson City RCMP. "When we got there, he started shooting at us and the bullet ended

up between me and the sergeant. Luckily it missed the helicopter blade!" Both he and his passenger were slightly injured by shrapnel, but Morrison was able to land successfully. "They ended up bringing a SWAT team in by DC-3 from Whitehorse, and he came out eventually with a white flag."[13]

RECONCILING THE PAST AND LOOKING TO THE FUTURE

While Morrison was brought in on this occasion, northern law enforcement agencies also had their own planes and pilots. The RCMP Air Section, for example, had been resurrected with new pilots (many RCAF trained) after the Second World War with two Beech 18s, a Grumman Goose, and its trusty Norseman, *The Falcon*.[14] Over the next two decades, these aircraft and others — notably Otters — became important for serving the Force's distant Arctic posts and patrolling the expanses north of 60. As Saunders notes regarding the mid-century, "a typical northern flight would leave Edmonton for far northern detachments carrying replacement members, fresh food, mail and other supplies." In the Commissioner's Report for March 1954, he wrote the Air Section was involved in "aerial searches for lost persons, escaped prisoners, wanted criminals, stricken vessels in coastal waters and occasionally stolen livestock and automobiles."

RCMP planes flew into communities to investigate crimes and transport bodies to the coroner, but the aircraft were also used to assist Department of Northern Affairs and sent on several mercy flights. In March 1956 several RCMP officers flew to Port Burwell in what is now Nunavut in a Beaver, CF-MPN, to investigate reports of starving Inuit there. They ended up flying in 135 kilograms of food and evacuating a young girl named Anatok to Fort Chimo (Kuujjuaq), Quebec for medical attention.[15] RCMP officers aboard an Otter, CF-MPP, also rescued four men who had forced-landed their Norseman on an ice floe in the Hudson Strait while en route from Coral Harbour to Nottingham Island. The Otter landed on the closest solid ice it could find, unpacked the collapsible boat it had on board, dragged it across three kilometres of snow to the ice's edge, and then paddled to the stranded men before reversing direction and getting them back to Coral Harbour safely.

By 1987 the RCMP Air Services — as the Air Section was renamed — had two pilots and one engineer at bases in Inuvik, Whitehorse, Yellowknife, and Iqaluit with Twin Otters at their disposal.[16] Those were later traded for nine-seat Pilatus PC XII aircraft based out of Yellowknife and Iqaluit. According to a 2000–01 report, Air Services flew twenty-five thousand hours each year, a significant portion of that in the North in the "world's biggest beat," as journalist Michael Vlessides dubbed the Northwest Territories "G" Division in an article. This territory, which included the Western Arctic and Nunavut, encompassed thirty-eight detachments, eight patrol cabins, and four satellite offices in 1998. RCMP Air Services pilots performed many of the same roles they always had since the earliest days, but increasingly the Force focused on community policing efforts and improving relationships with residents — especially indigenous ones — after decades of mixed experiences.[17]

The Roman Catholic and Anglican churches were also actively seeking reconciliation at the close of the residential school era, while also trying to serve their far-flung parishioners. Between 1982 and 1995, Bishop Ron Ferris regularly visited twenty-six mission points in the Yukon and northern British Columbia using a Cessna 172. "I shared the plane with the Catholic Bishop, who later died in a tragic accident in the plane," he notes.[18] The seventy-two-year-old Bishop Thomas Lobsinger, OMI, or "Lobby" as he was known to many, was en route to Dawson from Whitehorse with Brother Hoby Spruyt on April 15, 2000, when he crashed into Fox Lake. The "Flying Bishop" had been a popular figure, supporting healing initiatives among indigenous people who were abused at Church-run schools. He was also a pilot with thirty years of experience who was known to "drop into a lake and fish from the pontoons of his single-engine Piper Cub."

Aviation has become more commonplace in the North, with people and goods flowing in and out of town without the "big hubbub" experienced by Sandra Pikujak Katsak in Pond Inlet, Northwest Territories, in the 1980s. The plane would arrive at 8:00 p.m. and "Everyone would be out visiting after a plane came in," she says. "Sometimes it was the Akukitturmiut, the Greenlanders, who came in. Sometimes it was exchange students from the South, workers from Panarctic, sports competitors from other communities, or kids from the Iqaluit high school."[19] In September 1988 airplanes brought the "polls to the people" for the first time during the territory's elections. Pilots from Ptarmigan Airways and other Northwest Territories operators flew local election officials in Twin Otters from Yellowknife to Cambridge Bay (Iqaluktuuttiaq), Bay Chimo (Umingmaktok), and other points. In Bathurst Inlet (Kingoak), each of the settlement's five eligible voters turned out to take advantage of their democratic right.[20]

Residents may have appreciated fly-in elections, but by 1988 many women saw the need to examine the policy of flying out pregnant women to give birth. The availability of medevacs had certainly decreased infant and maternal mortality, but the system needed tweaking. Inuit women were sent out to Yellowknife or Iqaluit a month ahead of their expected delivery dates, forced to "billet with strangers, stay at a boarding house, impose on friends, or move in with relatives until the baby decides to arrive." It also meant leaving behind emotional support

and family. As journalist Joanne Irons noted, "It's not unheard of for an expectant mother to try to deceive the nurses about when her child is due, or to miss the flight that was to have taken her Out to the hospital."[21]

"It's different now with the surgeon up here," pilot Bob Heath noted of Inuvik, "but when I first came up anything more complicated than a breach birth — medevac. I've had a couple born on final here. One fellow that was born on the plane flies with Aklak regularly gets free airfare for life."[22]

Women wanted the choice of whether or not to fly out to give birth, but they also wanted the opportunity to enter northern aviation. Marlie McLaren Kelsey followed in the footsteps of her father, famous bush pilot and aviation businessman, Duncan McLaren. After joining CP Air to do Vancouver reservations in 1969, she says she "got very interested in getting ahead in the company. I met some of the agents in Whitehorse, and of course was fascinated with the idea of working north where my dad had flown. So in 1973 I put a bid in to transfer there and it was subsequently denied." Another male agent who had just finished the training course was given the position instead. "The union by then was in place and immediately disputed it and the company had to guarantee me a position. I was the only woman with twenty-two guys. Sounds enviable but actually it was very challenging and sometimes lonely." McLaren Kelsey notes that Whitehorse, the largest base in the "BC District," had had a revolving door of young male agents who would leave after their mandatory eighteen months were up. "I fell in love with the North and ended up staying six years," she says. One of the main reasons was the variety of work: "I got to do reservations, ticket office, cargo office, and all the

Marlie McLaren Kelsey

Marlie McLaren Kelsey, daughter of bush pilot and Pacific Western Airlines executive Duncan McLaren, worked for Canadian Pacific Airlines from 1969 to 1986. She was the first woman in the company allowed to bid for work in the North and became the agent at Whitehorse, the largest base in the "BC District," for six years.

positions at the airport including my favorite, doing the weight and balance of the aircraft. I felt that learning all these different jobs would give me a great background to move up into management."[23]

Soon, many northern companies had women pilots and co-pilots, flying in everything from small airplanes, like Cessna 185's, to Lear Jets and Jet Ranger helicopters. Judy Cameron was hired by Gateway Aviation of Edmonton in the mid-1970s as a co-pilot on a DC-3 out of Inuvik. "I think I pulled my weight, but I understand their concern about my strength," she says. "We carried drill parts, core samples, supplies to oil companies, and forty-five gallon

fuel drums — the DC-3 could take twenty-six.... We often had six thousand pounds of cargo, which we had to load and unload. I wore coveralls and boots with steel toes. I worked as hard as I could." Mireille Samson was another woman pilot who came of age during this period, and became the first woman to fly helicopters with the Canadian Coast Guard in May 1988; she now has several thousand hours on Bell Jet Ranger, Long Ranger, Twin Huey, and BO-105 helicopters. She has flown medevacs and SARs, but mostly her work has involved flying researchers, maintenance technicians, and doing ice patrols from ice-breakers in the Arctic Archipelago.[24]

In an interview in 1992, Lorna de Blicquy said her main regret was that she never flew for a major airline. "We just weren't allowed to then," she said. "They just never hired women. Back in the '50s, I had a pile of letters that said 'you're a nice girl, but we don't hire girls.'"[25] Even in the 1970s, Judy Cameron was told by the chief pilot at Gateway's Inuvik base "At least the airlines will never hire you, so we won't have to worry about losing you."[26] Until April 1973, that is, when Transair hired Rosella Bjornson as first officer on the Fokker F-28 Fellowship and she became the only woman airline pilot out of twenty-eight hundred men in Canada — and the first jet-qualified female first officer in North America.[27] She flew the F-28 until February 1979 when she moved to the twin turboprop NAMC YS-11. "We were based in Churchill a week at a time and we flew north to Rankin Inlet, Baker Lake, and Pelly Bay to service the north," she recalls. In 1987 she started flying the Boeing 737 for Pacific Western Airways, which had bought out Transair, and in 1990 she accomplished another first — the first female airline captain in Canada – when she was named airline captain for Canadian Airlines International.

Captain Rosella Bjornson (on the right) with her husband, First Officer Bill Pratt, in front of a Canadian North Boeing 737 on the Yellowknife Airport ramp, c. 1996. Bjornson was the first female jet captain in Canada and regularly flew all seven of the company's Boeing 737s.

GOLD, OIL, DIAMONDS, AND OTHER RICHES

One of the reasons doors opened to women aviators in the 1960s and 1970s (aside from changing attitudes) was the boom in northern resource exploration and extraction. There was the lead-zinc mine in Nanisivik near Arctic Bay on Baffin Island, and large corporations such as Echo Bay Mines operated the old Eldorado property at Port Radium until 1979 when it opened the Lupin gold mine at Contwoyto Lake.[28] It was oil in the Western Arctic that brought in $6.5 billion in exploration budgets and had helicopters and planes fanning out from Inuvik, Old Crow, and other northern points. "In the mid-1970s there were fifty Twin Otters operating in the Mackenzie Delta," said Bob Heath. "If you had an oil camp, you had a Twin Otter." When the Geological Survey of Canada estimated in the late 1970s that there were six billion barrels of oil in the Beaufort Sea reserves, worth $150 billion, it sounded like the company's investments were going to pay off.

The Canadian government also provided tax incentives to oil companies, and Dome Petroleum, Esso, Shell, and Petro-Canada were particularly active in the region. In particular, these companies wanted to build the Mackenzie Valley Pipeline, "the largest mega-project ever proposed in northern Canada" according to historian William Morrison. But things had changed from 1921, when Imperial Oil had swooped in unopposed to create Norman Wells, or from the Second World War and DEW Line eras, when militaries, governments, and civilian contractors had undertaken huge projects in the North. Local residents now wanted a say in how things would proceed — or whether they would go ahead at all.

Walter Sopher

Echo Bay Mines operated this Lockheed Hercules, C-FDSX, from 1980 to 1982. When the company began mining in the north, it found commercial carriers were not able to provide the service they required, so they created their own. They began by leasing a DC-3 (CF-CUG) in 1975, then a Convair 640 (C-FPWO). Once Lupin Mine was complete, it shifted to a Boeing 727, C-FPXD, which was in use until 1991.

At least one resident kept an eye on things and reported back to the community — and the world. In the late 1960s, "Here are the News" columnist Edith Josie commented on the comings and goings of aircraft from Bullock Helicopters, Okanagan Helicopters, and other operators on contract with oil exploration companies around Old Crow.[29] "One helicopter is here looking for oil and busy flying around every day. Andrew Charlie is working with them also Peter Lord he work for them," she noted. "Some people glad for oil company going to work for oil. Because the boys going to make good money." By October 1970, however, doubts had crept in about the effects on caribou and

the fragile local environment, despite the consortium's attempts to assuage their fears with town meetings and a tour over the proposed pipeline route. "They talk about Pipe line," she wrote, "if they put one close to Crow Mountain and if it ever broke the oil will go on the ground and they afraid the Caribou won't come to Old Crow, and so with water which they drink from the river it might get spoil." Josie's columns appeared not only in the *Whitehorse Star*, but often were printed in newspapers in Toronto, Edmonton, Alaska, and California; it was also translated into several European languages. People far beyond Old Crow could now read about the community's concerns.

This international attention helped when the Vuntut Gwitchin around Old Crow and other Gwich'in, Métis, and Inuvialuit in the Mackenzie Delta area began agitating for land claims negotiations in 1973. That year, the federal government, after a Canadian Supreme Court decision, declared the original Treaty 11 from the era of Imperial Oil's *Vic* and *René* null and void.[30] The government had not laid out reserves after the oil boom had ended in 1921 as it did not want to pay to fulfill the treaty promises to the Dene of this distant corner of the Dominion. The government also had never proposed treaties to the First Nations of the Yukon or Inuit in the rest of the Northwest Territories for this reason, and by the mid-1970s, Cree and Inuit had successfully negotiated the James Bay and Northern Quebec Agreement. With the money they received in return for the right to develop the hydroelectric potential of the region, Inuit set up the Makivik Corporation, which took over and expanded First Air (which was a descendant of Bradley Air Services). Air Inuit also got its start through the first phase of the massive James Bay Project with a single Beaver that flew negotiators and field workers between communities and construction sites.

In the Mackenzie Delta, however, many indigenous people opposed the pipeline and wanted development halted until land claims could be negotiated and the oil consortium could answer technical questions adequately. The Berger Inquiry (so-called because it was run by Justice Thomas Berger) was set up, and in January 1975, he and a commission began visiting thirty-five communities and hearing from one thousand witnesses. Two years later, he issued a report that recommended a ten-year moratorium on the project, and in July 1987 the Yukon created Herschel Island Territorial Park to protect the fragile ecological and historical site.

The Inuvaluit settled their land claims in 1984, and on April 22, 1992, the official signing of the Gwich'in Comprehensive Land Claim Agreement took place.[31] The political and cultural landscapes were shifting, and by 2002 Inuvik aviator Fred Carmichael became chair of the Aboriginal Pipeline Group after serving as president of the Gwich'in Tribal Council. In both these endeavours, he was a pragmatist who drew on his aviation business background. With his companies, he had always encouraged local people to pursue meaningful work opportunities and, in the absence of formal school programs, tried to give them an apprenticeship of sorts. "I tried to hire and help train local mechanics and flight attendants and office staff," he says. He saw, and continues to see, the pipeline as one way to bolster the local economy for the Gwich'in, Inuvialuit, and others living in the Western Arctic. "We're trying to get out from under the dependency on welfare," he notes. "We need to develop an economic base for our people. People are suffering, hanging on by the skin of their teeth."

"I really battle with the environmentalists," he continues. "There's a place for them, but they have to have some reality as well — to balance the needs of the human being. There's no other industry — if that's not good enough for you, then give us an alternative." Carmichael also argues there are the necessary agencies in place to control development and that industry is learning from indigenous peoples. "They can't take a bulldozer and clear trees anywhere they want. They don't throw garbage out on the roads like other northerners do. Industry, government, and Aboriginal people have all learned — 'Hey, we'd better look out for this environment.'"

Sue Bergren

Air North operated this DC-3, C-FIMA, from 1988 to 1998 out of Whitehorse. Nicknamed the *Yukon Musher* it was manufactured in 1942 as a C-47 Skytrain for the U.S. Army Air Force before being converted for civilian use. In 1998 it returned to the U.S. after being sold to Fly One out of New Mexico.

In an interview in 2010, Bob Heath agreed that since the Inuvaluit settled their land claims, "they have total environmental control over any project in the Inuvialuit Settlement Region and are very good at monitoring things. The days when an oil company could just point to a map and say we're going to build a camp here and we're going to start drilling tomorrow are over." He also noted that companies have to hire and train Inuvialuit people to do the various jobs, "and there's been a lot less resistance from the corporations than I thought would be there."[32]

In other parts of the North, especially around Dawson City, mineral exploration and extraction centred on placer gold mining. While journalist Larry Pynn argued that the 1990s gold rush in Northern British Columbia was "the realm of engineers with

helicopters and diamond drills backed by multimillion-dollar corporate ventures," in Dawson, activities were on a smaller scale, especially in earlier decades.[33] As Joe Muff recalls, there were "a lot of penny stock mining companies that had claims up here wanting to do exploration so they could prove their prospects and float the companies on that in the market/public offering." Even some pilots and mechanics tried their hand at it. Muff quit his engineer job at Great Northern the summer of 1970 to spend a few months in the bush with his geologist friend. "We were doing mostly mining staking and also geophysics and geochem sampling. I had studied some old maps all winter and so I was going to look for gold in the Dawson area, so I quit GN for this more exciting thing. But I figured

Henry M. Holden

"Buffalo" Joe McBryan in the cockpit of *Summer Wages*. This DC-3, C-GPNR, was involved in the Normandy invasion of the Second World War, according to McBryan, but since 1994 it has shuttled passengers and cargo around the Northwest Territories. It has also become a favourite at air shows and, since 2009, has appeared on the reality television series, *Ice Pilots NWT*.

they owed me a flight so I got them to fly me up to Old Crow."[34]

Joe Muff, who is now director of flight operations for Air North, knew resident Joe Sparling when they started their companies in 1971. "We were both in the bush," Muff says, "until I chased him out of the bush and he went into the big ones."[35] Sparling was born in the Yukon, and worked at his family's hotel where he did maintenance and counted cash. In 1972 he got his private pilot's licence and two years later his commercial ticket. Unlike most of his contemporaries, though, he also got his MBA from the University of British Columbia. In 1977 he and his partner, Tom Wood, acquired a charter operation, called it Air North, and started doing mineral exploration flights with single-engined Cessnas.

By 1981 Air North acquired DC-3s for its sked runs, and then brought in a DC-4 in the early 1990s. In 1998 Air North sold off its last DC-3 but, as Joe Sparling noted, he was not ready to call it the end of an era for the vintage aircraft. But it would be for the company, which permanently switched to Hawker Siddeley 748s for its scheduled passenger service. The "Gooney Bird" had been a fixture of northern transportation since the postwar years when Connelly-Dawson started landing on the gravel bars near Old Crow. The DC-3s had been used since to haul people, cargo, and smoke-jumpers for multiple Yukon companies, and earned its place of honour as the biggest weathervane at the Whitehorse Airport in 1981. It was used just as much in the Northwest Territories. Bob Heath recalls Aklak had a Super DC-3 from 1993 to 2007–08. "What we realized is that the DC-3 and those kinds of aircraft fill a particular niche and you really can't replace them."

Another airline was not giving up on the old warbirds quite so soon. Buffalo Airways in Yellowknife had more in its fleet than any other operator north of 60 in 2000. Many had been in continuous operation since Joe McBryan took the company over from its original owner, the famous Barren Lands survivor Bob Gauchie in 1970.[36] McBryan had actually first taken an airline job because he wanted to fly a DC-3; he was hired on at Great Northern Airways in 1969 for the last DC-3 course after flying for people like Jim McAvoy. "I went for one year and wore the uniform," he says. "I flew 1,400 hours on DC-3s that year, but certain people aren't cut out for a large crew. But it was exceptional training." McBryan admits that Buffalo Airways was "done by mistake with no five-year plan." His brother found aircraft — DC-3s, DC-4s, C-46s — and brought them home, and McBryan put them to work. "We tried to make a living. I didn't know about the financial pitfalls of aviation — probably wouldn't have gone into it if I had."[37] Still, in the early 1990s when diamonds were found at Lac des Gras, Northwest Territories, Buffalo Airways became very busy flying passengers and cargo on non-stop "Koala Airlifts" for Australian giant BHP Minerals.[38]

HERCULEAN EFFORTS

Canada's Armed Forces largely switched priorities in the postwar period to peace-keeping operations, but they continued to have a useful and constant presence in the North. The RCAF base at Resolute became "the jumping-off point for researchers, explorers, and government agents travelling in the High Arctic" in the postwar years, and the RCAF provided transportation services for these groups at times.[39] As historian Peter Kikkert notes, between 1949 and 1951, the RCAF flew the National Museum of Canada as well as the Northern Insect Survey of the Department of Agriculture. Sometimes the RCAF conducted wildlife surveys itself while overflying the Arctic.

Crews also flew Lancasters and then the Argus while undertaking Northern Patrols (NORPAT) for photo reconnaissance, ice patrol, and sovereignty-boosting activities. As author Larry Milberry notes for the Cold War period, "some Lanc missions also reconnoitered Soviet activity in the Arctic islands." Departing Comox, Greenwood, Yellowknife, or Frobisher bases, these crews also kept an eye on corporate airstrips, industrial developments (checking for any illegal emissions), and even made "courtesy" over-flights of remote centres "just to let the inhabitants know that somebody down south cares." In the 1980s and 1990s, residents might catch a glimpse of Northern Operations Readiness Patrol flights by Aurora marine patrol aircraft as well.[40]

It was the C-130 Hercules, however, that became the centrepiece of the Air Force in the North. So much so that when the Department of Indian Affairs and Northern Development (DIAND) and the Department of National Defense (DND) improved Canada's Arctic airstrips and built new ones from the mid-1960s to 1979, they kept the takeoff and landing needs of the large, four-engined transports in mind. It also became an important symbol: throughout the 1970s and 1980s, Operation Santa Claus collected toy donations at the Parachute

Maintenance Depot in Edmonton and sent them by Hercules to Yellowknife. Crews would then pack them onto Twin Otter "sleighs" for remote Arctic communities. As Captain Sandy Antal from the Edmonton Depot noted in 1986, the children knew Santa came from the North Pole, but did not know "he [had] a southern partner, and he [flew] a Herc."[41]

In addition to the Canadian Air Force's Labrador helicopters and twin-engined DHC-5 Buffalos, the Hercs were central to Search and Rescue operations. In September 1973 the crew of one spotted the wreck of Aklavik Flying Services' Cessna 185, CF-CMH, which had been doing an aerial caribou survey for a Calgary oil pipeline company. The plane had gotten trapped in a box canyon just over the Alaska border and crashed, killing all on board.[42]

On October 20, 1991, it would be the crew and passengers of an Air Force Herc that would require rescuing. Hercules CAF 130322 was en route to the Alert Wireless Station, the northernmost permanently inhabited place in the world, on one of its semi-annual Boxtop resupply missions.[43] The pilot, who was apparently flying by sight rather than relying on instruments, crashed into a hill top on final approach to the airstrip. Four of the eighteen passengers and crew were killed instantly, while the captain died later from exposure. Rescue efforts by Canadian and American personnel from local bases as well as from Edmonton and Trenton, Ontario, were hampered by a fierce blizzard, temperatures nearing -70°C with the wind chill, and the mountainous terrain; it took thirty hours for the first rescuers to arrive.[44]

The Boxtop 22 rescue mission, as it was called, was the most decorated peacetime event in Canadian military history. The crash

investigation recommended all Hercs be retrofitted with ground proximity detectors and better Arctic survival equipment, and the media wondered if the Air Force had adequate aircraft for these types of operations. Just a month earlier, an anonymous military official was quoted in Peter Tadman's book about Marten Hartwell, *The Survivor*, as saying that "if a jumbo jet crashed in the far North today, rescue forces would be unable to airlift any casualties and could only comfort the survivors until they died." Major Don Blair, in command of the largest SAR unit disagreed: "Some of the equipment definitely is aged but I think we're in a good position to respond." Perhaps it said something, however, that the survivors were apparently airlifted by two American H-60 Black Hawk helicopters from Alaska.[45]

The Canadian military presence in the North was small, with only 120 regular, reserve, and civilian personnel spread out over the whole Canadian Forces Northern Area (CFNA) in 1998. The Air Force had officially left the Yukon thirty years earlier after integration, but the Yellowknife-based CFNA maintained a Headquarters Detachment in Whitehorse and conducted exercises with the various branches of the Canadian military — as well as its American allies. It also continued to rely on its northern reservists, the Canadian Rangers, to perform ground patrols, and transported them and their equipment using Hercules and Twin Otters.[46]

One of the reasons for the shrinking military presence in the Arctic was the gradual closing down of the staffed DEW Line sites. Beginning in 1985 the military began replacing them with the new Canadian-run, two-billion-dollar North Warning System (NWS). Brigadier General Duane Daly,

Peter Hill

Peter Hill flew Bradley Air Services' Twin Otters from 1977 to 1981 into spots such as this DEW Line site. He recalls that Bradley made its own approach plates with communications frequencies, navigations systems information, as well as the available length to land. As he says, some were ice strips that only had beacons when the oil rigs were there.

the Canadian Forces Northern Area commander, and the U.S. squadron leader were both on hand at Tuktoyaktuk in 1993 when the DEW Line site there was deactivated. Both agreed that the threat of an attack on North America through the Arctic was very low, but that the "potential exists."

Approximately fifty military personnel and civilians attended the decommissioning, but Aklak pilot Bob Heath recalls there was little local sadness in its closure.[47] "When the contractors came up — if you were from here you could be hired as a bear monitor — that is you were a guy with a gun outside, not exactly career enhancing," he

notes. "But the Inuit were largely bypassed or ignored or pushed out of the way when they were building the sites. When they decommissioned the last manned site up in Tuk they had a memorial but no one from the village came. The mayor said, well my dad used to work there and they didn't treat him very nice. I'm glad they're gone."

The DEW Line also left another legacy — garbage. At the time of construction in the mid-1950s, *Maclean's* writer Pierre Berton noted that places like Coral Harbour on Southampton Island "had become a gigantic garbage heap.... [because] it would cost too much to move any of the wartime refuse back to the civilized world." In the 1990s much of it was still there. "A lot of our work up here has been remediating all those things, because if it wasn't made from PCB or Asbestos they didn't want it on that site," Heath noted wryly. "Fuel drums from twenty or thirty years ago are just abandoned here, because who would ever think of contamination in a place that's four hundred miles away from the nearest road? For the last twenty years, for the most part our work has been undoing the industrial mistakes of the past."

PLUS ÇA CHANGE

British-born Peter Corley-Smith felt at times that he and other pilots in the Canadian North were the "vanguard of destruction," and envied the blissful ignorance of early bush pilots.[48] He recognized when he flew in survey parties in the 1960s it might lead to an open pit mine, and that passengers might spot a trophy grizzly or wolf to "bag" as he ferried them, disregarding all fair chase laws. In the years since, aviation has continued to be central to the resource economy of the region, but northerners like Fred Carmichael have fought for sustainable development. They have also argued for self-determination in these economic and environmental decisions, decisions that do not always line up with what southerners would choose for the North and its peoples.

Aviation in the North, like the industry in the rest of Canada, has struggled through booms and busts, through recessions, skyrocketing inflation, privatization, and deregulation.[49] There has been a continuous changing of the guard as well, with personnel and aircraft shuffled around as companies expanded, contracted, and even went under. Pilot, engineer, and manager Adam Morrison remembers in the 1970s and 1980s "you knew everybody." He was talking about Whitehorse, but it could easily extend throughout the northern airlines and bush operators, especially since many of the companies had "satellite bases" in places like Inuvik or Cambridge Bay. They were like a big complicated family: they would compete for clients, have (usually friendly) rivalries, divvy up routes, and so on.

As with any family saga there has been drama and death. Even with vast improvements in navigation, equipment, and training, and much more stringent government regulations — aviation accidents happened in Canada's North on the eve of the twentieth century as they did elsewhere in the world. People and airplanes could also still go missing even with modern search and rescue strategies and communications technologies.

As the territories prepared for a new political reality after the creation of Nunavut in 1999, the North was poised for success on its own terms. The Ekati diamond mine had just opened, gold mining around Dawson City was taking off again, and Inuit and Inuvialuit had just bought a new airline, Canadian North. Its founding companies — Canadian Airlines, Pacific Western Airlines, Transair, and Nordair — had been involved in decades of DEW Line flights, scheduled runs Outside, and were themselves made up of the building blocks of smaller northern air services. Canadian North's slogan, "Your North. Your Airline" spoke to the company's commitment for the future and the peoples of the region. A new century of northern flight was about to begin with new generations of pilots, passengers, and planes.

"I'd Like to Do It All Over Again"

The North is more accessible than ever before to tourists, extreme adventurers, government officials, business people, and military personnel — for better or worse. Despite its remoteness from other parts of the world (or perhaps because of it) people regularly fly to the Yukon, Northwest Territories, and since 1999, the territory of Nunavut. And for those who cannot go in person, they can now experience the area and live vicariously through characters — fictional and real — on aviation-themed TV shows like *Ice Pilots NWT*, *Arctic Air*, and *Alaska Air*.

In many ways, southerners hold on to a romantic view of aviation in the North, but for those who live "up here" it continues to be a vital part of daily life. "Buffalo" Joe McBryan and the Buffalo Airways crews continue to act as a supply line to northern communities with their sked routes and cargo runs, and also provide fire suppression services — even

as they have become international celebrities. They are not alone. The "other Joe," Joe Sparling, president of Air North, continues to focus on his Yukon clients when it comes to choosing equipment, personnel, and routes. In 2000 the Vuntut Gwitchin First Nation of Old Crow bought a 49 percent stake in the company, and the tiny hamlet produced its first home-grown pilot in 2001, when Boyd Benjamin, the "Flying Gwitch'in Fiddler" received his fixed wing and helicopter licences and went to work at Air North and Alkan.[1] And while Air North operates Boeing 737s to fly from Whitehorse to southern destinations and recently added direct flights between Whitehorse, Yellowknife, and Ottawa, its local connections remain strong. In fact, as of 2014, Stephen Frost Sr. still meets the company's airplanes at Old Crow.[2]

These colourful characters of decades past continue to make people shake their heads — and make headlines. Leo and Rene Dionne of L & R Aircraft Repair operate out of the old BC-Yukon Air Services hangar in Watson Lake, doing inspections, float changeovers, and the odd field work for companies like Black Sheep Aviation. Over coffees they are happy to chat about the local pilot who flies a multi-coloured "Frankenstein" plane full of replacement parts, the fellow who took out the power lines at Dawson City, or the one who took up the local head RCMP officer on flights without a valid licence.

Technological advances, improved navigation systems, and better infrastructure have made flying in the North safer, but plane and helicopter crashes still occur with what can seem like alarming frequency. Even though a total of ten thousand flights on polar routes took place in 2010 — ten times more than in 2003 — the number of accidents and fatalities are actually going down.[3] Many pilots will remind you, however, that it is important to be vigilant and stay humble in the face of the North's unpredictable flying conditions.[4] Even the most careful companies and pilots can have accidents, though. Bob Heath, a legend of polar aviation with over twelve thousand hours on Twin Otters, was among three Kenn Borek Air pilots who lost their lives in 2012, when their Twin Otter crashed into one of Antarctica's highest mountains. Heath, who was fifty-five years old at the time, had met and married his wife on a plane, spent his career flying them, and shared his passion for the North and flying with all he met. Aviation was his life, and unfortunately it was his death as well.[5]

Despite its risks, aviation continues to save lives in the Arctic through medevac and military SAR activities (in conjunction with RCMP and other law enforcement agencies); local pilots keep an eye on their own backyards as well, either solo or through civilian organizations like CASARA. Fred Carmichael still goes out and looks for missing people in his Cessna 185, and recently he and his friend Doug Irish spotted a teenage girl who had almost died from exposure after her skidoo got caught in overflow. "You don't do these things for money or recognition, you're doing it for a fellow human being," he says. Even so, because of his mercy flights and other achievements, he was awarded the Order of Canada in 2010. He continues to work for his community and inspire a new generation of northern pilots.

These pilots, ground crew, and aviation professionals are more diverse than ever before, but many have a genetic predisposition to the industry. Bush pilot Don Hamilton's son, Fred, runs High Arctic Lodge, a fly-in fishing spot on Victoria Island in Nunavut, serviced by their own Beaver and Cessna 206s. His daughter, Lynn, is president and CEO of Air Spray Aviation Services out of Edmonton, the company he set up in 1967. Andy Williams now has his own glacier flying protégé — Phil Upton's son, Carl "Donjek" Upton — while Williams's daughter and son-in-law run his Icefields Discovery Camp in Kluane National Park. Williams still flies in visitors and supplies, and many climbers, but has not ascended Mount Logan himself: "I did touch a ski on the summit once. Just tapped the summit. That's good enough for me. I left my mark, and the next storm it was gone."[6]

The North has also wiped clues to many aviation mysteries clean. People are still searching off the coasts of Alaska, Yukon, and the Northwest Territories for the wreckage of the Russian DB-A transport plane that disappeared in 1937. Through Operation Mike, dozens of people are dedicated to uncovering the final resting place of the missing USAF Skymaster that vanished in 1950 with forty-four crew and passengers. Not a trace has been found of Don Bergren, the Air North pilot who was presumed drowned in 1996. The DC-4 he flew that day also disappeared for over a decade as the Iskut River shifted in the delta-like region of Northern British Columbia. It re-emerged in 2011, and a new mystery surfaced: the one million dollars of gold concentrate was gone. Was it stolen? Forgotten in the corporate shuffles of the gold mining industry? Or did the river water whisk it away? There was no time to answer these questions: by the fall of 2012 the Iskut had shifted again and entombed the plane once more.[7]

The search and extraction of gold and other natural riches — such as diamonds in the Northwest Territories — continue with the help of aviation. In a fascinating parallel with Klondike dreamers and schemers, there have even been recent proposals for new airships over the Arctic in the shape of futuristic blimps.[8] Debates over development and sustainability also persist, and almost forty years after it was first proposed, it remains to be seen if the Mackenzie Valley Pipeline Project will go ahead.[9] Many northern pilots and operators have embraced this tension, and Dan Reynolds uses aviation both to make a living exploiting natural resources and to

be a steward of his land. "I like it where it's at right now," he says. "It's not about money — but about having fun and managing the area at a sustainable level."

Northern resources have stimulated renewed sovereignty concerns that go far beyond the "usual" suspects of Arctic Circle neighbours like Russia, Denmark, and the U.S. Now that the Northwest Passage is opening up as the ice pack melts, even China wants a seat at the U.N. Arctic Council because of its vested shipping interests in the area. To assert claims over the seafloor there and any fossil fuels and minerals that might be found below, Canada has recently launched aeromagnetic flights over the North Pole. Canada's military and law enforcement divisions, such as the Rangers and RCMP air sections are also active in promoting the country's interests in the Arctic, and joint exercises such as Narwhal, Nanalivut, Nanook, and Nunakput ensure all branches of the Canadian Forces are ready for SAR operations, can support scientific research, and can defend the North against potential threats.

"Buffalo" Joe McBryan, who recently celebrated fifty years of flying in northern skies, says his greatest achievement has been gaining knowledge and passing it on to others. After all, he notes, the pilots of his childhood did it for him as he rode right-seat in old bush planes above the Northwest Territories. He may be gruff with new recruits as they learn how to fly vintage aircraft more than twice their age, but he knows the North does not suffer fools — or foolhardy pilots — and that many talented people and first-rate machines have been lost long before their time. McBryan, like other flyers, also knows how important aviation is to the people of the North, and he will not allow anyone in his company to let them down.

Since he played in a Fox Moth wreck at his father's mine, McBryan's life has been aviation, and despite many difficulties and dangers, he says it has been a good run. His thoughts mirror numerous others who have made their way north of 60 in everything from hot air balloons to airships to open-cockpit biplanes to jet airliners. People like Professor Leonard, Roald Amundsen, Wop May, Lorna de Blicquy, Fred Carmichael, and more who pushed the limits of human experience and knowledge in a century of flying the North. "I get to do what I want to do," McBryan says, scanning the sky, "and I'd like to do it all over again."

Glossary of Abbreviations and Acronyms

AAM	Alberta Aviation Museum
CARES	Civil Air Search and Rescue (Alberta)
CASARA	Civil Air Search and Rescue Association
CF	Canadian Forces
CFNA	Canadian Forces Northern Area
CPA	Canadian Pacific Airlines (also known as CP Air)
DCMA	Dawson City Museum Archives
DEW	Distant Early Warning
DHC	de Havilland Canada
DOT	Department of Transport
FAA	Federal Aviation Authority (U.S.)
GNA	Great Northern Airways
HBC	Hudson's Bay Company
HBCA	Hudson Bay Company Archives
LAC	Library and Archives Canada

NORAD	North American Aerospace Defense Command
NWSR	Northwest Staging Route
NWTA	Northwest Territories Archives
OMI	Oblates of Mary Immaculate
RCAF	Royal Canadian Air Force
RCN	Royal Canadian Navy
RCMP	Royal Canadian Mounted Police
SAR	Search and Rescue
TNTA	Trans North Turbo Air
USAAF	U.S. Army Air Force
VFR	Visual Flight Rules
VGFN	Vuntut Gwitchin First Nations
WCA	Western Canada Airways
WP&YR	White Pass & Yukon Route
YA	Yukon Archives

Notes

Chapter 1: Gold, Glory, and Spectacle

1. Information in the following paragraphs from Gray, *Gold Diggers*, 5, 11, 17–21, and 24–25.
2. Berton, *I Married the Klondike*, 107.
3. Winslow, *Big Pan-Out*, "Miners Pay Duty, Americans are Met by Customs Officers at Victoria," *Bellingham Bay Reveille*, July 30, 1897.
4. Teresa Earle, "Yukon's unique transportation heritage," *The Yukon News*, January 28, 2005.
5. Berton, *Klondike*, 119-20.
6. Milberry, *Air Transport in Canada, Vol. 1*, 12; and Vance, *High Flight*, 1. This had taken place August 10, 1840 in Saint John, New Brunswick when Louis Anselm Lauriat ascended in his *Star of the East*.
7. Nelson, "Airships in the Arctic," 278. A full account of Andrée's exploits can be found in P.J. Capelotti's *By Airship to the North Pole: An Archaeology of Human Exploration* (Piscataway, NJ: Rutgers University Press, 1999).
8. Les McLaughlin, "To the Klondike, James – by airship!" *Whitehorse Star*, March 13, 2009, 15.
9. Information in the previous paragraph from "By Air Ship to Klondike," *New York Times*, August 30, 1897.
10. "Klondike Airship Scheme," *New York Times*, November 26, 1897.
11. McLaughlin, "To the Klondike," *Whitehorse Star*.
12. Berton, *Klondike*, 120.
13. Ibid.
14. "Canadians for Klondike," *New York Times*, September 26, 1897, 4. Sources at the time vary the spelling of de l'Etoile considerably: the *New York Times* article spells his name J. De L. Etoiler, and in a letter dated September 27, 1886 to the Minister of Defence

and Militia in which he makes the proposition, his name is written L'Etoile. However, there is a Joseph de L'Etoile listed at 526 King St. in the Ottawa City Directory for 1897–98, and this spelling is the one used most often.

15. "By Air Ship to Klondike," *New York Times*, August 30, 1897.

16. "Canadians for Klondike," *New York Times*.

17. Obituary of Dr. Anthony Variclé in the *New York Times*, July 27, 1907. Antoine is often anglicized in the accounts of the day as "Antony" or "Anthony."

18. "In Search of Andrée," *Victoria Daily Colonist*, June 5, 1898, 3.

19. Antony Variclé, "My First Aerial Stampede," *Northern Light*, 12–15.

20. "News of the Week," *San Juan Islander*, April 14, 1898; and "To Klondyke [sic] in a Balloon," *Wanganui Herald* [New Zealand], May 31, 1898.

21. "In Search of Andrée," *Victoria Daily Colonist*.

22. On March 5, 1903, Variclé was listed in the Dental Register for Dawson and paid the annual fee until 1907. W. S. Dill's *The Long Day* (Ottawa: The Graphic Publishers Ltd., 1926), mentions Diamond Tooth Gertie specifically.

23. The term "Professor" was used by performers of the day to give themselves more credibility and allure with audiences. Milberry, *Air Transport in Canada, Vol. 1*, 13.

24. "Prof. Leonard Back in North," *Dawson Daily News*, June 17, 1903.

25. Information in this paragraph from "Balloon Ascension," *Weekly Star*, May 30, 1903; and "An Airship's Flight," *Dawson Daily News*, August 30, 1899.

26. Berton, *Klondike*, 354.

27. Vance, *High Flight*, 7.

28. Ibid., 2.

29. Coates and Morrison, *Land of the Midnight Sun*, 10 and 15.

30. "Balloon Ascension," *Weekly Star*.

31. "Attractions Up To Date of All Kinds and Nature, Even to Ballooning," *Dawson Daily News*, September 9, 1899.

32. John Leonard to John Newman (Colorado), December 2, 1899. University of Washington Special Collections — Digital Collections. John Emmett Berns Papers, Accession no. 740-1 Box 1.

33. "Up in a Balloon — Professor Leonard Makes a Successful Flight on Saturday," *Dawson Daily News*, May 27, 1900.

34. Information in this paragraph from: "Leonard's Balloon Destroyed," *Dawson Daily News*, May 28, 1900, 4; and "The Baloon [sic] Burned," *Daily Klondike Nugget,* May 28, 1900.

35. Information in preceding paragraph from: "Up in a Balloon," *Daily Klondike Nugget*, June 8, 1900; "Tonight the Balloon," *Daily Klondike Nugget*, June 9, 1900; "Did Not Ascend," *Daily Klondike Nugget*, June 11, 1900; and "A Successful Ascension," *Daily Klondike Nugget*, June 12, 1900.

36. Information in following section from: "Balloon Ascension," *Weekly Star*; "Aeronaut Falls Into the River Leonard Sends Thrills of Excitement Through Crowd on First Avenue," *Yukon Sun*, June 26, 1903; and "Prof. Leonard Back in North," *Dawson Daily News*, June 17, 1903.

37. "Prof. Leonard," *Dawson Daily News*, May 2, 1904[?].

38. "Northern News Budget," *Victoria Daily Colonist*, February 15, 1900, and "To Klondyke in a Balloon," *Wanganui Herald*.

39. Grierson, *Challenge to the Poles*, 41; and Nelson, "Airships in the Arctic," 278.

40. "In Search of Andrée," *Victoria Daily Colonist*, June 5, 1898, 3.

41. Grierson, *Challenge*, 40–42; and Nelson, "Airships in the Arctic," 278.

42. Information in the previous paragraph from: Grant, *Polar Imperative*.

43. "International Yukon Polar Institute," Dawson, Yukon Territory, Founded August 5, 1905," University of California — Berkley Internet Archive.

44. Davies and Ellis, *Seattle's Commercial Aviation*, 13. One of his sons, Roger, ended up becoming a pilot in Seattle and "conducted test flights in the so-called 'Flying Bed Post' by Eugene Romano in 1911 and 1912."

45. Nelson, "Airships in the Arctic," 279.

46. Grierson, *Challenge*, 23.

47. Nelson, "Airships in the Arctic," 279; Rob Mulder, "In the air with Roald Amundsen," *www.europeanairlines.no* (accessed May 17, 2014); and Kenneth P. Czech, "Roald Amundsen and the 1925 North Pole Expedition," *Aviation History*, published online June 6, 2009, *http://www.historynet.com/roald-amundsen-and-the-1925-north-pole-expedition.htm* (accessed May 15, 2014).

48. Nelson, "Airships in the Arctic," 280; and Wittreich, *Forgotten First Flights*, 260.

49. Nelson, "Airships in the Arctic," 279–80.

50. McAllister, *Wings Above the Arctic: A Photographic History of Arctic Aviation*, 9–16.

51. Information in the following three paragraphs from: Nelson, "Airships in the Arctic," 280–83.

52. Information in the previous paragraph from: Henry, *Uncharted Skies*, 124; and Milberry, *Air Transport in Canada, Vol. 1*, 83.

Chapter 2: The Era of Expeditions

1. Information in this section from: Berton, *I Married the Klondike*, 35–36, 40–41, 97–99; and "1909 Government Publication on transportation, Yukon Territory: Its History & Resources," in the clippings folders at the Dawson City Museum.

2. Gov 2492 File 3, City of Whitehorse fonds, Yukon Archives. As with many names at the time — especially non-Anglophone ones — there are a variety of spellings in the records. This appears to be the most likely spelling.

3. "Klondike Joins in the Fun: Dawson has an aeroplane enthusiast now hard at work," *Dawson Weekly News*, September 23, 1910; and "Airship for Yukoners," *Whitehorse Weekly Star*, April 18, 1918.

4. Weicht, *Air Route to the Klondike*, 111 and 257; and Ruotsala, *Pilots of the Panhandle*.

5. Grierson, *Challenge to the Poles*, 49. For the details of the flight from New York to Alaska and back, please see Grierson, 50–56 and F.H. Ellis, "New York to Nome and back," *The Beaver* (September 1949), 28–32.

6. Tim Sims, "Navigation and the Early Bush Pilot," *Journal of the Canadian Aviation Historical Society* (Winter 1976), 125.

7. Letter of agreement between Howard

T. Douglas, Captain, ASA to Robert Lowe signed June 17, 1920, Newmarch Collection, MacBride Museum.

8. Information in preceding paragraph from Ellis, "New York to Nome and back," 28–32.

9. Berton, *I Married the Klondike*, 133, 135, 141–42.

10. Frances Watson to Mrs. McTurnan, February 20, 1930, Gov 2492, File 9, Yukon Archives.

11. The information about the flights to Dawson is from: Berton, *I Married the Klondike*, 143; "Red Letter Day in Yukon's History," *Weekly Star*, August 30, 1920; Archie Gillespie, "The Day the First Planes Came to Dawson," *Yukon News*, May 26, 1965.

12. The information about Prest's journey up to Dawson City and his performance there from: "Flyer Prest arrives in Dawson City," *Dawson Daily News*, July 12, 1922; "Many will be here to see Prest perform," *Dawson Daily News*, July 14, 1922; "Flyer Prest at Selkirk — Here Tomorrow," *Dawson Daily News*, July 10, 1922; "Flyer Prest just missed a big storm," *Dawson Daily News*, July 11, 1922; Weicht, *Air Route to the Klondike*, 115; and McAllister, *Wings Over the Yukon*, 12–13.

13. Information about Prest's journey from Dawson to Fairbanks: "Flyer will take letters from Dawson," *Dawson Daily News*, July 14, 1922; "Welcome to flier," *Dawson Daily News*, July 10, 1922; "Prest started cross-country — no trace," *Dawson Daily News*, July 18, 1922; "Flyer Prest's own story of notable trip," *Dawson Daily News*, July 21, 1922; "Aviator Prest is safe — landed in tundra," *Dawson Daily News*, July 20 1922; "Luck 'O Prest," *Dawson Daily News*, July 21, 1922; and Weicht, *Air Route to the Klondike*, 258–60.

14. "Airplane in Yukon," *Dawson Daily News*, July 12, 1922.

15. Zaslow, *The Northward Expansion of Canada*, 22.

16. Main, *Voyageurs of the Air*, 36–37; and Ken M. Molson, "The Rene and Vic," *Journal of the Canadian Aviation Historical Society* (Summer 1982), 41–55. First-hand accounts were published by all four Imperial Oil employees involved as well as three people on-site. As can be expected, they occasionally gave conflicting accounts; I have gone with the most commonly accepted — and probable — course of events.

17. Grant, *Polar Imperative*, 224; "What happened at Fort Simpson, NWT, during winter 1921?" *The Beaver* (July 1921); and Zaslow, *Northward*, 23–24.

18. Paul Miller, "Keep 'em flying," *Imperial Oil Review* (Autumn 1999), 26–30; Molson, "The Rene and Vic," 44; and "The Wilderness is Shrinking," *The Beaver* (February 1921).

19. For a full account of May and Gorman's preparations, please see Molson, "The Rene and Vic," 42–44. Molson concedes, however, that dates and the exact purpose of this September flight are unknown.

20. Main, *Voyageurs of the Air*, 38.

21. Account of flights to NWT gleaned from: Molson, "The Rene and Vic," 44–46; Godsell, *Pilots of the Purple Twilight*, 32–33, 37–38; and F.C. Jackson, "Homemade HBC propellers bring back Ft. Norman planes," *The Beaver* (May 1921).

22. Grant, *Polar Imperative*, 224–25. For an in-depth exploration of the tensions between Inuit and Canadian cultural understandings during this period, please see: Grant, *Arctic Justice*. For more information on Logan, Bernier, and the 1922 patrol please see: Ernest Cable, "Air Force - a Leader in the Arctic" (paper, Air Force Historical Workshop, Montreal, 2010).

23. Information on Logan's 1922 reconnaissance mission and findings: Thomson, *Skyview Canada*, 38–39; Ellis, *Canada's Flying Heritage*, 217–20; Douglas, *Creation of a National Air Force*, 106.

24. Account of MacMillan Expedition from: A.E. Ted Hill, "Arctic Curtain Raiser," *CAHS Journal* (winter 1985), 122–23; Ellis, *Canada's Flying Heritage*, 220–22; Grierson, *Challenge to the Poles*, 93–98; Grant, *Polar Imperative*, 227–37; and Erik Watt, "Pushing the Frontier Back," *Up Here* (May/June 1995), 51.

25. Aviation historians have written extensively on this operation. Please see: A/V/M T.A. "Tommy" Lawrence, "The Hudson Strait Expedition," *CAHS Journal* (Fall 1982), 83–88; Grierson, *Challenge to the Poles*, 138–43; Ellis, *Canada's Flying Heritage*, 221–27; and Main, *Voyageurs of the Air*, 76–81.

26. Milberry, *Sixty Years*, 33; Gibson-Sutherland, *Canada's Aviation Pioneers*, 22; Ellis, *Canada's Flying Heritage*, 232–34; Milberry, *Air Transport in Canada*, Vol. 1, 71; Bernt Balchen, "My Introduction to Canada," *CAHS Journal* (Summer 1976), 39.

27. Information in this paragraph from: Cable, "Air Force – a Leader in the Arctic"; Douglas, *Creation of a National Air Force*, 106; and Thomson, *Skyview Canada*, 39.

28. Preceding story taken from: Flt. Lt. E.P. Wood, "Northern Skytrails, part 9," *The Roundel* (July 1949); Milberry, *Sixty Years*, 33; and Cable, "Air Force — a Leader in the Arctic." Bobby's last name is absent from most accounts, save Frank Ellis's works, "The Aerial Survey of Hudson Strait 1927–8," *The Roundel* (May 1965) and *Canada's Flying Heritage*, 224. Many Inuit did not use last names until Project Surname in 1969.

29. Zaslow, *Northward*, 39; Milberry, *Sixty Years*, 33; and E.P. Wood, "Northern Skytrails," *The Roundel* (November 1948), 31.

30. Information in this paragraph from: Zaslow, *Northward*, 102.

31. Several books have mistakenly called it *The Bouncing Bronco*. Jack's son, Colin Caldwell, and the majority of early sources note that it was in fact "Bruno," although none suggest where the nickname originated.

32. This story pieced together from: Ellis, *Canada's Flying Heritage*, 213; Milberry, *Air Transport in Canada, Vol. 1*, 54–55; Watt, "Pushing the Frontier Back," 51; and Erik Watt, "Those Magnificent Men and their flying machines," *Up Here* (June/July 1993), 27.

33. Zaslow, *Northward*, 104. Other early Northern Aerial Mineral Exploration Ltd (NAME) examples can be found in: Millberry, *Air Transport in Canada*; and Moar, *A Collection of Bush Flying Stories*.

34. Information for this section taken

from: Henry, *Uncharted Skies*, 31; and Sims "Navigation and the Early Bush Pilot." For other instances of aerial prospecting during this era, please see: Watt, "Those Magnificent Men and their flying machines;" Milberry, *Air Transport in Canada*, 35–38, 72–75; Ellis, *Canada's Flying Heritage*, 243–46; and S. R. (Stan) McMillan, "My Flying Career: A Legendary Northern Pilot recalls the adventurous side of a lifetime in aviation," *CAHS Journal* (Spring 2002), 4–15 and 36–37.

35. Much has been written about the Mac-Alpine expedition, as well as the subsequent search and rescue operations. I used the following sources for this section: Milberry, *Aviation in Canada*, 39–40; Melady, *Pilots*, 65–67; Milberry, *Air Transport in Canada, Vol. 1*, 81–83; Main, *Voyageurs of the Air*, 69–72; Ellis, *Canada's Flying Heritage*, 246–47, and 253–62; Zaslow, *Northward*, 105–7; Henry, *Uncharted Skies*, 33–37 and 59; McMillan, "My Flying Career," 51; and a Western Canada Airways report reprinted in two parts in the *Journal of the Canadian Aviation Historical Society* (Summer and Fall 1977). For a highly readable, detailed account, please see: Karram, *Four Degrees Celsius*.

36. Melady, *Pilots*, 52.

37. Information in this paragraph is from: Vance, *High Flight*, 38, 75, and 109.

Chapter 3: Hope in the Sky

1. Information in this paragraph is from: Coates and Morrison, *Land of the Midnight Sun*, 166; Watt, "Pushing the Frontier Back," 52; and Erik Watt,

"History and Mystery," *Up Here* (January/February 1999), 87.

2. For more on these ventures, please see: Mallory, *Coppermine*; Peter C. Newman, *Merchant Princes* (Toronto: Penguin Books Canada, 1991), 238; Ellis, *Canada's Flying Heritage*, 248–49; Zaslow, *Northward*, 180–82; and Milberry, *Air Transport in Canada*, Vol.1, 132.

3. Information in the previous paragraph from Mallory, *Coppermine*, 173, and 176–92.

4. Details in this paragraph from: "Farthest North Pipeline," *Canadian Aviation* (July 1937), 29; and McLaren, *Bush to Boardroom*, 29.

5. Mallory, *Coppermine*, 188, 199, 222 and 226; and McLaren, *Bush to Boardroom*, 31.

6. McLaren, *Bush to Boardroom*, 12, 15, and 18.

7. Reid, *Wings of a Hero*, 69.

8. McLaren, *Bush to Boardroom*, 20.

9. Henry, *Uncharted Skies*, 190.

10. Ibid., 160.

11. McMillan, "My Flying Career," 13 and 36.

12. Henry, *Uncharted Skies*, 155. This account spells his name "Meilike" but all other sources have the spelling I have used here.

13. Ibid., 100.

14. Watt, "Pushing the Frontier Back," 52.

15. McLaren, *Bush to Boardroom*, 23.

16. Information for this paragraph and next taken from: Reid, *Wings of a Hero*, 69; McLaren, *Bush to Boardroom*, 13; McAllister, *Wings Above the Arctic*, 124; Watt, "Those Magnificent Men," 28.

17. Mallory, *Coppermine*, 202.

18. Yukon Government Records, YRG 1, Series 1, GOV 1679, f. 17, Yukon Archives.

19. For a discussion of these attempts, please see: Bennett, *Yukon Transportation*, 121.

20. Author interview with Kerry Karram, August 26, 2013; Lunny, *Spirit of the Yukon*; Watt, "Those Magnificent Men," 27; Ellis, *Canada's Flying Heritage*, 240–43; and Watt, "Pushing the Frontier Back," 52.

21. The fascinating story of these air companies, and the colourful characters who ran them, has been ably told by other authors. For more detailed explorations, please see: Cameron, *Yukon Wings*; Ellis, *Canada's Flying Heritage*; Main, *Voyageurs of the Air*; and McAllister, *Wings Over the Yukon*.

22. Bennett, *Yukon Transportation*, 122.

23. Bennett, *Yukon Transportation*, 122; Weicht, *Air Route to the Klondike*, 100–01; and McMillan, "My Flying Career," 11. For more information on United Air Transport/Yukon Southern Air Transport and Grant McConachie, please see: Keith, *Bush Pilot with a Briefcase*.

24. Information and quotes in this section are from: Ellis, *Canada's Flying Heritage*, 248; Melady, *Pilots*, 56–60; Milberry, *Aviation in Canada*, 42; Henry, *Uncharted Skies*, 63–64; Watt, "Pushing the Frontier Back," 52; and Watt, "Those Magnificent Men," 28.

25. "Civil Aviation Statistics for 1929," *Canadian Aviation*, (April 1930), 46.

26. Bonnie Dickie, "The Flying Santas Remember," *Up Here* (December/ January 1986), 45; Reid, *Wings of a Hero*, 65–68; and McLaren, *Bush to Boardroom*, 9.

27. "Mail by Airplane," *[Whitehorse] Weekly Star*, July 6, 1918; Frank Ellis, "Early Northern Air Mail." *The Beaver* (Winter 1954), 12–15; and Berton, *I Married the Klondike*, 135.

28. The story of the Lindberghs' flight across the Arctic is detailed in: Lindbergh, *North to the Orient*, 10, 22, 26–27, and 77–78. Additional information from: Grierson, *Challenge to the Poles*, 304–06; Trevor Lloyd, "Aviation in Arctic North America and Greenland," *Polar Record*, Vol. 5, Issue 35–36 (December 1948), 166; McAllister, *Wings Above the Arctic*, 41–42

29. Information in this section is from: "The HBC Packet," *The Beaver* (December 1934), 5–8; and Grierson, *Challenge to the Poles*, 7, and 314–25. Modifications to the aircraft are listed on page 315 of that book.

30. These early Russian attempts to fly over the North Pole are outlined in: Baidukov, *Over the North Pole*; Smith-Matheson, *Lost*, 35–64; McAllister, *Wings Above the Arctic*, 37; and Grierson, *Challenge to the Poles*, 446–86.

31. For accounts of how Canadians co-operated in 1937–38 search, please see: McAllister, *Wings Above the Arctic*; and "Our Search for Levanevsky as told to Canadian Aviation by Air Commodore H. Hollick-Kenyon," *Canadian Aviation* (October 1937), 3–4, 34. As Smith Matheson details in *Lost*, during the late 1980s and early 1990s several hobbyists made attempts to find the downed plane without success.

32. Mayo Historical Society, *Gold & Galena*, 194. The story is related in

Karram's *Four Degrees*, and according to her, it was also the first fatality for Western Canada Airways.

33. "The Fur Trade," *The Beaver* (March 1937), 56–59; Armour Mackay, "Mercy Flight," *The Beaver* (March 1948); Fuller, *125 Years of Canadian Aeronautics*, 207; Herb Britton, "Days gone by — Bill Catton 1899 — 1974" Headingly Headliner; Henry, *Uncharted Skies*, 181; McAllister, *Wings Over the Yukon*, 109; and Morrison, *True North*, 126.

34. Information in previous section from: Smith and Vuntut Gwitchin First Nation, *People of the Lakes*, xlviii and lvii; Charlie Peter Charlie interviewed by Elaine Shorty, Yukon Archives Collection, VGFN, March 11, 1993; Newman, *Merchant Princes*, xiv–xv, and 207–12; and Morrison, *True North*, 53 and 124.

35. Charlie Thomas interviewed by Jane Montgomery, VGFN, July 24, 2004; and Dick Nukon interview with Marilyn Jenson, VGFN, August, 9, 1994.

36. "Down North with the Governor," *The Beaver* (December 1932), 131–35; "The Fur Trade," *The Beaver* (March 1935), 61–62; "The Fur Trade," *The Beaver* (March 1937), 56–59; and Newman, *Merchant Princes*, 240–41.

37. The information in the following section is from: "Floats: A Flying Episode Off Eskimo Point, Hudson Bay," *The Beaver*, (June 1933), 48–52.

38. The details in this paragraph are from: "The HBC Packet," *The Beaver*, (December 1934), 5; "The Fur Trade," *The Beaver* (March 1937), 57; "Floats: A Flying Episode," 48.

39. The next section draws on: Smith, *The Mad Trapper*, 36, 50, 143; and Zaslow, *Northward*, 133.

40. Alfred Charlie interview, January 20, 1995, VGFN, published in Smith, *People of the Lakes*, 247.

41. The information in the following section is taken primarily from: Denny May and Owen Brierley, "The Chronicles of W.R. (Wop) May," *www.wopmay.ca* (last accessed May 21, 2014); Dick North, "Interview with Earle Hersey," *Yukon Magazine* (October 1969); Garry Saunders, "Air Services' 50th Anniversary," *Royal Canadian Mounted Police Gazette*, Vol. 49, No. 10 (1987), 5; Reid, *Wings of a Hero*, 70–7; Milberry, *Air Transport in Canada, Vol. 1*, 83; Smith, *People of the Lakes*, 250; and Gibson-Sutherland, *Canada's Aviation Pioneers*, 42.

42. Dick Nukon interview on August 9, 1994, Marilyn Jenson Collection, VGFN; and La Pierre House Oral History (March 1994). This information was also published in Smith, *People of the Lakes*, 248–49.

43. Quotes in the following paragraphs are from: "The Hunt for the Mad Trapper of Rat River – as told by 'Wop' May to the 12th Calgary Scout Troop, Feb 19, 1952," *http://www.nwtandy.rcsigs.ca/stories/may.htm* (last accessed May 21, 2014).

44. Smith, *The Mad Trapper*, 106.

45. La Pierre House Oral History (March 1994); Dollie Moses interview, March 19, 1994; Smith, *People of the Lakes*, 249–50; and T. Shawn Giilck, "Mad Trapper Chase Recalled," *Northern News Services*, February 21, 2013.

Chapter 4: The Northern Front

1. The information for this section is from: Kikkert "Creating a Role: The Royal Canadian Air Force in the Arctic, 1945–1953," (paper, De-Icing Required! The Historical Dimension of the Canadian Air Force's Experience in the Arctic, Sainte-Anne-de-Bellevue, QC, June 2010); Wood, "Northern Skytrails: Part Two," *The Roundel* (December 1948), 22; Wood, "Northern Skytrails," 31; Wood, "Northern Skytrails: Part VII," *The Roundel*, (May 1949), 24; Wood, DFC, "Northern Skytrails: Part Three," *The Roundel*, (January 1949), 30–31; Wood, DFC "Northern Skytrails: Part IV," *The Roundel* (February 1949), 22–30; Wood, "Northern Skytrails: Part V," *The Roundel* (March 1949), 26–28; Shaw, *Photographing Canada from Flying Canoes*, 129–35; McCaffery, *Bush Planes and Bush Pilots*, 25; Milberry, *Sixty Years*, 32 and 35; Milberry, *Air Transport in Canada*, *Vol. 1*, 153–55.

2. Much of the information in the following section is from: Saunders, "Air Services' 50th Anniversary," 5–10.

3. Wood, "Northern Skytrails: Part V," 22–28.

4. Quoted material in this section from: Wood, "Northern Skytrails: Part V," 22–24.

5. Saunders, "Air Services' 50th Anniversary," 12. The author says only three of the Dragonflies were drafted, the fourth was kept in storage at "N" Division.

6. Milberry, *Air Transport in Canada*, *Vol. 1*, 153; and Wood, "Northern Skytrails," 31.

7. Newman, *Merchant Princes*, 240.

8. "News of the Fur Trade," *The Beaver* (June 1940), 53; and "H.B. Beech — B.M.I. On Long Hop," *Canadian Aviation* (March 1940), 56.

9. "News of the fur trade," *The Beaver* (June 1940), 53; and Newman, *Merchant Princes*, 240.

10. Information in this paragraph from: "Single-Engined Beech for H. Bay Company," *Canadian Aviation* (July 1940), 50; "Fur Trade News," *The Beaver*, (May 1940), 56; "Winter Packet," *The Beaver* (December 1941); "Winter Packet," *The Beaver* (December 1943); and "War and the Company," *The Beaver* (December 1939).

11. Morrison, *True North*, 127 and 130. Otto Nordling, a long-time Yukoner, compiled a list of approximately ninety-seven people who gave a Yukon address upon enlisting in all branches of service in the Second World War.

12. "Gordon McIntyre's War Tale," *Whitehorse Star*, November 10, 1977. McIntyre ended up in the First Survey Regiment of the Royal Canadian Artillery.

13. Information and quotes in the following paragraph are from: Norm Hartnell (compiled by Sherron Jones), "Memories," *Moccasin Telegraph — Special Edition*, (April 14, 2004); and interview with John Gould, December 10, 2010, Dawson City, Yukon.

14. Information in this paragraph on women's participation in the war effort is from: Dawn Dorothy Nickel, "Realities and Reflections: Women and the Yukon Frontier During the Alaska Highway Period," (master's thesis, University of Alberta, Fall

1998); Smith, *Warplanes to Alaska*, 202; Lackenbauer, "Introduction," in *Aboriginal Peoples and the Canadian Military: Historical Perspectives*, eds. P. Whitney Lackenbauer, Craig Mantle, and Scott Scheffield (Kingston: Canadian Defence Academy Press, 2007); P. Whitney Lackenbauer and R. Scott Sheffield, "The Historiography on Canadian Native Peoples and the World Wars," in *Aboriginal Peoples and the Canadian Military*; and Grace Poulin, "Invisible Women: Aboriginal Servicewomen in Canada's Second World War," in *Aboriginal Peoples and the Canadian Military*, 137–69.

15. Details on northern indigenous participation from: Scott Scheffield, "'Of pure European Descent and of the White Race': Recruitment Policy and Aboriginal Canadians, 1939–1945," *Canadian Military History*, Vol. 5, No. 1 (Spring 1996), 11–15; P. Whitney Lackenbauer, John Moses, R. Scott Sheffield, Maxime Gohier, "Chapter Five," *Aboriginal People in the Canadian Military*, http://www.cmp-cpm.forces.gc.ca/dhh-dhp/pub/boo-bro/abo-aut/chapter-chapitre-05-eng.asp (last accessed May 21, 2014); and Chuck Tobin, "Yukoners remember those who served," *Whitehorse Star*, November 10, [2009].

16. Information in this paragraph from: Tobin, "Yukoners remember"; "Yukon has reached the quota," *Dawson Weekly News*, June 12, 1941; Smith, *People of the Lakes*, LIX; and Alfred Charlie interviewed by Robert Bruce Jr., June 10, 2011, Vuntut Gwichin Oral History Project.

17. The majority of the following section on the Lend-Lease program and the creation on the Northwest Staging Route is from: Grant, *Polar Imperative*, 254; Smith, *Warplanes to Alaska*, 36, 45, 67–68, 85, 89–90, 94–95, 105–6, 120–23, 135, 137, 146, 156–57, 167, and 178–79; Main, *Voyageurs of the Air*, 171–73; Milberry, *Air Transport in Canada, Vol. 1*, 161–64; and Bennett, *Yukon Transportation*, 122.

18. Zaslow, *Northward*, 213; Grant, *Polar Imperative*, 271; and "Yukon Southern Planes Use Wheels Winter and Summer in North," *Canadian Aviation* (December 1940), 60.

19. "Improve Airport at Whitehorse," *Canadian Aviation* (1941).

20. "Yukon Route Now Defense Lifeline," *Canadian Aviation* (January 1942).

21. Flight Lieutenant Perkin noted this in April 1943 in the RCAF Daily Diary for North West Air Command Headquarters at Edmonton, Alberta. Copies of Department of National Defence microfilm at Yukon Archives.

22. "Building Airports to Yukon," *Canadian Aviation* (May 1942), 26.

23. French, "North-West Staging Route," *Shell Aviation News* (December 1957), 12–14.

24. RCAF North West Air Command Daily Diary, November 2–4, 1944. Yukon Archives microfilm.

25. RCAF North West Air Command Daily Diary, December 25, 1942. Yukon Archives microfilm.

26. McGinniss, "Weekly Progress Report," RCAF North West Command, August 26, 1944; French, "North-West Staging Route," 14; and Zaslow, *Northward*, 217 and 223.

27. Morrison, *True North*, 147.

28. "Troupers visit RCAF outposts on North Route," *Edmonton Journal*, April 1945.

29. Interview with Gordon Toole.

30. Smith, *Warplanes to Alaska*, 137.

31. "Winter Operation Hints from Experience in North," *Canadian Aviation* (December 1940), 50 and 53.

32. Smith, *Warplanes to Alaska*, 85.

33. Some of these crashes are outlined in: Smith, *Warplanes to Alaska*; McCaffery, *Bush Planes and Bush Pilots*; McAllister, *Wings Over the Yukon*; and French, "North-West Staging Route," 11–12.

34. Smith Matheson, *Lost*, 81.

35. "Russ Baker of CPA Completes ... Rescue Job, Northern Style ... Saving 24 U.S. Air Force Men," *Canadian Aviation* (October 1944).

36. McAllister, *Wings Over the Yukon*; French, "North-West Staging Route," 14–15; and Stanley W. Dzuiban, "Military Relations Between the United States and Canada, 1939–1945" (Washington, DC: United States Army, 1959), 203.

37. French, "North-West Staging Route," 15.

38. Sandy Babcock, "Operation CANON: A Case Study of Early RCAF Arctic Search and Rescue Capabilities" (paper, De-Icing Required! The Historical Dimension of the Canadian Air Force's Experience in the Arctic, Sainte-Anne-de-Bellevue, QC, June 2010).

39. Information in this paragraph from: P.S. Barry, "'Punch' Dickins and the Origins of Canol's Mackenzie Air Fields," *Arctic*, Vol. 32, No. 4 (Dec 1979), 366–373; Smith, *Warplanes to Alaska*, 49, 52, 54; and Leigh, *And I Shall Fly*. CANOL stands for Canadian American Norman Oil Line.

40. Details in this paragraph from: Morrison, *True North*, 134; and Thomson, *Skyview Canada*, 98.

41. This paragraph draws on the following sources: John T. Greenwood, "General Bill Hoge and the Alaska Highway," in *The Alaska Highway: Papers of the 40th Anniversary Symposium*; and Heath Twichell, "The role of the Public Roads Administration," *The Alaska Highway*; and French, "North-West Staging Route," 16.

42. Information in this section is from: Russell, *Tales of a Catskinner*, 4, 8, 20, 69, 85.

43. Morrison, *True North*, 134 and 144.

44. "CP Air Lines Rushes Essential Workers into North," *Canadian Aviation* (September 1943).

45. "Mercy Flight under Sub-Zero Weather Piloted by Les Cook Saves Soldier's Life," *Whitehorse Star*, December 4, 1942. In a sad twist of fate, this article appeared the day he and two engineers, Donald Dickson and Kenneth McLean, died when the Norseman they were test-flying crashed on a Whitehorse street. In 1944, the U.S. awarded him the U.S. Air Medal for several mercy flights he made for them. For a full account, please see: Cameron, *Yukon Wings*.

46. Zaslow, *Northward*, 227; and Grant, *Polar Imperative*, 272.

47. Information on the Canol project is from: Morrison, *True North*, 133–37, 149; Main, *Voyageurs of the Air*, 175–80; Zaslow, *Northward*, 222; Grant, *Polar Imperative*, 261 and 273; "Oil for the Planes of Alaska," *The Beaver* (September 1943); and Richard S. Finnie, "The Origin of Canol's

Mackenzie Air Fields," *Arctic*, Vol. 33, No. 2 (June 1980), 273–79.

48. This paragraph draws on information from: Morrison, *True North*, 134 and 145; Grant, *Polar Imperative*, 148 and 279–80; Zaslow, *Northward*, 223 and 227; and Coates and Morrison, *The Alaska Highway in World War II*, 4–6 and 11.

49. Joanne MacDonald, "General Store in Champagne thrived during 1940s," [publication unknown]. From clippings file at Yukon Archives.

50. Information on epidemics and the environment during this period drawn from: Morrison, *True North*, 138–42; Alison Reid, "For Native people, life changed forever," *The Optimist* (June 1992), 6–7; Cruikshank, *Life Lived Like a Story*; "Oil for the Planes of Alaska"; and Mabel Braaethen interview stored at the NWT Archives.

51. Info for this section on the Eldorado mine is from: *Edmonton Bulletin* (Saturday Nov 17, 1945), 22; Grant, *Polar Imperative*, 274; Henry, *Uncharted Skies*, 50–51; Watt, "Pushing Back the Frontiers," 55; and Canadian Broadcast Corporation, "Mining for a bomb," *http://www.cbc.ca/history/ EPISCONTENTSE1EP14CH2PA3LE. html* (last accessed May 21, 2014).

52. "Two thousand people take part in V-E Day Celebration here," *Whitehorse Star*, May 11, 1945.

Chapter 5: Arctic Threats

1. Information in this section from: Milberry, *Sixty Years*, 205; Kikkert, "Creating a Role"; Raymond Stouffer, "Military Culture and the Mobile Striking Force"; and Richard Goette, "The Roundel and Building RCAF Arctic Air Mindedness during the Early Cold War," all papers from the De-Icing Required! conference. Much of the Air Force's activities, strategies, and DEW Line work has been ably covered by Larry Milberry and P. Whitney Lackenbauer in their works.

2. This quote and the following one are from: D.J. Blain, "Sweetbriar Diary," *The Roundel* (December 1950), 37–46; and L.J. Nevin, "Operation Deep Freeze," *The Roundel* (August 1958), 20–23.

3. For more detailed explanations of these navigational phenomena, please see: Cable, "Air Force – a Leader in the Arctic"; and Bergquist, *Great Circles*.

4. Milberry, *Sixty Years*, 251; and Kikkert, "Creating a Role."

5. "Report on the Low Frequency LORAN Program," Privy Council Office, August 5, 1947, DHH 112.3m2.

6. Bud Laurin, "The end of an era as the Air Force leaves the Yukon," *Whitehorse Star*, May 13, 1968; and Rusty Erlam, "Now it can be told," *Whitehorse Star*, May 13, 1968.

7. Information in this paragraph from: W.H. Cleaver, "Operation Photo," *The Roundel* (February 1950), 14–17; and McAllister, *Wings Over the Yukon*, 20.

8. Correspondence with Fred Aldworth, December 9, 2010; and Sean M. Maloney, "Canada's Arctic Sky Spies: The Director's Cut," *Canadian Military Journal* (August 2008).

9. Theriault, *Trespassing in God's Country*, 33–36, 39, 41, 46–48, 52, 58, 62; and Milberry, *Sixty Years*, 396.

10. Information in this paragraph from: Milberry, *Sixty Years*, 217, 221, 224–25, and 228—30; and McAllister, *Wings Over the Yukon*, 92.

11. Information in this paragraph from: interview with Bryce Chase, April 13, 2011; Milberry, *Sixty Years*, 232; Grant, *Polar Imperative*, 272; Lackenbauer, "If it ain't broke, don't break it: expanding and enhancing the Canadian Rangers," 3; and Lackenbauer, "Canada's Northern Defenders," 355.

12. Grant, *Polar Imperative*, 258 and 276; P. Whitney Lackenbauer and Ryan Shackleton, "Inuit-Air Force Relations in the Qikiqtani Region during the Early Cold War," (paper, De-Icing Required! The Historical Dimension of the Canadian Air Force's Experience in the Arctic, Sainte-Anne-de-Bellevue, QC, June 2010).

13. Kikkert, "Creating a Role."

14. Morrison, *True North*, 165.

15. Rachel Lea Heide, "Frigid Ambitions: The Venture of the Alert Wireless Station and Lessons Learned for the Canada First Defence Strategy," (paper, De-Icing Required! The Historical Dimension of the Canadian Air Force's Experience in the Arctic, Sainte-Anne-de-Bellevue, QC, June 2010).

16. Berton, *Mysterious North*, 211–17.

17. Information in this paragraph from: Morrison, *True North*, 164–66; and L.C. Morrison, "NORAD – Only the name's the same," *The Roundel* (September 1963), 3–7.

18. The following section draws on: interview with Bryce Chase, April 13, 2011; and Dickie, "The Flying Santas Remember."

19. Information in this paragraph is from: Morrison, *True North*, 165; Newman, *Merchant Princes*, 241 and 245; Smith, *People of the Lakes*, 161; Wachowich, *Saqiyuq*, 270; Thrasher, *Skid Row Eskimo*, 55.

20. Newman, *Merchant Princes*, 248–49; and Sandra Martin, "James Houston and Kananginak Pootoogook," *Working the Dead Beat: 50 Lives that Changed Canada* (Toronto: House of Anansi Press, 2013), 157–65.

21. "Conditions Amongst the Eskimos — Resolute Bay, January 5, 1961," LAC, RG 18, Vol. 55, File TA 500-8-1-14.

22. Previous quotes and information from: Lackenbauer and Shackleton, "Inuit-Air Force Relations."

23. Dickson, *The Dew Line Years: Voices from the Coldest Cold War*, 35–36.

24. Berton, *Mysterious North*, 267.

25. Freeman, *Life Among the Qallunaat*, 52.

26. Following section from: Thrasher, *Skid Row Eskimo*, 71, 80, and 160–61.

27. Information in this paragraph from: Mary-Ellen Kelm, "Change, Continuity, Renewal," in *Colonizing Bodies: Aboriginal Health and Healing in British Columbia, 1900–1950* (Vancouver: UBC Press, 1998), 82; Meijer Drees, *Healing Histories*, 1 and 9.

28. Information and quotes in this paragraph from: Grant, *Arctic Justice*, 249; Drees, *Healing Histories*, 2–3; Morrison, *True North*, 164; Lackenbauer and Shackleton, "Inuit-Air Force Relations"; and Wachowich, *Saqiyuq*, 271.

29. The information in this paragraph is from: Thrasher, *Skid Row Eskimo*, 85; Kelm, "Change, Continuity, Renew-

al"; and Drees, *Healing Histories*, 30.

30. This paragraph and the following one draw on: Lyall, *An Arctic Man*, 165, 169, and 204–5; and Whyard, *Ernie Boffa*, 78.

31. Wachowich, *Saqiyuq*, 91–95.

32. The information in this paragraph comes from: Ann Meekitjuk Hanson, "Finding Hope and Healing in Memories of Our Past," *Above and Beyond* (March/April 2012), 23–29; and Lyall, *An Arctic Man*, 170.

33. The following section draws primarily on: Grant, *Arctic Justice*, 249. Drees, *Healing Histories*, 9–10, 14, 16, and 96.

34. David E. Pelly, "The Mysterious Disappearance of Father Buliard, OMI," *Above and Beyond* (July/August 2005).

35. Hamilton, *Flying Overloaded*, 134–35.

36. Callison, *Pack Dogs to Helicopters*, 153.

37. Lynn A. Hamilton email, November 25, 2013.

38. Following section taken from: Drees, *Healing Histories*, 79, 83, 93, 105, and 144.

39. Lyall, *An Arctic Man*, 200.

40. Drees, *Healing Histories*, 9.

41. Ibid., 23.

42. Meekitjuk Hanson, "Finding Hope and Healing."

43. Morrison, *True North*, 152.

Chapter 6: New Horizons

1. Information in this section primarily from an interview with Fred Carmichael, November 2010. Also draws on: Darielle Talarico, "The Flying Carmichaels," *Up Here* (June 1993), 20–21; and Erik Watt, "Freddie Carmichael: Flying into the future," *Northwest Explorer* (Spring 1989),

19–23.

2. Keith Billington, who was a nurse at Fort McPherson, writes about several of these medevacs in his book, *House Calls by Dogsled: Six Years in an Arctic Medical Outpost*.

3. Aviation Safety Network, *http:// aviation-safety.net/database/record. php?id=19721201-0* (last accessed May 20, 2014).

4. For more information on Max Ward and Wardair, please see: Melady, *Pilots*; and Ward, *The Max Ward Story*.

5. Render, *No Place for a Lady*, 50.

6. The information in this paragraph from: Render, *No Place for a Lady*, 51 and 53.

7. Details and quoted material in this paragraph from: "Canadian … Women in Aviation," *Canadian Aviation* (February 1940), 19–21, and 42.

8. "Pioneer CP Air Flight Attendant Jets North on Nostalgic Flight," *CP Air News*, July 7, 1980.

9. Interview with Gordon and Rose Toole, October 25, 2010.

10. Interview with Fran Phipps, August 2010. Additional information from: Peter Moon, "Whisky Whisky Papa," publication and date unknown, probably c. 1971; Avery, *Whiskey Whiskey Papa*, 4, 34, 36–37, 50, and 96; and Smith Matheson, *Flying the Frontiers*.

11. This paragraph draws on following sources: Render, *No Place for a Lady*, 365; email correspondence with Betty Campbell; Frank Flaherty, "Aerial Survey of Canada Immediate Postwar Need," *Canadian Aviation* (November 1943); Elizabeth A. Fleming, "Mapping a Northern Land: obtaining the high altitude photography required

for the completion of the mapping of Canada by the use of wartime aircraft (1951–1963)," *Geomatica*, Vol. 64, No. 4 (2010), 463–472; Avery, *Spartan*; and Robert N. Pettus, "Flying world-wide with Kenting Aerial Surveys," *CAHS Journal* (Summer 1999), 52–63, and 74.

12. This section uses following sources: Render, *No Place for a Lady*, 157, 160–61, and 163; and Smith Matheson, Flying the Frontiers, 196–69, and 201–12.

13. This section drawn from: interview with Dick de Blicquy; and Render, *No Place for a Lady*, 190.

14. Paul Bickford, "Flying for a living," *Northern News Services*, May 2, 2005.

15. Whyard, *Ernie Boffa*, 114–18; and Smith Matheson, *Flying the Frontiers* Vol. 3, 230–6.

16. Hamilton, *Flying Overloaded*, 103, and 154; and "Wolves kill horses," *Whitehorse Star*, March 28, 1963.

17. Bereza, *The Big Dipper Route*; Wheeler, *Skippers of the Sky*; Bereza and Shirlee Smith Matheson have profiled many of these pilots.

18. Louise Buffum diary from NWT Archives; Richard Finnie, "Treaty Time at Fort Rae" *The Beaver* (March 1940); and Edith Josie, "Here are the News," *Whitehorse Star*, August 29, 1968.

19. Lyall, *An Arctic Man*, 166–68.

20. This paragraph drawn from: Billington, *Housecalls by Dogsled*, 94, and 183; and interview with Stephen Frost Sr.

21. Quotes and information in this section from: "History of Old Crow, Yukon. Story by Mrs. Effie Linklater, Old Crow Resident"; Charlie Thomas, interview, Gwitchin First Nation oral history — "Recollections" Project; Interview with Stephen Frost Sr.; and Edith Josie, "The Best of Edith Josie: Old Crow News," A collection of Edith Josie from the columns of the Whitehorse Star. Yukon Territory, 1965, 1966–67, and 1969–70.

22. This paragraph drawn from: Main, *Voyageurs of the Air*, 307; Morrison, *True North*, 56; McLaren, *Bush to Boardroom*, 29; Louise Buffum's diary, September 14, 15, 18, and 19, 1939, NWT Archives; Smith Matheson, *Flying the Frontiers Vol II*, 149.

23. Information in this section from: Smith Matheson, *Flying the Frontiers Vol 2*, 150–53 and 161. William "Bill" Leising also detailed his experiences in his memoir, *Arctic Wings*, which was used to promote the Oblates' work in the North and raise funds for operations.

24. As Smith Matheson notes on page 162 of *Flying the Frontiers Vol. 2*, Leising would have liked to buy a DC-3 — and one was offered to him for one dollar at one point — but superiors thought it was too large as they were starting to close schools.

25. Leising, *Arctic Wings*, 193. After 1900, the Anglicans opened a school at Carcross, Yukon, and the Catholics opened one at Hay River, NWT. In June 1953, for example, Leising flew the Norseman ten hours a day for three weeks returning 250 children to their homes around the territory.

26. Information in this section from: Milberry, *Air Transport in Canada, Vol. 1*, 369; Smith Matheson, *Flying the Frontiers Vol 2*, 47 and 159; and Lyall, *An Arctic Man*, 185–57, and 224.

27. Information in this paragraph from

Hamilton, *Flying Overloaded*, 174–75.

28. Leising, *Arctic Wings*, 286; and Lyall, *An Arctic Man*, 188–89.

29. This paragraph draws on the following sources: Thrasher, *Skid Row Eskimo*, 3–4; Morrison, *True North*, 153–54; Newman, *Merchant Princes*, 245; Wachowich, *Saqiyuq*, 108.

30. Morrison, *True North*, 156 and 176; and Grant, Arctic Justice, 250. For an excellent discussion of the history of residential schools in Canada and their outcomes, please see: Milloy, *A National Crime*.

31. Milloy, *A National Crime*, xvi; Coates and Morrison, *Land of the Midnight Sun*, 287; Lyall, *An Arctic Man*, 185 and 230

32. Morrison, *True North*, 154.

Chapter 7: Miracles, Tragedies, and Just Plain Luck

1. Operation Mike: The Search for 2469, *http://www.operationmike.com/node/8* (last accessed May 21, 2014).

2. Smith Matheson outlines the story of Johnny Bourassa in *Lost: True Stories of Canadian Aviation Tragedies*.

3. This section drawn from an interview with George Popadynec and his collection of documents and clippings from the time, as well as Paul Koring, "The Watson Lake Triangle Incidents," *Yukon News*, February 25, 1976.

4. Following section: Mokler, *Aircraft Down*, 67 and 77; and Patrick Fahy, "History of CASARA Edmonton" (April 2007).

5. "Miracles Happen" section, unless otherwise indicated, from: Helen Klaben, *Hey, I'm Alive!*; "Hey, I'm Alive," *Whitehorse Star*, reprinted

June 16, 1990; Mokler, *Aircraft Down*, 92–93, 96–97, 103–7, and 109. Mokler never names Flores and Klaben but there are enough identifying details about the aircraft, location, and date to make the connection.

6. McCallum, *Tales of an Old Bold Pilot*, 90.

7. "Where are they now? Ties That Bond," *Whitehorse Star*, November 26, 1993.

8. McCallum, *Tales of an Old Bold Pilot*, 88 and 93.

9. Klaben called him Jack George while other accounts say his name was Frank George.

10. McCallum, *Tales of an Old Bold Pilot*, 89.

11. "Where are they now?" *Whitehorse Star*.

12. Flo Carter, "First plane crash pictures," *Whitehorse Star*, April 1, 1963.

13. Jimmy Smothers, "Young soldier's grandfather at center of famous survival tale," *Gadsden Times*, December 26, 2010.

14. Carter, "First plane crash pictures."

15. "Where are they now?"; and Mokler, *Aircraft Down*, 93.

16. "The 'Miracle' Survivors of a Yukon Air Crash Relive Their Ordeal," *People Magazine*, March 24, 1975.

17. *Whitehorse Star* editorial, March 28, 1963.

18. The information in the following section from: Gaffin, *Edward Hadgkiss*.

19. Section on Chuck McAvoy drawn from: Smith Matheson, *Lost*, 97; Mike W. Bryant, "Ghost Plane Found," *Northern News Services*, August 6, 2003; "Bodies, wreckage reveal fate of mystery plane," *CBC North*, August 6, 2003; Mike Bryant, "McAvoy plane comes home," *North-*

ern News Services, September 1, 2004.

20. Section on Bob Gauchie from: Mike W. Bryant, "Stranded 58 days," *Northern News Services*, April 6, 2007; Jennifer Pritchett, "Bush pilot remembers being stranded on the Northern barrens," *Northern News Services*, July 2, 1997; and "Bush pilot rescued after 58 days in NWT wilderness," *CBC Digital Archives http://www.cbc.ca/archives/categories/science-technology/aviation/pioneers-in-the-sky-bush-pilots-of-canada/bush-pilot-rescued.html* (last accessed May 21, 2014)

21. Travis-Henikoff, *Dinner with a Cannibal*.

22. The section on Marten Hartwell largely from: Tadman, *The Survivor*; and Stephen and Susan Hume, "It was the first day of his life," *Calgary Herald*, December 11, 1972.

23. Ed Logozar landed in the company's Twin Otter, and the two decided Hartwell would do the mercy flight.

24. There are several spellings of Kootook's first names, David Pisuriak and Davidie Pessurajak being the most common. I have decided to go with the most prevalent in reports at the time.

25. Tadman, *The Survivor*, 122–23 and 98. Also, the aircraft was apparently missing key equipment and Hartwell said he had complained about the instruments in the past.

26. Hume, "It was the first day of his life."

27. "Eskimo boy helped pilot survive in Arctic," *Calgary Herald*, December 11, 1972.

28. Milberry, *Sixty Years*, 402–3.

29. "MOT gets earful at Hartwell inquest," *Yellowknifer*, March 7, 1973; "Jury makes recommendations," *News of the North*, March 7, 1973; and Brian Thompson, "Better transportation links says NWT Chamber," *News of the*

North, March 7, 1973.

30. Svjetlana Mlinarevic, "Camp of a cannibal," *Northern News Services*, December 7, 2012.

Chapter 8: The Top of the World

1. Monty Alford, "Crossing the Kluane Park glaciers on skis," *Whitehorse Star*, 1980.

2. McAllister, *Wings Over the Yukon*, 159.

3. "High-level test in the Yukon," *Airborne* (March/April 1981), 41 and 60–62.

4. Information in the rest of this section is drawn from: an interview with Joe Muff; Andy Williams, "Philip P. Upton, 1919–1984," *Arctic Institute of North America*, Vol. 37, No. 3 (1984).

5. Jane Gaffin, "Bushed: From Kennedys to mine mechanics," *Yukon News*, October 11, 1996; Stephanie Waddell, "Aviation pioneer flew U.S. senator to Mt. Kennedy," *Whitehorse Star*, December 18, 2009.

6. McAllister, *Wings Above the Arctic*, 159.

7. Information in this section comes from: a transcript of an interview with Kurt Koken, May 27, 1978. Allen Wright fonds, Yukon Archives. MSS 131, #83/79 900-8-14; and Lord Hunt, "The Yukon Alpine Centennial Expedition — 1967," *Alpine Journal* (1968).

8. Lloyd Freese to Larry Tremblay, "Report on Rescue of John Lauchin's Party from the South West Ridge of Mount Logan — Kluane National Park," June 27, 1978, Yukon Archives.

9. The following story is from: Mark Hume, "Tears for fellow climbers," *Edmonton Journal*, June 18, 1982; "Rescue," *Whitehorse Star*, June 16, 1982; John Crump, "Rescued aren't upset Alouette helicopter wasn't avail-

able,' *Whitehorse Star*, June 17, 1982.

10. Avery, *Whiskey, Whiskey, Papa*, 102–4.

11. "Arctic flight for EXPO," *Canadian Aviation* (February 1967).

12. Royal Canadian Mounted Police, Aviation Section, *RCMP Air Division, 1937–1973* (Ottawa: Information Canada, 1973).

13. Avery, *Whiskey, Whiskey, Papa*, 112.

14. Ibid., 117.

15. Saunders, "Air services' 50th anniversary."

16. Avery, *Whiskey, Whiskey, Papa*, 113–14.

17. Moon, "Whisky Whisky Papa"; Avery, *Whiskey, Whiskey, Papa*, 114–15.

18. "People who go to the Pole," *Northwest Explorer*, Vol 3, No 1, (Winter 1984), 21–25.

19. Interview with Bob Heath, November 2010.

20. Kelly Cryderman, "The ice wasn't thick enough," *The Ottawa Citizen*, (nd, 1997).

21. Interview with Bob Heath, November 2010.

Chapter 9: The Old and the Bold

1. The information in this section largely taken from: the Coroner's report into the death of Don Bergren by the Province of British Columbia.

2. Larry Pynn, "The Golden Triangle," *Georgia Straight*, March 20, 1997.

3. Chuck Tobin, "Search for missing pilot is suspended," *Whitehorse Star*, August 15, 1996.

4. Interview with Bob Heath, November 2010.

5. Spring, *The Sky's the Limit: Canadian Women Bush Pilots*, 54–55; and Melady, *Pilots*, 218. Erik Vogel, the twenty-four-year-old pilot of Wapiti Airways twin-engined Piper Chieftan that crashed in northern Alberta on October 19, 1984, details the pressure he felt in Carol Shaben, *Into the Abyss: An Extraordinary True Story*.

6. Interview with Joe Muff, December 2010.

7. Erik Watt, "Don't worry doc, we'll make it," *Up Here* (October/November 1992).

8. "Flying bandit sleeps," *Northern News Services*, November 16, 2007.

9. Interview with Dan Reynolds, December 2010.

10. Interview with Helmut Schoener, December 2010.

11. Email from John Faulkner, January 6, 2011.

12. Appeal files in Rolls murder case," *Whitehorse Star*, May 8, 1978.

13. Interview with Adam Morrison, October 2010; and "Shots fired at helicopter," *Klondike Sun*, July 27, 1989.

14. The information in this paragraph is from: Main, *Voyageurs of the Air*, 307; McAllister, *Wings Over the Yukon*; Saunders, "Air Services' 50th Anniversary," 12; *RCMP Air Division, 1937–1973*; and Josie, "Here are the News," October 19, 1965.

15. This paragraph drawn from: E.P Gardiner, "The Winged Mounties," *The Journal of the CAHS*, Vol. 6, No. 4 (1968), 105–08; and *RCMP Air Division, 1937–1973*.

16. Saunders, "Air Services' 50th Anniversary."

17. Michael Vlessides, "Forever Red: RCMP Celebrate 125 years," *Above & Beyond* (Summer 1998), 24–30.

18. Email from Ron Ferris, April 27,

2010; "Yukon bishop killed in plane crash," *Western Catholic Reporter*, April 24, 2000; and "Yukon Bishop well-suited to life in remote diocese," *National Post*, April 19, 2000.

19. Wachowich, *Saqiyuq*, 245.

20. Nancy McLeod, "Democracy takes wing," *Up Here*, (December/February 1988).

21. Joanne Irons, "Getting a baby," *Up Here*, September/October 1988.

22. Interview with Bob Heath, December 2010.

23. Email correspondence with Marlie McLaren Kelsey.

24. This paragraph from: Render, *No Place for a Lady*, 273, and 299–301.

25. Stephanie Myles, "Female pilot recognized as pioneer," *Ottawa Citizen*, May 30, 1992.

26. Melady, *Pilots*, 217–18.

27. Render, *No Place for a Lady*, 288 and 291; and email correspondence with Rosella Bjornson.

28. The information in this paragraph taken from: Erik Watt, "History and Mystery," *Up Here* (January/February 1999); Braden, *On Good Ice*; Bob Heath interview; Morrison, *True North*, 169–72; and Coates and Morrison, *Land of the Midnight Sun*, 147.

29. This paragraph drawn from: Josie, "Here are the News," 1968–70; and Evans, *From Fox Moths to Jet Rangers*, 62 and 179.

30. The information for this section comes from: Western Arctic Handbook Committee, *Canada's Western Arctic*, 37 and 220; Adam Johnson, "The past, re-examined," *Northern News Services*, August 28, 2006; Morrison, *True North*, 152, 170–72 and

181; Coates and Morrison, *The Land of the Midnight Sun*, 147–48; and The Dene Nation's website *http://www.denenation.com/history.html* (accessed May 14, 2014).

31. *Canada's Western Arctic*, 221; and Fred Carmichael interview.

32. Bob Heath interview.

33. Pynn, "The Golden Triangle."

34. Joe Muff interview.

35. Section on Air North from: Joe Muff interview; McAllister, *Wings Over the Yukon*, 147, 150; and Chuck Tobin, "Last DC-3 soars off into history," *Whitehorse Star*, May 6, 1998.

36. John Valliant, "Buffalo Joe and his amazing frozen flying machines," *Sports Afield* (March 2000), 68.

37. Ice Pilots NWT, Season 3, Episode 13 "Coming Home" — interview with Joe McBryan. Filmed July 2011.

38. Knight, *Buffalo Airways*, 143 and 149.

39. McAllister, *Wings Above the Arctic*, 86; Kikkert, "Creating a Role"; and Lackenbauer and Shackleton, "Inuit-Air Force Relations."

40. Milberry, *Sixty Years*, 405.

41. Dickie, "The flying Santas remember."

42. Yukon Air Crash Site Inventory.

43. Heide, "Frigid Ambitions."

44. Clyde H. Farnsworth, "After a Plane Crash, 30 Deadly Hours in the Arctic," *New York Times*, November 5, 1991.

45. Milberry, *Air Transport in Canada Vol 2.*, 923–27.

46. Kikkert, "Creating a Role"; and Pascale Dion, "Patrolling Canada's High Arctic to maintain sovereignty," *Up Here* (July/August 2004).

47. Following section drawn from: interview with Bob Heath; Patricia

Saunders, "Dew Line closing signals end of era," *Inuvik Drum*, July 22, 1993; and Berton, *Mysterious North*, 184.

48. Corley-Smith, *10,000 Hours*, 222.
49. Bruce, *The Pig That Flew*.

Epilogue: "I'd Like to Do It All Over Again"
1. "Boyd Benjamin — Windspeaker Confidential," *Windspeaker*, Vol. 27, Issue 4 (2009).
2. Stephanie Waddell, "Air North plans a moderate flight path," *Whitehorse Star*, March 26, 2010.
3. Transportation Safety Board of Canada, "Aviation Statistics — 2010," *http://www.tsb.gc.ca/eng/stats/aviation/2010/ss10.asp* (accessed January 2, 2014).
4. Carol Shaben, "Fly at your own risk," *The Walrus* (November 2009); and *Into the Abyss*.
5. Chris Purdy, "Recovery in doubt for remains of Canadian plane-crash victims in Antarctica," *Globe and Mail*, October 6, 2013.
6. Teresa Earle, "High flyer," *Explore* (June 2009), 43–47, and 60–61.
7. Eva Holland, "What happened on the Iskut?" *Up Here* (November/December 2012).
8. Tristin Hopper, "NWT aviation company plans for fleet of futuristic blimps to haul cargo," *National Post*, August 31, 2011.
9. Margo McDiamid, "Mackenzie Valley pipeline facing possible revival," *CBC News*, October 25, 2013.

Selected Bibliography

What follows is a list of books along with scholarly articles, papers, and dissertations used in the creation of this book. For the sake of brevity, references to archival materials, newspaper and magazine articles, websites, personal interviews, and correspondence can be found in the notes.

Abel, Kerry and Ken S. Coates, eds. *Northern Visions: New Perspectives on the North in Canadian History*. Toronto: University of Toronto Press, 2001.

Anderson, James F. *Outlaw Pilot: True Adventures of Jimmy Midnight Anderson*. Canada: privately published, 1993.

Avery, Norman. *Spartan Air Services: Seven Letters that Spanned the Globe*. Ottawa: privately printed, 2009.

———. *Whiskey Whiskey Papa: Chronicling the Exciting Life and Times of a Pilot's Pilot*. Ottawa: M.O.M. Printing, 1998.

Babcock, Sandy. "Operation CANON: A Case Study of Early RCAF Arctic Search and Rescue Capabilities." Paper, De-Icing Required! The Historical Dimension of the Canadian Air Force's Experience in the Arctic, Sainte-Anne-de-Bellevue, QC, June 2010.

Baidukov, George. *Over the North Pole*. Translated by Jessica Smith. New York: Harcourt, Brace and Company, 1938.

Balchen, Bernt. *Come North with Me: An Autobiography*. New York: E.P. Dutton & Co., 1958.

———. "My Introduction to Canada," *CAHS Journal* (Summer 1976), 35–38.

Barry, P.S. "'Punch' Dickins and the Origins of Canol's Mackenzie Air Fields." *Arctic*, Vol. 32, No. 4 (December 1979): 366–373.

Bennett, Gordon. *Yukon Transportation: A History. Canadian Historic Sites: Occasional Papers in Archaeology and History No. 19*. Ottawa: Parks Canada, 1978.

Bereza, Danny. *The Big Dipper Route: A Canadian Arctic Adventure Book*. Courtenay, BC: Solaster Publishing, 2005.

Bergquist, Kathy. *Great Circles: The Keith Greenaway Story*. Canada: privately printed, 2008.

Berton, Laura Beatrice. *I Married the Klondike*. Toronto: McLelland & Stewart, 1961.

Berton, Pierre. *Klondike: The Last Great Gold Rush, 1896–1899*. Toronto: McClelland & Stewart, 1972.

———. *The Mysterious North*. New York: Knopf, 1956.

———. *Prisoners of the North*. New York: Caroll & Graf, 2004.

Billington, Keith. *House Calls by Dogsled: Six Years in an Arctic Medical Outpost*. Madeira Park, BC: Harbour Publishing Co., 2008.

Blanchet, Guy. *Search in the North*. Toronto: The MacMillan Company of Canada, 1960.

Boer, Peter. *Bush Pilots: Canada's Wilderness Daredevils*. Edmonton: Folklore Publishing, 2004.

Braun, Don C. with John C. Warren. *The Arctic Fox: Bush Pilot of the North Country*. Excelsior, MN: Back Bay Press, 1994.

Breynat, Gabriel Joseph Elie and Alan Gordon Smith. *The Flying Bishop: Fifty Years in the Canadian Far North*. London: Burns & Oates, 1955.

Byer, Doug. *Northern Service*. Calgary: Detselig Enterprises, 1997.

Cable, Ernest. "Air Force — a Leader in the Arctic." Paper, De-Icing Required! The Historical Dimension of the Canadian Air Force's Experience in the Arctic, Sainte-Anne-de-Bellevue, QC, June 2010.

Callison, Pat. *Pack Dogs to Helicopters: Pat Callison's Story*. Vancouver: Evergreen Press, 1983.

Cameron, R.B. *Yukon Wings*. Calgary: Frontenac House, 2012.

Capelotti, P.J. *By Airship to the North Pole: An Archaeology of Human Exploration*. Piscataway, NJ: Rutgers University Press, 1999.

Cashman, Tony. *Gateway to the North*. Edmonton: Duval House Publishing, 2002.

Coates, Kenneth and William R. Morrison. *The Alaska Highway in World War II: The U.S. Army of Occupation in Canada's Northwest*. Norman: University of Oklahoma Press, 1992.

———. *Land of the Midnight Sun: A History of the Yukon*. Montreal & Kingston: McGill-Queen's University Press, 2005.

Corley-Smith, Peter. *10,000 Hours: Reminiscences of a Helicopter Bush Pilot*. Victoria: Sono Nis Press, 1985.

Condit, John. *Wings over the West: Russ Baker and the Rise of Pacific Western Airlines*. Madeira Park, BC: Harbour Pub., 1984.

Crouch, Tom. *Lighter Than Air: An Illustrated History of Balloons and Airships*. Baltimore: Johns Hopkins University Press, 2009.

Cruikshank, Julie. *Do Glaciers Listen? Local Knowledge, Colonial Encounters, & Social Imagination*. Vancouver: UBC Press, 2005.

———. *Life Lived Like a Story: Life Stories of Three Yukon Native Elders*. Vancouver: UBC Press, 2002.

Czech, Kenneth P. "Roald Amundsen and the 1925 North Pole Expedition." *Aviation History*, published online June 6, 2009. *http://www.historynet.com/roald-amundsen-and-the-1925-north-pole-expedition.htm* (accessed May 15, 2014).

Davies, Ed and Steve Ellis. *Seattle's Commercial Aviation: 1908–1941*. Charleston, SC: Arcadia Publishing, 2009.

Dickson, Frances Jewel. *The DEW Line Years: Voices from the Coldest Cold War*. Lawrencetown Beach, NS: Pottersfield Press, 2007.

Dill, W. S. *The Long Day*. Ottawa: The Graphic Publishers, 1926.

Dobrowolsky, Helene. *Law of the Yukon: a Pictorial History of the Mounties.* Whitehorse, YT: Lost Moose, 1995.

Douglas, W.A.B. *Creation of a National Air Force: The Official History of the Royal Canadian Air Force*, vol. 2. Ottawa: University of Toronto Press and Supply and Services Canada, 1986.

Dunbar, Moira and Keith R. Greenaway. *Arctic Canada from the Air.* Ottawa: Canada Defence Research Board, 1956.

Dzuiban, Stanley W. *Military Relations between the United States and Canada, 1939–1945.* Washington, DC: United States Army, 1959.

Ellis, Frank H. *Canada's Flying Heritage.* Toronto: University of Toronto Press, 1954.

———. *In Canadian Skies.* Toronto: Ryerson Press, 1959.

Evans, Harvey. *Fox Moths to Jet Rangers: A Bush Pilot's Life.* Madeira Park, BC: Harbour Publishing, 2009.

Fergus, Grant J. "North to the Yukon by Air." *Canadian Geographic Journal.* August, 1937.

Fleming, Elizabeth A. "Mapping a Northern Land: obtaining the high altitude photography required for the completion of the mapping of Canada by the use of wartime aircraft (1951–1963)." *Geomatica,* Vol. 64, No. 4 (2010): 463-472.

Foster, Tony. *The Bush Pilots: A Pictorial History of a Canadian Phenomenon.* Toronto: McClelland & Stewart, 1990.

Francis, Daniel. *National Dreams: Myth, Memory, and Canadian History.* Vancouver: Arsenal Pulp Press, 2005.

Fuller, G.A, J.A. Griffin and K.M. Molson. *125 Years of Canadian Aeronautics: 1840–1965.* Willowdale, ON: Canadian Aviation Historical Society, 1983.

Fumoleau, René. *Way Down North: Dene Life — Dene Land.* Montreal: Novalis, 2010.

Gaffin, Jane. *Edward Hadgkiss: Missing in Life.* Whitehorse, YT: Word Pro, 1989.

Gardiner, E.P. "The Winged Mounties." *CAHS Journal,* Vol. 6, No. 4. (1968): 105–108.

Gibson-Sutherland, Alice. *Canada's Aviation Pioneers: Fifty Years of McKee Trophy Winners.* Toronto: McGraw-Hill Ryerson, 1978.

Glines, Carroll V. *Polar Aviation.* New York: F. Watts, 1964.

Godsell, Philip H. *Pilots of the Purple Twilight: The Story of Canada's Early Bush Flyers.* Toronto: Ryerson Press, 1955.

Grant, Robert S. *Bush Flying: The Romance of the North.* Surrey, BC: Hancock House Publishers, 1995.

Grant, Shelagh D. *Arctic Justice: On Trial for Murder, Pond Inlet 1923.* Montreal & Kingston: McGill-Queen's University Press, 2002.

———. *Polar Imperative: A History of Arctic Sovereignty in North America.* Vancouver: Douglas & McIntyre, 2010.

Gray, Charlotte. *Gold Diggers: Striking it Rich in the Klondike.* Toronto: HarperCollins, 2011.

Greenaway, K.R. and M.D. Gates. *Polar Air Navigation — A Record.* Ottawa: printed privately, 2009.

Greenwood, John T. "General Bill Hoge and the Alaska Highway." In *The Alaska Highway: Papers of the 40th Anniversary Symposium*, edited by Kenneth Coates. Vancouver: UBC Press, 1985.

Grierson, John. *Challenge to the Poles: Highlights of Arctic and Antarctic Aviation.* Hamden, CT: Archon Books, 1964.

———. *High Failure: Solo Along the Arctic Air Route.* London: Hodge & Co., 1936.

Hamilton, Donald F. *Flying Overloaded: Adventures of a Canadian Arctic Pilot.* Canada: privately printed, 2007.

Hancock, Lyn. *Winging it in the North.* Lantzville, BC: Oolichan Books, 1996.

Heide, Rachel Lea. "Frigid Ambitions: The Venture of the Alert Wireless Station and Lessons Learned for the Canada First Defence Strategy." Paper, De-Icing Required! The Historical Dimension of the Canadian Air Force's Experience in the Arctic, Sainte-Anne-de-Bellevue, QC, June 2010.

Helmericks, Harmon "Bud." *Arctic Bush Pilot.* Leicester: Brockhamton Press, 1957.

Henry, Walter and eds. *Uncharted Skies: Canadian Bush Pilot Stories.* Edmonton: Reidmore Books, 1983.

Hesketh, Bob, ed. *Three Northern Wartime Projects: Alaska Highway, Northwest Staging Route, Canol.* Edmonton: Canadian Circumpolar Institute, Historical Society of Alberta, Edmonton and District Historical Society, 1996.

Hill, A.E. "Arctic Curtain Raiser," *CAHS Journal* (Winter 1985): 122–4.

Hine, Harold R. *Yukon Antics.* Surrey, BC: Hancock House, 1987.

Hotson, Fred W. *deHavilland in Canada.* Toronto: CANAV Books, 1999.

Hunt, C. W. *Dancing in the Sky: The Royal Flying Corps in Canada.* Toronto: Dundurn, 2009.

Josie, Edith. "A Short Autobiography." Old Crow Home of the Vuntut Gwitchin. *http://www.oldcrow.ca/edith.htm* (accessed February 27, 2014).

Karram, Kerry. *Four Degrees Celsius: A Story of Arctic Peril.* Toronto: Dundurn, 2012.

Keith, Ronald A. *Bush Pilot with a Briefcase: The Happy-Go-Lucky Story of Grant McConachie.* Don Mills, ON: PaperJacks, 1972.

Kelley, Thomas P. *Rat River Trapper: The Story of Albert Johnson, the Mad Trapper.* Don Mills, ON: Paperjacks, 1972.

Kelm, Mary-Ellen. *Colonizing Bodies: Aboriginal Health and Healing in British Columbia, 1900–1950.* Vancouver: UBC Press, 1998.

Kikkert, Peter. "Creating a Role: The Royal Canadian Air Force in the Arctic, 1945–1953." Paper, De-Icing Required! The Historical Dimension of the Canadian Air Force's Experience in the Arctic, Sainte-Anne-de-Bellevue, QC, June 2010.

Klaben, Helen. *Hey, I'm Alive!* New York: McGraw-Hill, 1963.

Knight, Darrell. *Buffalo Airways: Diamonds, DC-3s and 'Buffalo Joe' McBryan.* Calgary: Alberta Publishing, 2010.

Lackenbauer, P. Whitney, Craig Mantle, and Scott Scheffield, eds. *Aboriginal Peoples and the Canadian Military: Historical Perspectives.* Kingston, ON: Canadian Defence Academy Press, 2007.

———. "Canada's Northern Defenders: Aboriginal Peoples in the Canadian Rangers, 1947–2005. In *Calgary Papers in Military and Strategic Studies. Canadian Arctic Sovereignty and Security: Historical Perspectives,* ed. P. Whitney Lackenbauer. No. 4 (2011).

———. "If It Ain't Broke, Don't Break It: Expanding and Enhancing the Canadian Rangers." Working Papers on Arctic Security No. 6, March 2013. Munk School of Global Affairs .

———. "The Canadian Rangers: Supporting Canadian Sovereignty, Security, and Stewardship since 1947." *Above & Beyond* (September/October 2012): 31–36.

Lackenbauer, P. Whitney and Ryan Shackleton. "Inuit-Air Force Relations in the Qikiqtani Region during the Early Cold

War." Paper, De-Icing Required! The Historical Dimension of the Canadian Air Force's Experience in the Arctic, Sainte-Anne-de-Bellevue, QC, June 2010.

Larson, Erik. *The Devil in the White City: Murder, Magic, and Madness at the Fair that Changed America.* New York: Vintage Books, 2003.

Leigh, Z. Lewis. *And I shall Fly: The Flying Memoirs of Z. Lewis Leigh.* Toronto: CANAV Books, 1985.

Leising, William A. *Arctic Wings.* Garden City, NY: Doubleday & Company, 1959.

Lloyd, Trevor. "Aviation in Arctic North America and Greenland." *Polar Record,* Vol. 5, Issue 35–6 (December 1948): 163–71.

Lopaschuk, William. *They call me Lopey: A Saga of Wilderness Flying.* Smithers, BC: Creekstone Press, 2009.

Lunny, June. *Spirit of the Yukon.* Prince George, BC: Caitlin Press, 1992.

Lyall, Ernie. *An Arctic Man: The Classic Account of Sixty-Five Years in Canada's North.* Goodread Biography, 1983.

Maloney, Sean M. "Canada's Arctic Sky Spies: The Director's Cut." *Canadian Military Journal* (August 2008), published on National Defence and the Canadian Armed Forces website, *http://www.journal.forces.gc.ca/vo9/no1/11-maloney-eng.asp.* Accessed March 10, 2014.

McLaren, Duncan D. *Bush to Boardroom: A Personal View of Five Decades of Aviation History.* Winnipeg: Watson & Dwyer Publishing, 1992.

Main, J.R.K. *Voyageurs of the Air: A History of Civil Aviation in Canada, 1858–1967.* Ottawa: Queen's Printer, 1967.

Mallory, Enid L. *Coppermine: The Far North of George M. Douglas.* Peterborough, ON: Broadview Press, 1989.

Martin, Sandra. *Working the Dead Beat: 50 Lives that Changed Canada.* Toronto: House of Anansi Press, 2013.

May, Denny. *More Stories about "Wop" May.* Edmonton: Maycroft, 2011.

May, Denny and Owen Brierley. *The Chronicles of W.R. (Wop) May. http://www.wopmay.com.* Accessed February 27, 2014.

Mayo Historical Society. *Gold & Galena: A History of the Mayo District.* Mayo, Yukon: Mayo Historical Society, 1990.

McAllister, Bruce. *Wings above the Arctic: A Photographic History of Arctic Aviation.* Boulder, CO: Roundup Press, 2003.

———. *Wings over the Alaska Highway: A Photographic History of Aviation on the Alaska Highway.* Boulder, CO: Roundup Press, 2001.

———. *Wings over the Yukon: A Photographic History of Yukon Aviation.* Boulder, CO: Roundup Press, 2008.

McCaffery, Dan. *Bush Planes and Bush Pilots.* Toronto: J. Lorimer, 2002.

McCallum, Jack. *Tales of an Old Bold Pilot Who Lived to Tell His Story of Flying the North.* Sicamous, BC: J.E. McCallum, 2004.

McCartney, Denny. *Picking up the Pieces.* Victoria: Trafford, 2002.

McGrath, T.M. *History of Canadian Airports.* Toronto: Lugus and Transport Canada and the Canadian Govt. Pub. Centre, 1992.

McMillan, S. R. (Stan). "My Flying Career: A Legendary Northern Pilot recalls the adventurous side of a lifetime in aviation." *CAHS Journal* (Spring 2002): 4–15 and 36–7.

Meijer Drees, Laurie. *Healing Histories: Stories from Canada's Indian Hospitals.* Edmonton: The University of Alberta Press, 2013.

Melady, John. *Pilots: Canadian Stories from the Cockpit.* Toronto: McClelland & Stewart, 1989.

Milberry, Larry. *Air Transport in Canada, Vol. 1 and 2.* Toronto: CANAV Books, 1997.

———. *Aviation in Canada.* Toronto: McGraw-Hill Ryerson, 1979.

———. *Canada's Air Force: At War and Peace.* Toronto: CANAV Books, 2000.

———. *Sixty Years: the RCAF and CF Air Command, 1924–1984.* Toronto: CANAV Books, 1984.

Milloy, John S. *A National Crime: The Canadian Government and the Residential School System, 1879–1986.* Winnipeg: The University of Manitoba Press, 1999.

Moar, Jack and Kitty Moar. *A Collection of Bush Flying Stories.* Victoria, BC: privately printed, 1991.

Mokler, R. J. *Aircraft Down: A Personal Account of Search, Survival, and Rescue in the Canadian North.* New York: Exposition Press, 1968.

Molson, K.M. *Pioneering in Canadian Air Transport.* Winnipeg: J. Richardson, 1974.

———. "The Rene and Vic," *CAHS Journal* (Summer 1982): 41–55.

Morrison, William R. *True North: The Yukon and Northwest Territories.* Don Mills, ON: Oxford University Press, 1998.

Morritt, Hope. *Land of the Fireweed: A Young Woman's Story of Alaska Highway Construction Days.* Edmonds, WA: Alaska Northwest Pub. Co, 1985.

Morrow Lindbergh, Anne. *North to the Orient.* New York: Harcourt, Brace and Co. 1937.

Mulder, Rob. "In the air with Roald Amundsen." *www.europeanairlines.no.* Accessed May 17, 2014.

Myers, Patricia A. *Sky Riders: An Illustrated History of Aviation in Alberta, 1906–1945.* Saskatoon, SK: Fifth House Publishers, 1995.

Myles, Eugenia Louise. *Airborne from Edmonton: Being the True Tale of How Edmonton, a Remote Frontier City in Northwestern Canada, Became the Plymouth of a New Age of Air Discoveries and Air Conquests and Air Commerce, and of How the Dreams of her Pioneer Pilots Were to Be Realized a Thousandfold.* Toronto: Ryerson Press, 1959.

Nelson, Stewart B. "Airships in the Arctic." *Arctic.* Vol. 48, No. 3 (September 1993): 278–83.

Nickel, Dawn Dorothy. "Realities and Reflections: Women and the Yukon Frontier During the Alaska Highway Period." Master's thesis, University of Alberta, Fall 1998.

Oswald, Mary, ed. *They Led the Way: Members of Canada's Aviation Hall of Fame.* Altona, MB: Friesens, 1999.

Parsons, H.P. "Hank." *Trail of the Wild Goose: A Story of a Bush Pilot.* Kelowna, BC: Alex Wilson Publications, 1978.

Payne, Stephen. Ed. *Canadian Wings: A Remarkable Century of Flight.* Toronto: Canada Aviation Museum and Douglas & McIntyre, 2006.

Pettus, Robert N. "Flying world-wide with Kenting Aerial Surveys." *CAHS Journal* (Summer 1999): 52–63, 74.

Pigott, Peter. *Flying Colours: A History of Commercial Aviation in Canada.* Toronto: Douglas & McIntyre, 1997.

Polunin, Nicholas. *Arctic Unfolding: Experiences and Observations during a Canadian Airborne Expedition in the Arctic.* London: Hutchinson & Co, 1949.

Regan, Paulette. *Unsettling the Settler Within: Indian Residential Schools, Truth Telling, and Reconciliation in Canada.* Vancouver: UBC Press, 2010.

Reid, Sheila. *Conquer the Sky: Flying Ace Wop May.* St. Catharines, ON: Vanwell Publishing, 2008.

———. *Wings of a Hero: Canadian Pioneer Flying Ace Wilfrid Wop May*. St. Catharines, ON: Vanwell Publishing, 1997.

Render, Shirley. *Double Cross: The Inside Story of James A. Richardson and Canadian Airways*. Vancouver: Douglas & McIntyre, 1999.

———. *No Place for a Lady: The Story of Canadian Women Pilots, 1928–1992*. Winnipeg: Portage & Main Press, 1992.

Royal Canadian Mounted Police, Aviation Section. *RCMP Air Division, 1937–1973*. Ottawa: Information Canada, 1973.

Ruotsala, Jim. *Pilots of the Panhandle: Aviation in Southeast Alaska. Vol. 1 Early Years 1920–35*. Juneau, AK: Seadrome Press, 1996.

Russell, Chester. *Tales of a Catskinner: A Personal Account of Building the Alaska Highway, the Winter Trail, and Canol Pipeline Road in 1942–43*. North Bend, OR: Wegferds' Printing and Publications, 1999.

Saunders, Garry. "Air Services' 50th Anniversary," *Royal Canadian Mounted Police Gazette*, Vol. 49, No. 10 (1987): 4–21.

Scheffield, Scott. "'Of pure European Descent and of the White Race': Recruitment Policy and Aboriginal Canadians, 1939–1945." *Canadian Military History*, Vol. 5, No. 1 (Spring 1996): 11–15.

Shaben, Carol. *Into the Abyss: An Extraordinary True Story*. New York: Grand Central Publishing, 2012.

Shaw, S. Bernard. *Photographing Canada from Flying Canoes*. Burnstown, ON: General Store Publishing House, 2001.

Sims, Tim. "Navigation and the Early Bush Pilot." *CAHS Journal* (Winter 1976): 125.

Smith, Blake W. *Warplanes to Alaska*. Surrey, BC: Hancock House, 1998.

Smith, Philip. *It seems like only yesterday: Air Canada, the first 50 years*. Toronto: McClelland & Stewart, 1986.

Smith, Shirleen and Vuntut Gwitchin First Nation. *People of the Lakes: Stories of Our Van Tat Gwich'in Elders*. Edmonton: University of Alberta Press, 2010.

Smith Matheson, Shirlee. *Amazing Flights and Flyers*. Calgary: Frontenac House, 2010.

———. *Flying the Frontiers: A Half-Million Hours of Aviation Adventure*. Saskatoon, SK: Fifth House, 1994.

———. *Flying the Frontiers, Volume II: More Hours of Aviation Adventure*. Calgary: Detselig Enterprises, 1996.

———. *Flying the Frontiers, Volume III: Aviation Adventures Around the World*. Calgary: Detselig Enterprises, 1999.

———. *Lost: True Stories of Canadian Aviation Tragedies*. Saskatoon, SK: Fifth House, 2005.

Spring, Joyce. *The Sky's the Limit: Canadian Women Bush Pilots*. Toronto: Natural Heritage, 2006.

Tadman, Peter. *The Survivor*. Hanna, AB: Gorman & Gorman, 1991.

Terpening, Rex. *Bent Props and Blow Pots: A Pioneer Remembers Northern Bush Flying*. Madeira Park, BC: Harbour Pub., 2003.

Theriault, George. *Trespassing in God's Country: Sixty Years of Flying in Northern Canada*. Chapleau, ON: Treeline Pub., 1994.

The Western Arctic Handbook Committee. *Canada's Western Arctic Including the Dempster Highway*. Vancouver: Gordon Soules Book Publishers, 2002.

Thomson, Don W. *Skyview Canada: A Story of Aerial Photography in Canada*. Ottawa: Energy, Mines and Resources Canada, 1975.

Thrasher, Anthony Apakark. *Thrasher: Skid Row Eskimo.* Toronto: Griffin House, 1976.

Travis-Henikoff, Carole A. *Dinner with a Cannibal: The Complete History of Mankind's Oldest Taboo.* Solana Beach, CA: Santa Monica Press, 2008.

Turner, Dick. *Wings of the North.* Saanichton, WA: Hancock House, 1976.

Twichell, Heath. "The role of the Public Roads Administration." In *The Alaska Highway: Papers of the 40th Anniversary Symposium,* ed. Kenneth Coates. Vancouver: UBC Press, 1985.

Vance, Jonathan. *High Flight: Aviation and the Canadian Imagination.* Toronto: Penguin Books, 2002.

Wachowich, Nancy. *Saqiyuq: Stories from the Lives of Three Inuit Women.* Montreal & Kingston: McGill-Queen's University Press, 1999.

Ward, Max. *The Max Ward Story: A Bush Pilot in the Bureaucratic Jungle.* Toronto: McClelland & Stewart, 1991.

Weicht, Christopher. *Air Route to the Klondike: An Aviation History.* Sechelt, BC: Creekside Publications, 2006.

———. *North by Northwest.* Sechelt, BC: Creekside Publications, 2004.

———. *Yukon Airways.* Sechelt, BC: Creekside Publications, 2007.

Wheeler, William. *Skippers of the Sky: The Early Years of Bush Flying.* Calgary: Fifth House Publishers, 2000.

Whyard, Florence. *Ernie Boffa: Canadian Bush Pilot.* Whitehorse, YT: Beringian Books, 1984.

Winslow, Kathryn. *Big Pan-Out: The Klondike Story.* London: Phoenix House Ltd, 1952.

Williams, A.R. (Al). *Bush and Arctic Pilot.* Surrey, BC: Hancock House, 1998.

Wittreich, Paul. *Forgotten First Flights.* Bloomington, Indiana: Xlibris Corporation, 2009.

Zaslow, Morris. *The Northward Expansion of Canada, 1914–1967.* Toronto: McClelland & Stewart, 1988.

Index

66–70, 100–1, 107–9, 111, 119, 122–23

early contact with aviation, 38, *39*, *42*, 62; residential schools, 123; search and rescue, 129, 133, 136, 165; sovereignty, 44, 179

Royal Canadian Navy, 93, *94;* HMCS *Labrador*, 94

Russell, Chester, 84

Russia, 28, 30–31, 43, *78*, 81, 89–90, 92, 95, 179

Ryan B-1 Brougham, 56

Ryder, Lloyd, 129, 146

Sachs Harbour (Northwest Territories), 115, 122

Sagiuktuk, Charlie, *99*

Saint Elias Range, 19, 142, 144, *145,* 146–47, 149, *150*

Savoia-Marchetti S.55, 31

Schlachter, Eliane Roberge, 111

Schoener, Helmut, 162

Search and Rescue (SAR), 125–128, 178; CASARA, 127; CARES Alberta, 127; military SAR, 127, 129, 139, 167, 174; Rescue Coordination Centre in Edmonton, 129; unofficial, 109, 111

Second World War: Alaska Highway and Canol Pipeline, 83–86; Aleutian campaign, 83–84, 86; fear of Japanese attack, 82–83, 86; HBC pilots joining up, 74–75; impact on North, 86–89; northerners joining up, 75–77; Northwest Staging Route, 77– 83

Selkirk (Yukon), 38

Sheardown, Ron, 138

Shell, 168

Short Range Navigation (SHORAN), 91–93

Short-takeoff-and-landing (STOL), 143, *153*

Simmons, George, 56, 142

Sims, Tim, 48

Skagway (Alaska), *23*, 25, 28, 34, 38, 58

Slager, Paul, *14*

Slemon, C.R., 70

Snag (Yukon), 81, 125

Snip Mine, 158

Soviet Union. *See* Russia

Sparling, Joe, 159, 172, 177. *See also* Air North

Spartan Air Services, 95, *97*, 114

Spence Bay (Northwest Territories), 101, 106, 118, 122–23, 139

Spitsbergen (Norway), 28, 30, *31*, 95

Spruyt, Hoby, 165

Standard J-1 biplane, 37, *39*

Stefansson, Vilhjalmur, 61

Stevens, Glen, 138

Stevens Jr., Leo (Don Carlos Stevens), 22

Stewardess. *See* flight attendant

Stinson 108 Voyager, *105*, 107–9, 119

Streett, St. Clair "Bill," *35*, 36

Strickland, John, 152

Super Beech 18, *110*

Taku Air Transport, 163

Tamney, Melba, 113

Teemotee, Joe, 103

Terpening, Rex, *53*, 61–62

Territorial Airways, 163

Terry, N.C., 45–46

Teslin (Yukon), *77, 86*

The Pas (Manitoba), 45

Theriault, George, 92

Thomas, Charlie, 63, 119

Thompson, George, 41

Thrasher, Anthony Apakark, 100–1, 123–24

Tidd, Claude, *74*

Tlingit, 25, *86*

Tomlinson, Sammy, 52

Toole, Gordon, 80–81, 113

Toole, Rose, 113

Torp, Douglas, *137*

Torrie, Horace, 61